THE CURIOUS FEMINIST

Cynthia Enloe

THE CURIOUS FEMINIST

Searching for Women in a New Age of Empire

UNIVERSITY OF CALIFORNIA PRESS

Berkeley   Los Angeles   London

University of California Press
Berkeley and Los Angeles, California

University of California Press, Ltd.
London, England

Library of Congress Cataloging-in-Publication Data

Enloe, Cynthia H., 1938–
    The curious feminist : searching for women in a new age
of empire / Cynthia Enloe.
        p. cm.
    Includes bibliographical references and index.
        ISBN 0-520-24235-1 (cloth : alk. paper) —
    ISBN 0-520-24381-1 (pbk. : alk. paper)
        1. Feminism. 2. Sex role. 3. Women and the military.
4. Women and war. I. Title.
HQ1155.E55 2004
305.42 — dc22   2004010904

Manufactured in the United States of America
13   12   11   10   09   08   07   06   05
10   9   8   7   6   5   4   3   2

The paper used in this publication meets the minimum
requirements of ANSI/NISO Z39.48-1992 (R 1997) (*Permanence
of Paper*).

B+T NA/55

For
Gilda Bruckman
and
Judy Wachs

Contents

Introduction

Being Curious about Our Lack of Feminist Curiosity

Being curious takes energy. It may thus be a distorted form of "energy conservation" that makes certain ideas so alluring. Take, for instance, the loaded adjective "natural." If one takes for granted that something is "natural" — generals being male, garment workers being female — it saves mental energy. After all, what is deemed natural hasn't been self-consciously created. No decisions have to be made. The result: we can imagine that there is nothing we need to investigate. We can just feel sympathy with women working in sweatshops, for instance, without bothering to figure out how they got there or what they think about being women sewing there.

"Tradition" serves much the same misguided energy-saving purpose. If something is accepted as being "traditional" — inheritance passing through the male line, incoming officials swearing on a Bible — then it too can be swathed in a protective blanket, making it almost immune to bothersome questioning.

A close cousin of "traditional" is "always." Warning lights now start flashing in my head whenever I hear someone wielding "always." Too often it is used to cut short an awkward discussion. "Americans have always loved guns." "Women have always seen other women as rivals." A variant on "always" is "oldest" — as in the glib declaration "Prostitution is the oldest profession." As if prostitution were timeless, without a history. As if the organizing of certain women's sexuality so that it can serve simultaneously commercial and masculinized functions had "always" existed, everywhere. Thank goodness, the fans of "always" imply, now we don't have to invest our scarce energy in exploring that topic. Phew.

During the eight years that it has taken me to think through the essays included here — the last was written during the continuing U.S. occupation of Iraq — I have become more and more curious about curiosity and its absence. As an example, for so long I was satisfied to use (to think with) the phrase "cheap labor." In fact, I even thought using the phrase made me sound (to myself and to others) as if I were a critically thinking person, someone equipped with intellectual energy. It was only when I began, thanks to the nudging of feminist colleagues, to turn the phrase around, to say instead "labor *made* cheap," that I realized how lazy I actually had been. Now whenever I write "labor made cheap" on a blackboard, people in the room call out, "By whom?" "How?" They are expanding our investigatory agenda. They are calling on me, on all of us, to exert more intellectual energy.

The moment when one becomes newly curious about something is also a good time to think about what created one's previous *lack* of curiosity. So many power structures — inside households, within institutions, in societies, in international affairs — are dependent on our continuing lack of curiosity. "Natural," "tradition," "always": each has served as a cultural pillar to prop up familial, community, national, and international power structures, imbuing them with legitimacy, with timelessness, with inevitability. Any power arrangement that is imagined to be legitimate, timeless, and inevitable is pretty well fortified. Thus we need to stop and scrutinize our lack of curiosity. We also need to be genuinely curious about others' lack of curiosity — not for the sake of feeling self-satisfied, but for the sake of meaningfully engaging with those who take any power structure as unproblematic.

Why is a state of uncuriosity about what it takes to produce a pair of fashionable sneakers so comfortable? What is there about being uncurious about how any military base affects the civilians living in base towns that seems so reasonable? I've come to think that making and keeping us uncurious must serve somebody's political purpose. I also have become convinced that I am deeply complicit in my own lack of curiosity. *Un*curiosity is dangerously comfortable if it can be dressed up in the sophisticated attire of reasonableness and intellectual efficiency: "We can't be investigating everything!"

What is distinctive about developing a *feminist* curiosity? One of the starting points of feminism is taking women's lives seriously. "Seriously" implies listening carefully, digging deep, developing a long attention span, being ready to be surprised. Taking women — all sorts of women, in disparate times and places — seriously is not the same thing as valorizing women. Many women, of course, deserve praise, even awe; but many women we need to take seriously may appear too complicit in violence or in the oppression of others, or too cozily wrapped up in their relative privilege to inspire praise or compassion. Yet a feminist curiosity finds all women worth thinking about, paying close attention to, because in this way we will be able to throw into sharp relief the blatant and subtle political workings of both femininity and masculinity.

"Military spouses," "child soldiers," "factory managers," "sweatshop workers," "humanitarian aid workers," "rape survivors," "peace activists," "warlords," "occupation authorities." Each of these conventional ungendered terms serves to hide the political workings of masculinity and femininity. Each dampens our curiosity about where women are and where men are, about who put women there and men here, about who benefits from women being there and not someplace else, about what women themselves think about being there and what they do with those thoughts when they try to relate to men and to other women. Any time we don't pursue these questions, we are likely to miss patriarchy. It will glide right by us like an oil tanker on a foggy night. The fog is uncuriosity. Yet if we miss patriarchy when it is in fact operating as a major structure of power, then our explanations about how the world works will be unreliable.

Patriarchy — patriarchy is the structural and ideological system that perpetuates the privileging of masculinity. All kinds of social systems and institutions can become patriarchal. Whole cultures can become patriarchal. That is a reality that has inspired feminist movements to become national in scope, mobilizing energies on so many levels simultaneously. Families, town halls, militaries, banks, and police departments are among those sites of ordinary life perhaps especially notorious for their inclinations toward patriarchal values, structures, and practices. Scores of hospitals, schools, factories, legislatures, political parties, museums, newspapers, theater companies, television networks, religious organizations, corporations, and courts — no matter how modern their outward trappings — have developed ways of looking and acting toward their own members and clients and toward the world around them that derive from the presumption that what is masculine is most deserving of reward, promotion, admiration, emulation, agenda prioritization, and budgetary line. Patriarchal inclinations can also be found in peace and justice movements, as well as in the offices of progressive magazines, enlightened foundations, and globally sensitive nongovernmental organizations — each of them can be, and have become, patriarchal.

Patriarchal systems are notable for marginalizing the feminine. That is, insofar as any society or group is patriarchal, it is there that it is comfortable — unquestioned — to infantilize, ignore, trivialize, or even actively cast scorn upon what is thought to be feminized. That is why a feminist curiosity is always directed not only at the official or public discourses and behaviors of people in groups or institutions, but also at their informal, private, casual conversations, at the shared jokes, gestures, and rituals — all of which help to glue relationships together. The feminist investigator always arrives before the meeting begins to hear the before-the-meeting offhand banter and is still wide awake and curious when the meeting-after-the-meeting continues among a select few down the corridor and into the pub.

No patriarchy is made up just of men or just of the masculine. Far from it. Patriarchal systems have been so enduring, so adaptable, precisely because they make many women overlook their own marginal positions and feel instead secure, protected, valued. Patriarchies—in militias, in labor unions, in nationalist movements, in political parties, in whole states and entire international institutions—may privilege masculinity, but they need the complex idea of femininity and enough women's acceptance or complicity to operate. To sustain their gendered hierarchies, patriarchal law firms, for example, need not only feminized secretaries and feminized cleaners, but also feminized law associates and feminized paralegals. Patriarchal militaries need feminized military wives and feminized military prostitutes. Patriarchal corporations need feminized clerical workers and feminized assembly-line workers. Every person who is pressed or lured into playing a feminized role must do so in order to make the masculinized people seem to be (to themselves as well as everyone else) the most wise, the most intellectual, the most rational, the most tough-minded, the most hard-headed.

One of the reasons that feminists have been so astute in exposing patriarchy as a principal cause for so many of the world's processes—empire-building, globalization, modernization—is that feminists have been curious about women. By taking women seriously in their myriad locations, feminists have been able to see patriarchy when everyone else has seen only capitalism or militarism or racism or imperialism. It will be clear in the chapters that follow, I think, that I have become more and more convinced—as I have been tutored by others—that patriarchy must always be on the analytical couch.

Patriarchy is not old hat. And it is not fixed. The structures and beliefs that combine to privilege masculinity are continuously being modernized. Nowadays there are so many feminists and other women's advocates internationally sharing information, insights, and strategies that the enterprise of updating patriarchy is perhaps less assured of success than it has ever been.

Still, every new constitution drafting, every new economic planning, every new treaty negotiation provides at least the opportunity for those who benefit from the privileging of masculinity to equip patriarchy with a deceptive "new look." Patriarchy, consequently, can be as fashionable as hiring Bechtel, Lockheed, and other private military contractors to carry on the tasks of foreign occupation. That is, as the U.S. government's strategists seek to give their postwar reconstruction steps in Iraq and Afghanistan the look of something that is the opposite of old-fashioned dictatorships and imperialism, in practice they are paying some of the most profoundly masculinity-privileging organizations to carry out this imperial agenda. What is allegedly new thus may be reproducing something that is all too familiar. Patriarchy can be as ubiquitous as nationalism, patriotism, and postwar reconstruction.

So it is always risky to assume that the only power structures and related ideological justifications to be on the look out for are capitalism, militarism, racism, and imperialism. The question I have come to think we must always pose is: How much of what is going on here is caused by the workings of patriarchy? Sometimes patriarchy may be only a small part of the explanation. Other times patriarchy may hold the causal key. We will never know unless we ask, unless we seriously investigate how and why masculinity is privileged — and how much of that privileging depends on controlling women or drawing them into complicity.

The newest path down which my feminist curiosity has been taking me is marked "Girlhood." My own girlhood, to be exact.

Part 4 in this book is a small sampling of what I'm discovering as I take a fresh look at my own girlhood in a wartime New York suburb. As I dig away, I am becoming curious about how a middle-class American girlhood, even that of a "tomboy," was subtly feminized. At the same time I am trying to see if I can figure out how my girlhood was militarized — in the games my friends and I played on Aldershot Lane, in the songs I diligently memorized off of vinyl records, in the ways I imagined the lives of my mother and my father during those wartime and postwar years. This exploration is a work-in-progress. At the moment, as you will see, I have more questions than answers. But I'm learning a lot about the feminization and militarization of a seemingly ordinary girlhood by just being curious. Even the format I've chosen is different, unlike any other I've ever tried. I think because my whole stance in this effort is not one of explaining, but one of quizzicalness, the lines come to me in abbreviated form. The usual lengthy expository prose just doesn't seem right for this newest "dig."

At the same time, as I have been seeking to look at one girlhood afresh, I have been asking new questions about what it takes — how much dismantling of patriarchal relations between women, men, and states it takes — to achieve genuine and lasting *de*militarization. Some of the most exciting feminist questioning being done today is by feminists working to support women in what are often called now "postconflict zones." They have been generous in teaching me about the often surprising layers of masculinized public and private relationships that need to be exposed and unpacked in order to effect more than superficial demilitarization. I am fortunate to count among these feminist demilitarizing teachers/ thinkers/activists Cynthia Cockburn, Dyan Mazurana, Carol

Cohn, Felicity Hill, Vanessa Farr, Angela Raven-Roberts, Sandra Whitworth, Wenona Giles, Nic Marsh, Suzanne Williams, Laura Hammond, and Vijaya Joshi.

Among those people who recently have done the most to make me more curious about the ways in which patriarchy and militarization work together in American women's and men's lives have been feminists in Japan, Korea, and Turkey. Japanese, Korean, and Turkish feminists are not just living with, and revealing, the gendered effects of U.S. patriarchal militarism. They also are energetically exploring precisely how the workings of their own homegrown varieties of patriarchy and militarization combine with those of the United States to create and sustain the sorts of international alliances that deepen the privileging of certain forms of masculinity. These Turkish, Korean, and Japanese feminists warn against imagining that any brand of nationalism uninformed by feminist understandings can, by itself, effectively dismantle the operations of militarization and masculinized privilege in women's lives. I am particularly grateful to Ruri Ito and her feminist colleagues in Tokyo at Ochanomizu University's Institute for Gender Studies, as well as Japanese feminists in Kyushu and Okinawa; to Eun Shil Kim, Insook Kwon, the editorial group of *If* magazine, and their feminist colleagues in Seoul; and to Ayse Gul Altinay and the other brave feminist thinkers and activists throughout Turkey. They each have been stretching me to ask new questions; all have energized me so that I won't be comforted by too-easy answers.

For more than a decade now Naomi Schneider of the University of California Press has been my editor, sounding board, and friend. I am fortunate indeed. Sue Heinemann, Sierra Filucci, and all the wonderful people of the Press are real "pros."

Joni Seager is a leading feminist geographer and author of the astounding *Penguin Atlas of Women in the World*, whose new edition she has just published (2003). As a partner, Joni has been wonderfully generous, sharing with me with her Canadian consciousness, her worldly inquisitiveness, her genius for finding just the right turn of phrase, and her mischievous irreverence.

My ever-stretchy local reading and writing friends include Serena Hilsinger, Lois Brynes, Laura Zimmerman, Julie Abraham, Amy Lang, Wendy Luttrell, Robert Shreefter, Madeline Drexler, and E. J. Graff. This book is dedicated to Gilda Bruckman and Judy Wachs, my longest feminist best pals, so curious, generous, and witty. Friendship matters.

PART ONE

Sneakers, Silences, and Surprises

The Surprised Feminist

Predicting never has been my preferred vocation. Friends have to bribe me to go with them to sci-fi movies. Reading academic "ten-year plans" almost never puts me on the edge of my seat. So, I confess, I am quite daunted at the prospect of responding to an enticing invitation from the feminist journal *Signs* to spell out even tentative hunches about where feminist scholarship — especially activist-minded scholarship — will be heading in the twenty-first century.

Surprise. I have come to think that the capacity to be surprised — and to *admit* it — is an undervalued feminist attribute. To be surprised is to have one's current explanatory notions, and thus one's predictive assumptions, thrown into confusion. In both academic life and activist public life in most cultures, one is socialized to deny surprise. It is as if admitting surprise jeopardized one's hard-earned credibility. And credibility, something necessarily bestowed by others, is the bedrock of status. To deny surprise, to sweep confusion under the rug, thus may be especially tempting for feminists, since in societies ranging from Serbia to the United States, from Vietnam to Italy, our purchase on status is insecure early in this new millennium. Better to assume the "Oh, well, of course it would turn out like that" pose.

This, however, seems to me to be an increasingly risky, if understandable, inclination. Being open to surprise, being ready to publicly acknowledge surprise, may be among the most useful attitudes to adopt to prepare one's feminist self for what now lies ahead.

For all of my daily attempts to listen to and mull about the world, I did not predict, did not anticipate these late-twentieth-century occurrences:

the NATO-ization of human rights

the fall of Indonesia's Suharto

the collapse of the Brazilian economy

the Canadian Inuits' adoption of a gender-equality principle for their new territorial Nunavut parliament

the recruitment of girl children into the Sierra Leone rebel army

the rise of the Kosovo Liberation Army

the British arrest of Chilean ex-dictator Augusto Pinochet

Harvard's decision to award male scholars scarce fellowships at Radcliffe's Bunting Institute

All of these events and the dynamics that brought them about are deeply gendered. That is, women and men played different roles in them. Moreover, they have had quite different effects on ideas about femininity and masculinity. The ways particular women of distinct citizenship statuses, social classes, ethnic groups, and

In Liberia fifteen-year-old Rachel Wesseh joined one of the country's insurgent armies a year after her mother was raped. She told *Washington Post*
reporter Emily Wax, "I was hurting so deeply. So I became a fighter. What
was I doing with my life here, anyway?" The male officer watching her
here called himself Rachel's "boyfriend." Other girls who have joined (or
been abducted by) insurgent and government forces have reported sexual
abuse by the men in those forces. (Photo by Michel Ducille, © 2003, *The
Washington Post*, reprinted with permission)

racialized identities respond to each of these events is certain to
determine the respective depth or shallowness of its long-term
consequences in the twenty-first century. My surprise at Suharto's
1998 fall suggests that I underestimated the breadth of Indonesians' political disaffection, even though I was trying hard to
chart the organizing efforts of Nike's Indonesian women sneaker-
factory workers. My surprise at Ottawa officials' 1999 agreement
to establish Nunavut and at local Inuits' decision to institutional-
ize a fifty-fifty female/male legislative representation reveals the
inadequacy of my long-standing curiosity about the politics of

Native Canadian women. Being caught off guard by the Kosovo Liberation Army's militarized emergence is a result of having paid insufficient attention to the impacts of the oppressive policies of Slobodan Milosevic, Yugoslavia's 1990s president, on Kosovar young men's ethnicized sense of their own masculinity.

The list of embarrassments goes on. My feminist eyebrows went up at:

- the success of the U.S. Women's National Basketball Association
- the post-bubble economy corporate layoffs of Japanese clerical "office ladies"
- the reemergence of butch/fem role-playing among many young American lesbians
- the rising number of Mexican men working in border *maquiladoras* (assembly plants)
- the appearance of Russian women in the brothels of Thailand and Israel

Admitting my surprise is the only way I am going to be able to take fresh stock of my feminist analyses of developments both far afield and close to home. If I worked hard enough, I probably could manage to fit the rising unemployment of Japanese clerical workers into my existing concepts of the sexual division of labor. I could explain Japanese corporate executives' decisions to lay off some of their most feminized labor not in terms of the classic workings of cheapening labor but in terms of those executives' acceptance of equally classic notions that privilege men's employment in times of economic depression. Likewise, I might be able to explain the success of the American women's professional basketball league in terms of patriarchy's famed adaptiveness. After all, at the same time gifted women athletes are gaining a thin slice of ESPN's prime-time television coverage, Reebok and Nike are commodifying those same women's bodies, and more and more men are vying to coach those women's (and their younger school-girl sisters') sports teams. That is, whenever one is surprised, one most likely can manage to squeeze the new development into a comfortable, worn conceptual shoe. And this effort is worth the try. Maybe an existing idea does satisfactorily explain the surprising phenomenon. Certainly, sexual divisions of labor and adaptive patriarchy are not concepts that any feminist should rush to dump. But one needs to make that explanatory effort in a spirit of willingness to let go, willingness to think afresh.

It is often in the classroom that a feminist academic is most routinely tested in her commitment to acknowledging surprise. Say I have just made a point — about Canadians' political culture or about the role of misogyny in fueling the Rwandan genocide — when a student raises her hand and describes something she has observed that doesn't jibe at all with my analytical argument. What do I do? I am tempted to commend the student for her interesting contribution but then to move right into reworking it so that it somehow confirms my point. What I need to do, though, is to pause and say, "Gee, that's surprising. Let's all think about what this new information does to my earlier analysis." It is amazing how much guts, or at least stamina, it takes to do this. It may take even a larger dose of these resources to do it on a prestigious conference panel or in an intense strategy session.

At the time when I was drafting this short essay in early 1999, I had to practice the art of admitting surprise at a number of developments:

the Columbine High School massacre in Colorado

nightly televised images of Kosovo refugee "women and
children"

British prime minister Tony Blair's outmilitarizing all of his
NATO colleagues

learning about a strand of Tibetan culture that celebrates
male warriors

the Pentagon's decision to extend its Junior ROTC military
training program into middle schools

When the latest news is so dismayingly patriarchal, it is natural
for anyone with a hint of feminist consciousness to think, "Here
we go again." Yet there is a very fine line, sometimes, between a
sharp vision that can see clearly the perpetuating dynamics of patriarchal structures and a cynicism that dulls curiosity — curiosity
about exactly why two Colorado boys used guns and explosives to
express their masculinized adolescent alienation or about precisely what gender rearrangements occurred in an Albanian tent
city. Seeing patriarchy, even misogyny, is not enough. In each instance, we need to know exactly how it works and whether, even
if continuing, it has been contested. At a gross level of analysis
the patriarchal outcomes may seem to be more of the same, but
discovering what is producing them may come as a surprise.

Thus, as we go forward in the twenty-first century, feminists
inside and outside academia need to be on our guard against a
cynical form of knowing. We need to send the roots of our curiosity down ever deeper. We need to stand ready to be surprised — to admit surprise and build on it. It is bound to enliven
our teaching, broaden our conversations, and make our strategies
more savvy.

CHAPTER 2

Margins, Silences, and Bottom Rungs

How to Overcome the Underestimation of Power in the Study of International Relations

When I think about what it is that seems so unrealistic (yes, that loaded term) in most formal analyses of international politics, what strikes me is how far their authors are willing to go in *under*estimating the amounts and varieties of power it takes to form and sustain any given set of relationships between states. This conclusion, of course, rings oddly. So many analysts, after all, profess to be interested chiefly in power — who has it, how they got it, what they try to do with it. Their profession notwithstanding, I believe that by concentrating so single-mindedly on what is referred to euphemistically as the "center," scores of analysts have produced a naive portrait of how international politics really (there's that tricky concept again) works.

No individual or social group finds itself on the "margins" of any web of relationships — a football league, an industry, an empire, a military alliance, a state — without some other individual or group having accumulated enough power to create the "center" somewhere else. Beyond its creation, there is the yearly and daily business of maintaining the margin where it currently is and the center where it now is. It is harder for those at the alleged center to hear the hopes, fears, and explanations of those on the margins, not because of physical distance — the margin may be two blocks from the White House, four stops on the Paris metro from the Quai d'Orsay — but because it takes resources and access to be "heard" when and where it matters. Consequently, those who reside at the margins tend to be those deemed "silent." They are either imagined to have voices that simply cannot be heard from so far away or portrayed as lacking language and articulateness altogether: the taciturn Indian, the deferential peasant, the shy woman.

None of this amounts to an earth-shattering revelation, but let's continue. Traveling from the center to the margins is not traversing a horizontal plane, even if one does move horizontally from Jakarta to West Irian or from London to Aberystwyth. It is making a journey along a vertical relationship, from the top of a political pyramid down to its base. Those apparently silent on the margins are actually those at the bottom of the pyramid of power. Thus it is that people of West Irian have more in common politically with African Americans living in row houses a stone's throw from the White House than they do with the ethnic Javanese military commander whose headquarters is uncomfortably close by. Thus, too, a manager of a large fruit farm in the south of Chile is more likely to have his (no pronoun is casually employed) needs taken seriously in that country's center of power than is the maid who lives a mere lung-clogging half-hour bus ride away from La Moreda, Chile's presidential palace.

Margins, silences, and bottom rungs — these descriptors express different qualities, but they have as a common denominator lack of public power and being the object of other people's power.

Fine. That isn't too hard to accept. But one might still argue that that does not mean that those people lacking significant public leverage, living on the margins, whose voices are hard to hear at the center, are inherently interesting. Perhaps socialist scholars in Britain's History Workshop interviewing East London garment workers or African feminist oral historians working in the Western Cape will devote scarce time and recording tape to the powerless. But that is because they apparently are committed to a democratic sort of scholarly practice that presumes value in human experience for its own sake: if a person dwells on this planet, she or he is worthy of being recorded; to be recorded assigns dignity; all humans, because of their humanity, possess dignity, or should.

This is a woefully incomplete sketch of both socialist and feminist scholarly motivation, but my guess is that it is one widely held.

Such a humanitarian, populist approach, whatever motivates it, is still not, it is argued, what a formal analysis of international politics is all about. Or, rather, most international relations analysts feel ambivalent toward the relevance of human dignity and democracy to their own intellectual enterprise. They derive from the tradition of the European Enlightenment a belief in the human capacity to reason and, with that reason, the possibility of uncovering untainted universal truths. This is the same conviction that has permitted so many people to imagine that democratic forms of governance are within human grasp — at least for those, the Enlightenment's inheritors would caution, who have realized their human potential for reason, that is men who have been thoroughly assimilated into the culture of Western Europe.[1] Still, as practiced, this same Enlightenment-derived faith espouses a scientific pursuit "free" of the burdens of identity and space. So few mainstream academic international relations analysts would admit that they are designing their research self-consciously to accord with democratic values of either the social-ist or feminist sort. The raison d'être for studying international politics, instead, is *explanation*. One is on the trail of cause and effect. And when sorting out cause and effect, one has to be eco-nomical, discriminating. Everything is not the cause of some one thing. Likewise, something does not cause every single thing. For an explanation to be useful, a great deal of human dignity has to be left on the cutting-room floor.

By definition, people on the margins, those who are silenced, those perched on the bottom rung, are precisely those who, for whatever reason — and the reasons may be grossly unjust — lack what it takes to have a meaningful impact on the course of those particular events that together cause certain regional or world patterns to take the shape they do. Silenced marginalized people hovering on the lower rungs of any international hierarchy may be able to find the voice to sing while doing their laundry, may be able to affect the local patterns of intermarriage, may even be able to create micro-pyramids of inequality. Not everyone on the bottom rung has a zinc roof; some only have thatched. Not everyone at the bottom carries equal weight when the decision is made whether to use a condom in bed at night. Yet none of these distinctions is of a potency that can be decisive in determining flows of weapons trade, patterns of investment, rules for interstate peace. Thus conventional analysts of international affairs feel justified in ignoring them.

"Thank goodness for the anthropologists," these analysts might sigh. "Let *them* listen to the laundry lyrics, let *them* meticulously chart those mind-boggling kinship patterns and the local mal-distribution of zinc roofs. They can afford," the busy cause-and-effect rationalist might say, "to be open to the sort of populist values imported by socialists and feminists. None of them has to shoulder the heavy responsibility of finding economical explanations for the workings of entire international systems."

To study the powerful is not autocratic. It is simply reasonable. Really?

There is, I think, a serious flaw in this analytical economy, and in the common research strategy that flows from it. It presumes that margins, silences, and bottom rungs are so naturally marginal, silent, and far from power that exactly how they are *kept* there could not possibly be of interest to the reasoning, reasonable explainer. A consequence of this presumption is that the actual amount and the amazing variety of power that are required to keep the voices on the margins from having the right language and enough volume to be heard at the center in ways that might send shivers up and down the ladder are never fully tallied. Power, of course, only exists within a relationship. So omitting myriad strands of power amounts to exaggerating the simplicity of the entire political system. Today's conventional portrait of international politics thus too often ends up looking like a Superman comic strip, whereas it probably should resemble a Jackson Pollock painting.

A second consequence of this presumption — that margins stay marginal, the silent stay voiceless, and ladders are never turned upside down — is that many orthodox analysts of international politics are caught by surprise. If one imagines that unequal power relationships — the ones that allow the analyst the luxury of focusing only on the people at the top, the decision-makers with foreign policy portfolios — are natural (well, almost natural, so firmly anchored in place that they might as well be natural), then one is very likely to be uncomfortably jolted by any tremors that jeopardize those unequal power relationships.

Let's take the Mayan Indians of Chiapas, the southern state of Mexico. Here may be one of the groups that an efficient international politics realist could quintessentially afford to "leave to the anthropologists" — or to the socialists or the feminists. No explanatory risks here. Keep your hotel reservations restricted to the capital. Fly down (one is unlikely to be flying up) to Mexico City with a stopover in Tijuana or Juarez perhaps. Maquiladora managers (Mexican, American, and Japanese) in these sprawling border cities have become too vocal and visible to be defined as inhabiting the margins, even if geographically that is precisely where they reside. Rent a Hertz car in the capital later and drive up to talk to some of the bankers in the commercially important city of Monterrey for a couple of days if necessary.

Chiapas fits all the criteria of a classically marginal political space. Mexico City seems a world away from the farms, villages, and (disappearing) forests of Chiapas, bordering Guatemala. To border on Guatemala certainly is different from bordering on the United States. The latter bordering existence magnifies political voice, the former muffles it. As poor peasants, many of whom are ethnic Indians from a multiplicity of distinct communities too easily labeled "Mayan," in a society that accords influence to agribusiness entrepreneurs, joint venture industrialists, and senior state technocrats with ties to the long-ruling Institutional Revolutionary Party (the PRI), the majority of Chiapas residents rarely have had their voices heard in the rooms where national decisions were being made. Indian motifs may decorate Diego Rivera's heroic murals, but being painted on a public wall does not amount to having a voice in Mexican affairs. Octavio Paz, Mexico's Nobel laureate, knew what he was talking about when he said that the Spanish conquistadors and their bourgeois mestizo successors each adopted the Aztec pyramid as their model for a political order.[2] No one has been more unarguably shoved to the modern Mexican pyramid's base than poor Indian-dialect-speaking rural Chiapans.

So it made little sense for international relations specialists to devote any thought in the 1990s to Chiapas when they were seeking to explain why the North American Free Trade Agreement (NAFTA) was being negotiated when it was and in the fashion that it was. Not paying any attention to the Mohawks and Cree of Canada hadn't cost analysts anything when trying to explain the origins and outcome of NAFTA's precursor, the U.S.-Canada Free Trade Agreement, had it? No more than not wondering whether the French-speaking Quebecois women who provided the swing vote in the earlier Quebec separatist referendum would do so again when the vote was retaken in 1995. No more than had neglecting Asian Canadian women sewing in garment factories along Toronto's Spadina Avenue.[3]

"Mexico" never negotiated with "the United States," any more than four years earlier "Canada" had negotiated with "the United States." Particular officials of particular ruling regimes conducted these complex negotiations under the more or less credible pretense that the states they spoke for were functioning and durable.

Even though we all know this, we frequently slip into using these misleading lazy shorthands. They may save breath, but they disguise the artifice that is the ultimate foundation of every state. In disciplinary terms, international relations analysts rest too heavily on the presumptions derived from their comparative politics colleagues without examining them very closely. Maybe international relations specialists need to do more of their own homework. Maybe they need to make their own assessments about the modes of power it is taking at any time to keep these fictions — "Mexico," or "Canada" or "the United States" — glued together. By leaving it all to their friends in comparative politics — who in turn typically rely heavily on the observations of anthropologists — international relations analysts (1) underestimate the amount and varieties of power operating in any interstate relationship and (2) mistakenly assume that the narrative's "plot" is far more simple and unidirectional than it may in truth be. Taking seriously the experiences and responses — even explanatory understandings — of people living voiceless out on the margins, down at the bottom, is one of the most efficient ways I know to accurately estimate just how fragile that artifice is, just how far off the mark it is to describe "Mexico" as negotiating NAFTA with "the United States."

Actually, scholarly commentators specializing in Mexico have been trying for several decades, especially since the capital city massacre of 1968, to alert their colleagues to the fragility of the artifice that is the Mexican state.[4] They have tried to reveal just how much power and of what sorts it took not just to keep the PRI (and the party's leading figures, the *Priistas*) in control of the state from 1929 to the end of the twentieth century, but what consequences this had for Mexican state evolution. Until 1994, the skill and dexterity poured into this state construction and maintenance enterprise matched those of Japan's long-ruling Liberal Democrats and Italy's long-ruling Christian Democrats.

Rosario Castellanos gave us a finely drawn portrait of Chiapas political subtleties in her famous novel *The Nine Guardians.*[5] Castellanos herself grew up in the 1930s as a child of cattle-ranching, coffee-growing hacienda owners. Writing in the 1950s, she looked back at this decade in the political evolution of the Mexican *Priista* state, believing that inspection of intimate routines and tensions woven into the lives of Chiapas Indians and their Hispanicized local *patrons* could expose the gendered and racialized contradictions running through that state system even then, even at the moment in the 1930s that commentators typically point to as the moment when the current Mexican state system was successfully consolidated. It was the decades-long perpetuation of this particular statist formula — with regular infusions of pragmatic refinements always far short of radical change — crafted by the PRI under populist president Lázaro Cárdenas that made the NAFTA negotiations possible in the early 1990s. Assuming that this formula remained fundamentally unassailable led the post–Cold War analysts to imagine that neglecting marginalized Chiapas seemed reasonable and efficient.

Castellanos introduces us to 1930s Chiapas politics by putting us in the shoes of a white young Mexican girl who feels closer to her Mayan nanny than to her privileged mother and father.

> I go to the kitchen where Nana is heating coffee. . . . I sniff in the larder. I like to see the colour of the butter and to touch the bloom of the fruit, and peel the onion skins. . . .
> "Just look what they've done to me."

Pulling up her *tzec*, Nana shows me a soft reddish wound disfiguring her knee. . . .

"Why do they hurt you?"

"Because I was brought up in your house. Because I love your parents, and Mario, and you."

"Is it wicked to love us?"

"It's wicked to love those that give orders and have posses-
sions. That's what the law says. . . ."

I go away, sad because of what I've just heard. My father dismisses the Indians with a gesture, and lies on in the ham-
mock reading. I see him now for the first time. He's the one who gives the orders and owns things.[6]

Rosario Castellanos is describing a racialized 1930s political economy that is being challenged both by a new generation of Mayans who have traveled outside Chiapas and have learned Spanish, the patrons' language, and by PRI president Cárdenas, who is fashioning a new populist mantle for his party, a mantle he hopes will end the peasants' revolution yet domesticate the generals and keep the loyalty of both the new commercial class and the old landowning rural elite. For Cárdenas and the emergent Mexican state elite the stakes are not merely national; they are continental, even hemispheric. Woodrow Wilson's American military incursion across the border is still fresh in Mexicans' minds. Only if the PRI's strategy for state consolidation succeeds, at least minimally, can the statist boundaries within the hemisphere gel along lines that will keep American imperialism at bay.[7] It will take more than the taming of bandits and the nationalizing of foreign-
owned oil companies; it will, Cárdenas believes, require co-opting the *patrons*, channeling the resentments of their Indian employees. Listening to women of any class? Perhaps this will not be neces-

sary at this juncture in the hemisphere's statist stabilization, so long as husbands and fathers can keep "their women" confined to the margins of public affairs.

Nana, herself ambivalent and seemingly powerless, nonetheless has aided the Cárdenas state-building, hemispherically transformative enterprise. She has caused a little white girl to see her own father with new racially conscious eyes. Still, Castellanos's fictional hacienda-owning father is confident he can play his own *patron's* shell game. Few states are so powerful that policies issued at the center can be assured faithful implementation on the margins, especially if the state itself depends on the continuing support of these very people, people with privilege derived from accumulating the resources on the margins, it is calling upon to sacrifice a good portion of their income and their sense of class honor. Thus Castellanos puts these confident words into the father's mouth:

> "Go on, Jaime, you almost scared me. When I saw you arrive with that hang-dog look I thought there really had been some disaster. But this [the government's new requirement that hacienda owners build and staff schools for their Indian employees] isn't important. You remember when they fixed the minimum salary? Our hearts went into our boots. It was the end of everything. And what happened? We're slippery lizards and they can't catch us as easily as all that. We discovered a ruse by which we didn't have to pay."
>
> "No Indian's worth seventy-five *centavos* a day. Nor even a month."
>
> "Besides, I ask you, what would they do with the money? Only get drunk."[8]

And, of course, the hierarchical relationships that undergirded the region's political system and thus the contradiction-ridden state itself are not based on cattle and coffee alone. Not even on language. There's always the politics of sexuality.

Castellanos, raised in a privileged Spanish-speaking, landowning white family, but learning the local Mayan language by listening to her nanny, employed a feminist imagination to create credible renditions of Mayan Indians' political discussions. She did not lump all Chiapas Indians together in a single ungendered literary stew; she refrained from putting political thoughts into the minds and mouths of Indian men alone; nor did she turn all her Indian women characters into activist popular heroes, as if they were unfettered by the oppressive interplay of Mayan and Hispanicized patriarchal expectations. It had taken not just racialized class hierarchies but also daily reinforcement of complementary notions about ranchers' wives and peasants' wives to sustain the political systems of Chiapas, and thus of Mexico, for generations. To ignore those political structures, Rosario Castellanos implied, would be to present a far too naive analysis of the chances of President Lázaro Cárdenas's success.[9]

> Felipe rocked with laughter. His wife watched him terrified, thinking he'd gone off his head.
>
> "I'm remembering what I saw in Tapachula. There are whites so poor they beg and drop with fever on the streets."
>
> The rest hardened their eyes unbelieving.
>
> "It was in Tapachula that they gave me the paper to read, and it speaks well, I understood what it says: that we're equal to white men. . . . On the oath of the President of the Republic. . . ."
>
> Felipe's wife slipped silently to the door. She couldn't go on listening. . . .
>
> Juana had borne no children. . . . In vain she pounded the herbs the women recommended. . . . Shame had fallen upon

her. But in spite of everything, Felipe did not want to leave
her. Whenever he went away — for he seemed to be a rolling
stone — she stayed sitting with clasped hands as if she had
said goodbye to him forever. Yet Felipe always returned.
But this time, coming back from Tapachula, he wasn't the
same anymore. His mouth was full of disrespectful words
and bold opinions. She, being humble and still full of gratitude to him, did not repudiate him in front of the rest but
kept her thoughts silent and secret. She feared this man
whom the lands of the seacoast had thrown her back, bitter
and harsh as salt, a trouble-maker. . . . She longed for him
to be off once again. Far, far away. And that he'd never come
back.[10]

Hierarchies are multiple, because forms of political power are
diverse. But the several hierarchies do not sit on the social land-
scape like tuna, egg, and cheese sandwiches sitting on an icy cafe-
teria counter, diversely multiple but unconnected. They relate to
each other, sometimes in ways that subvert one another, sometimes in ways that provide each with its respective resiliency. The
bedroom's hierarchy is not unconnected to the hierarchies of the
international coffee exchange or of the foreign ministry. The
questions to pose, then, are: When and how exactly are these hierarchies connected? With what consequences for the lives lived
in bedrooms, on trading floors, and around diplomatic tables?

For instance, a male rancher's ability to bargain with central
state officials over land reform and tariff proposals depends in no
small part on his confidence — and his credibility in the eyes of
the state official — in his ability to control his ranch employees,
his confidence that they won't be able to bargain with that same
official behind his back, his confidence that they, or at least most
of them, wouldn't even imagine that bargaining independently

with the state was in their own interests. Part of that confidence, and thus part of the male rancher's political arsenal, derives from his ongoing sexual access to the women among his employees and their families. Part of the weakening of his employees' sense of their own agency in dealings with state officials comes from the humiliation or even confusion that such masculinized access sows. The male state official, for his part, is likely to accept the rancher's confident political stance — and thus be more receptive to his arguments about land politics and their implications for international trade negotiations — precisely because he shares the rancher's masculinized version of how race and class hierarchies are effectively sustained. The official sees those unequal sexual encounters as so natural that he never even imagines they require discussing, except perhaps as a basis for common masculine bonding to create mutual comfort between the two men before the "real" political bargaining begins.

Castellanos had spent years eavesdropping on masculinized conversations among the white landowning Mexican men who dominated Chiapas.

> Cesar and Ernesto went down the steps from the veranda to the farmyard. They mounted, and at a slow trot put the house behind them. . . . The women, kneeling on the ground to pound the grain, stopped their tasks and sat quietly with arms rigid, as if rooted into the stone of their mortars, their slack breasts hanging loose in their blouses. They watched the two men pass. . . .
>
> "There are the Indian women to do your bidding, Ernesto. We'll be looking out for one of these brats to turn up with your complexion. . . . Beggars can't be choosers. I'm talking from experience."
>
> "You?"

"Why so surprised? Yes, me. Like everyone I've a sprin-
kling of children among them."

It was doing them a favor, really, because after that the
Indian women were more sought after and could marry
where they liked. The Indian always recognized this virtue
in his woman, that the *Patron* had found pleasure in her. And
the children among those that hung about the big house and
served there faithfully.[11]

Unless, that is, the state could expand its civil service broadly
enough to absorb some of those offspring, especially the sons, the
"godsons." In the 1930s, the postrevolutionary Mexican state was
indeed expanding. The ruling party, the party that Cárdenas was
attempting to provide with lasting access to this state, was (and is)
called the *Institutional* Revolutionary Party.

"Don't you recognize me, Don Cesar?"

Cesar scrutinized him. The swart face and bushy eyebrows
awakened no memory.

"I'm Gonzalo Utrilla, son of Georgia that was."

"You? But why did no one tell me? Look, Zoraida, it's my
godson. . . . And now you're a fine strapping man."

"All thanks to your care, Godfather."

Cesar decided to ignore the irony in this. . . .

"I work for the Government. . . ."

All enemies are big ones, Cesar thought. If only he'd been
kinder to this Gonzalo when he was a bit of an Indian lad! . . .

"What exactly is your work?"

"I'm an agrarian inspector."[12]

Even this unfair excerpting of Castellanos's richly textured
novel offers up a variety of forms of power that is quite mind-
boggling. Bureaucratic co-optation, racial intimidation, exclusive

access to the language of the state, marital pressures, elite connections, land proprietorship, denial of access to schooling, sexual imposition, ownership of models for sexual emulation, employment patronage. And this list still omits the distribution of
formal voting rights to some (men), while withholding them
from others (women would not manage to win the vote until
1953, almost four decades after the Mexican revolution, during
which anticlerical revolutionary men argued that women would
use their votes to support the Church). The list also still omits
access to private armies' force and to federal police and military
force. When was the last time one saw an analysis of an international trade negotiation — and its implications — that gave serious
attention to landowners' private armies (called *mapaches* in 1930s
Chiapas, *guardias blancas* in 1990s Chiapas)?[13] What is the equivalent omission in the study of the European Union, of the emergence of Asia's newly industrializing "tigers"?

The surprising Chiapas peasant rebellion launched in January
1994 was led by an unknown organization whose members called
themselves the Zapatista National Liberation Army (ZNLA).
Officials of the PRI-dominated government of President Carlos
Salinas initially tried to portray the ZNLA as urban intellectuals,
communist agitators, outsiders, hiding under bandannas and ski
masks while opportunistically exploiting the still-potent legend
of Mexico's peasant revolutionary hero Emiliano Zapata. This
state portrayal soon had to be abandoned. It was too clear that
the majority of the rebels were poor peasants, many identifying
themselves as Mayan Indians, though this is a many-sided and
fluid identity. The Zapatistas and their less organized supporters
were the economically, culturally, and politically disenfranchised
of Chiapas, people who remembered the unfulfilled revolution-

legitimizing promises of 1910 and the unfulfilled *Priista* state-legitimizing promises of the 1930s.[14]

The Zapatista rebels' selection of January 1994 as a moment for direct confrontation with the Chiapas PRI-rancher alliance, the federal military, and the central regime of President Carlos Salinas apparently was based in part on their assessment of diminishing local alternatives. Their selection of early 1994, however, also seemed to stem from their monitoring of the government's half-hearted electoral reforms in preparation for the crucial August 1994 nationwide election of Salinas's presidential successor as well as their accounting of the NAFTA negotiations, its winners and losers. These peasant farmers of Chiapas were doing what so many international relations commentators were not: tracing causal connections between local political economies, state system contradictions, and emergent interstate relationships. They connected the Mexican state's bowing to the U.S. state's pressure to the lowering and eventual abandoning of state corn price subsidies and to the fall in international oil prices, on which many male Indians had come to depend as part-time petroleum workers. They connected those trends to the escalating violence wielded by *guardias blancas* hired by wealthy Chiapas landowners who thought that by driving Indians off land carved out of the rainforest they could attract U.S. investors into joint cattle-raising NAFTA-fueled ventures. In their sophisticated international analysis, the Zapatistas went still further: they contended that none of these moves would have been possible were not the PRI able to control the national political system through an electoral process that ensured that poor peasants' voices could not have an impact on state decision-making.[15]

In their formal communiqué, the ZNLA leadership spoke a

great deal about the structural conditions for marginalized people gaining a "voice":

> To the People of Mexico:
> To the Peoples and Governments of the World:
> To the national and international Press:
> Brothers:
> . . . When the [ZNLA] was only a shadow, creeping through the mist and darkness of the jungle, when the words "justice," "liberty" and "democracy" were only that: words; barely a dream that the elders of our communities, true guardians of our dead ancestors, had given us in the moment when day gives way to night, when hatred and fear began to grow in our hearts, when there was nothing but desperation; when times repeated themselves, with no way out, with no door, no tomorrow, when all was injustice, as it was, the true men spoke, the faceless ones, the ones who go by night, the ones who are jungle, and they said:
> ". . . Let not the voices of the few be silenced, but let them remain in their place, waiting until the thoughts and hearts become one in what is the will of the many and opinion from within and no outside force can break them nor divert their steps to other paths."
> Our path was always that the will of the many be in the hearts of the men and women who command. . . . Thus was born our strength in the jungle, he who leads obeys if he is true, and he who follows leads through the common heart of true men and women. Another word came from afar so that this government was named and this work gave the name "democracy" to our way that was from before words travelled.
> . . . We see that it is the few now who command, and they command without obeying, they lead commanding. And among the few they pass the power of command among

themselves, without hearing the many . . . the word comes
from afar says they lead without democracy, without the
command of the people, and we see that this unreason of
those who lead commanding, directs the road of our sorrows
and feeds the pain of our dead.

. . . We are despised, we are small, our word is muffled,
silence has inhabited our houses for a long time, the time has
come to speak for our hearts, for the hearts of others, from
the night and from the earth our dead should come, the face-
less ones, who are the jungle, who dress with war so their
voice will be heard, that their word later falls silent and they
return once again to the night and to the earth, that other
men and women may speak, who walk other lands, whose
words carry truth, who do not become lost in lies.[16]

The rebellion surprised everyone — almost: not the local
human rights monitors, not the liberation theology priests working in this southernmost state, not those farmers imprisoned for
petitioning the PRI governor for access to arable land, instead of
to the dregs that usually were handed out in the state's sporadic
land title distributions. Their voices had not been heard, or if
heard, not taken seriously, not heard as if what they had to say
mattered in the larger scheme of Mexican state affairs, not heard
as if their messages mattered for the evolution of continental politics, as if they mattered for understanding the tendencies in the
fluid post–Cold War international system. Instead, virtually all
the commentators had been recording the successes of *Salinismo*,
crediting the president's own brand of state refinement with not
only warding off serious electoral challenges but with navigating
the ship of state through the shoals of unequal continentalism
and into the safe post–Cold War harbor of NAFTA.[17]

What had been underestimated by most analysts, most of those following the making of the new "globalized" system in which trade apparently was replacing nuclear targeting as the medium of state security and interstate stability, was that the Mexican state system was in a condition of creeping crisis. While much attention had been focused, with good reason, on President Carlos Salinas's deft refurbishing of the PRI's famous patronage machine, too little attention had been paid by academic and media observers to the state's reliance on repression. Mexican human rights groups had been documenting the uses of coercion — state and parastate — yet these documents rarely were deemed relevant to international relations analysis.[18] Human rights reports opened a window into the ways in which male Chiapas large landowners, the grandsons (not the grandgodsons), had managed to weather the Cárdenas state-building innovations of the 1930s without surrendering much of their power. Human rights documents, when read along with Rosario Castellanos's novel, provided ample clues that the "Mexico" that was represented at the NAFTA bargaining table in the early 1990s had earned those inverted commas.

The Grupo Rosario Castellanos is one of the recent civic organizations that has provided the means for achieving such a surprising level of political mobilization in Chiapas.[19] It is one of several groups that women have organized to assess the relationships among patriarchal male practices, the *Priista* state formula, the Chiapas political economy, and NAFTA. It is no more adequate today to analyze international politics from the margins as if those politics were ungendered than it was in the 1930s when Rosario Castellanos was absorbing her early lessons about how political power is constituted. The Cold War was created and sustained by the flows of gendered forms of power; so too now are its endings — at the centers, on the margins, along the borders. And as in the previous international system, of 1946 to 1989, so too today, those forms of power are not always easy to see, their contestations not always easy to delineate. Via electronic mail, the Zapatista National Liberation Army distributed in the mid-1990s a document entitled "Women's Revolutionary Law." It declares that women "regardless of their race, creed, color or political affiliation" may be incorporated into the revolutionary struggle, so long as they "meet the demands of the exploited people." Among the ZNLA's principles spelled out in this document are women's "right to work and receive a just salary," women's right to "decide the number of children they have and care for," women's right "to be free of violence from both relatives and strangers" ("Rape will be severely punished"), women's right "to occupy positions of leadership in the organization and hold military ranks in the revolutionary armed forces."[20]

Precisely who wrote this and out of what process and with whose commitment of support is not yet clear. Early and sketchy reports suggested that the drafting of "Women's Revolutionary Law" was begun months before the open revolt in January 1994. These same reports described a woman member of the ZNLA's coordinating body, the Indigenous Revolutionary Clandestine Committee (CCRI), who went only by the name "Susana," as developing women's demands by "making the rounds of dozens of communities, speaking with groups of women to pull their ideas together"[21]

Mayan communities are described by outside anthropologists as being infused with a democratic culture, though they are also sustained in their present forms by patriarchal practices. Sometimes impressed by the former, a visitor can be tempted to overlook the latter. Thus a visiting *New York Times* reporter, trying to understand why so many Mayan peasants who did not take part in the 1994 uprising nonetheless voiced support for the ZNLA's objectives, spent time in El Carrizal, an Indian village whose members had been trying for over a decade to find a way to make the government respond to their legal land claims.

"In the afternoon, after the men return from the fields and the women are busy preparing the evening meal, a kind of assembly occurs in El Carrizal," the American observed.[22] Has the reporter prepared for his visit by reading Rosario Castellanos? Will he listen for who does not speak?

> The men sit on two benches made from tree trunks. These people do not vote in regular elections (it costs 50 cents to take the bus into town and it is just not worth it they say) but here all decisions are made democratically.
> This day they discussed the land conflict, again. . . . Those who want to speak leave the bench and sit on a rough white rock at the other end of the parallel rows, their hats at their feet.
> One old man in a ragged knit shirt placed his hat on the ground. "All of the newspapers all say that Mexico is at peace, that everyone now is happy because the fighting is over, they are wrong," he said. "Companions, it is true that in Mexico we are almost all equal. But what is equality here? It is that nobody has anything."[23]

Maybe "Susana" managed to get the village men to share a seat on the white rock with their wives and daughters when she came to formulate the Zapatista women's demands.

Looking at NAFTA from Chiapas, giving Mayan Indian women and men voices and visibility in an analysis of this major post–Cold War political construction, is not a matter of simply choosing post-positivist *Rashomon* over Enlightenment-inspired *Dragnet*. *Rashomon* was the highly acclaimed Japanese film that told the story of a highway robbery and abduction not just from the omnipotent — "true" — perspective of the filmmaker, but from the multiple — perhaps all "true" — perspectives of several of the characters. *Dragnet* was one of American television's most popular shows in the era of the small black-and-white screen. Joe Friday, the series' male protagonist, was a laconic police detective. His style was persistent and deadpan. Taking Chiapas landless peasants seriously does more than open questions about detective hero Joe Friday's "Just the facts, Ma'am" approach to international politics, though it certainly does do that. It does indeed appear to make far more sense to adopt a *Rashomon* posture, to assume that people playing different roles in any international phenomenon will understand its causes and its meanings differently. For instance, Benedict Kerkvliet and Resil Mojares have revealed how, by looking at the "February Revolution" that overthrew the Philippines' autocrat Ferdinand Marcos in 1986 not just from Manila and not just from the vantage point of Marcos and his chief elite allies and opponents, but from the multiple perspectives of provincial elites and ordinary citizens throughout the archipelago, we can gain a much clearer sense of exactly what cost the Marcos regime its legitimacy.[24] For students of international relations this *Rashomon* approach improves one's clarity of vision. One can more fully explain how the fall of Marcos led to the U.S. military being forced to give up its giant Subic Bay naval base, an installation constructed as pivotal to the American government's hegemony in the Pacific.

Similarly, if we take seriously the interplays of power in Chiapas when we explore post–Cold War attempts to integrate three North American political economies, we will, I think, comprehend the meanings of that complex process more fully. But this is only half the story. I believe that the 1994 Chiapas rebellion and its ripples that spread now throughout the Mexican political system — to press reporters' relations with the state, to the opposition parties' relations with electoral officials, to citizens' sense of their political capacities — reveal that those "facts" that are relevant to explaining any given international phenomenon are buried far deeper down in any political system than is typically imagined by academia's *Dragnet* afficionados. It is only by delving deeper into any political system, listening more attentively at its margins, that we can accurately estimate the powers it has taken to provide the state with the apparent stability that has permitted its elite to presume to speak on behalf of a coherent whole in interstate trade bargaining sessions. Only with this explicit political accounting can we explain why the evolving international system takes the turns it does today.

This effort is likely to reveal that there is much more power and many more forms of power in operation in international relations than is conventionally assumed. What has it taken to keep Mayan women off the white rocks? The answer to that question is pertinent to explaining the international politics of beef, oil, and coffee, and thus to explaining the newly competitive intrastate politics of parties and elections in Mexico, and therefore to making sense of the continental politics of NAFTA and consequently the politics of the post–Cold War world.

Sound far-fetched? I don't think so. As students of international politics, we need to become less parochial, more energetic, more curious. Joe Friday, the Enlightenment's policeman, may have gotten his man, but he probably underestimated the crime.

CHAPTER 3

The Globetrotting Sneaker

Four years after the fall of the Berlin Wall marked the end of the Cold War, Reebok, one of the fastest-growing companies in recent United States history, decided that the time had come to make its mark in Russia. Thus it was with considerable fanfare that Reebok's executives opened their first store in downtown Moscow in July 1993. A week after the grand opening, store managers described sales as well above expectations.

Reebok's opening in Moscow was the perfect post–Cold War scenario: commercial rivalry replacing military posturing, consumerist tastes homogenizing heretofore hostile peoples, capital and managerial expertise flowing freely across newly porous state borders. Russians suddenly had the freedom to spend money on U.S. cultural icons like athletic footwear, items priced above and beyond daily subsistence: at the end of 1993 the average Russian earned the equivalent of $40 a month. Shoes on display were in the $100 range. Almost 60 percent of Russia's single parents, most of whom were women, were living in poverty. Yet in

Moscow and Kiev, shoe promoters had begun targeting children, persuading them to pressure their mothers to spend money on stylish Western sneakers. And as far as strategy goes, athletic shoe giants have, you might say, a good track record. In the United States many inner-city boys who see basketball as a "ticket out of the ghetto" have become convinced that certain brand-name shoes will give them an edge.

But no matter where sneakers are bought or sold, the potency of their advertising imagery has made it easy to ignore this mundane fact: Shaquille O'Neal's Reeboks are stitched by someone; Michael Jordan's Nikes are stitched by someone — so are your roommate's, so are your grandmother's. Those someones are women, mostly Asian women who are supposed to believe that their "opportunity" to make sneakers for U.S. companies is a sign of their country's progress — just as a Russian woman's chance to spend two months' salary on a pair of shoes for her child allegedly symbolizes the new Russia.

As the global economy expands, sneaker executives are looking to pay women workers less and less, even though the shoes that they produce are capturing an ever-growing share of the footwear market. By the end of 1993 sales in the United States alone had reached $11.6 billion. Nike, the largest supplier of athletic footwear in the world, posted a record $298 million profit for 1993 — earnings that had nearly tripled in five years. And still today sneaker companies continue to refine their strategies for "global competitiveness" — hiring supposedly docile women to make their shoes, changing designs as quickly as we fickle customers change our tastes, and shifting factories from country to country as trade barriers rise and fall.

The logic of it all is really quite simple; yet trade agreements such as the North American Free Trade Agreement (NAFTA) and the World Trade Organization (WTO) are often talked about in a jargon that alienates us, as if they were technical matters fit only for economists and diplomats. The bottom line is that all companies operating overseas depend on trade agreements made between their own governments and the regimes ruling the countries in which they want to make or sell their products. Korean, Indonesian, and other women workers around the world know this better than anyone. They are tackling trade politics because they have learned from hard experience that the trade deals their governments sign do little to improve the lives of workers. Guarantees of fair, healthy labor practices, of the rights to speak freely and to organize independently, will usually be left out of trade pacts — and women will suffer. The 1990s passage of both NAFTA and WTO ensured that a growing number of private companies would now be competing across borders without restriction. The result? Big business would step up efforts to pit working women in industrialized countries against much lower-paid working women in "developing" countries, perpetuating the misleading notion that they are inevitable rivals with each other in the global job market.

All the "New World Order" really means to corporate giants like athletic shoemakers is that they now have the green light to accelerate long-standing industry practices. In the early 1980s the field marshals commanding Reebok and Nike, which are both now U.S.-based, decided to manufacture most of their sneakers in South Korea and Taiwan, hiring local women. L.A. Gear, Adidas, Fila, and Asics quickly followed their lead. In a short time, the coastal city of Pusan, South Korea, became the "sneaker capital of the world." Between 1982 and 1989 the

United States lost 58,500 footwear manufacturing jobs to cities like Pusan, which attracted sneaker executives because its location facilitated international transport. More to the point, in the 1960s to mid-1980s South Korea's government was a military government, and, as such, it had an interest in suppressing labor organizing. This same military government also had a comfortable military alliance with the United States government. Korean women at the time seemed accepting of Confucian philosophy, which measured a woman's morality by her willingness to work hard for her family's well-being and to acquiesce to her father's and husband's dictates. Their acceptance of Confucian values, when combined with their sense of patriotic duty, seemed to make South Korean women the ideal labor force for modern export-oriented factories.

U.S. and European sneaker company executives were also attracted by the ready supply of eager Korean male entrepreneurs with whom they could make profitable arrangements. This fact was central to Nike's strategy in particular. When they moved their production sites to Asia to lower labor costs, the executives of the Oregon-based company decided to reduce their corporate responsibilities further. Instead of owning factories outright, a more efficient strategy, Nike executives decided, would be to subcontract the manufacturing to wholly foreign-owned — in this case, South Korean — companies. The new American managerial attitude was: Let Korean male managers be responsible for workers' health and safety. Let them negotiate with newly emergent unions. Nike officials, safely ensconced in their Oregon offices, would retain control over those parts of sneaker production that gave them the greatest professional satisfaction and the ultimate word on the product: design and marketing. Although Nike was following in the historic footsteps of garment and textile manufacturers, it set the trend for the rest of the athletic footwear industry.

At the same time, nevertheless, women workers were developing their own strategies. As the South Korean pro-democracy movement grew throughout the 1980s, increasing numbers of women rejected traditional notions of feminine duty. Women began organizing in response to the dangerous working conditions, daily humiliations, and low pay built into their work. Such resistance was profoundly threatening to the government, since South Korea's emergence as an industrialized "tiger" had depended on women accepting their feminized role in growing industries like sneaker manufacture. If women reimagined their lives as daughters, as wives, as workers, as citizens, it wouldn't just rattle their Korean employers and those men's foreign corporate clients; it would shake the very foundations of the whole political system. At the first sign of trouble, factory managers called in government riot police to break up employees' meetings. Troops sexually assaulted women workers, stripping, fondling, and raping them "as a control mechanism for suppressing women's engagement in the labor movement," reported Jeong-Lim Nam of Hyosung Women's University in Taegu.[1] The heavy-handed coercion didn't work. It didn't work because the feminist activists in groups like the Korean Women Workers Association (KWWA) helped women factory workers understand and deal with the assaults. The KWWA held consciousness-raising sessions in which notions of feminine duty and respectability were tackled along with wages and benefits. They organized independently of

Korea's male-led labor unions to ensure that women's issues would be taken seriously, both in labor negotiations and in the pro-democracy movement as a whole.

The result was that women were at meetings with management, making sure that in addition to issues such as long hours and low pay, sexual assault at the hands of managers and women workers' health care were on the table. Their activism paid off: not only did they win the right to organize women's unions, but their earnings grew. In 1980 South Korean women in manufacturing jobs earned 45 percent of the wages of their male counterparts; by 1990 they were earning more than 50 percent. Modest though it was, the pay increase represented concrete progress, given that the gap between women's and men's manufacturing wages in Japan, Singapore, and Sri Lanka actually widened during the 1980s. Last but certainly not least, women's organizing was credited with playing a major role in toppling South Korea's military regime and forcing open elections in 1987.

Having lost that special kind of workplace control that only an authoritarian government could offer, American and European sneaker executives knew that it was time to move. In Nike's case, its famous advertising slogan — "Just Do It" — proved truer to its corporate philosophy than its women's "empowerment" ad campaign, designed to rally women's athletic (and consumer) spirit. In response to South Korean women workers' newfound activist self-confidence, the sneaker company and its subcontractors began shutting down a number of their South Korean factories in the late 1980s and early 1990s. After bargaining with government officials in nearby China and Indonesia, many Nike subcontractors set up new sneaker factories in those countries, while some went to Thailand. In the 1990s China's government remained only nominally communist; in Indonesia the country's ruling generals were only toppled in the late 1990s. The regimes were authoritarian regimes. Both shared the belief that if women can be kept hard at work, low-paid, and unorganized they can serve as a magnet for foreign investors. Each of these regime attributes proved very appealing to American and European sneaker company executives as they weighed where next to set up their factories.

Where does all this leave South Korean women — or any woman who is threatened with a factory closure if she demands the right to organize, decent working conditions, and a fair wage? They face the dilemma confronted by thousands of women from dozens of countries. The risk of job loss is especially acute for women working in relatively mobile industries; it is easier for a sneaker, garment, or electronics manufacturer to pick up and move the factory than it is for an automaker or a steel producer. In the case of South Korea, poor women had moved from rural villages into the cities in the 1960s searching for jobs to support not only themselves, but parents and siblings. The late 1980s exodus of sneaker-manufacturing jobs forced more women into the growing "entertainment" industry. The kinds of bars and massage parlors offering sexual services that mushroomed around U.S. military bases during the Cold War now opened up across the country.

Yet despite facing this dilemma, many women throughout Asia are organizing, knowing full well the risks involved. Theirs is a long-term view; they are taking direct aim at companies' nomadic advantage by building links among workers in countries targeted for "development" by multinational corporations. Through sustained grassroots efforts, women are developing the skills and confidence that will make it increasingly difficult to keep their labor cheap. Many looked to the United Nations conference on women in Beijing, China, in September 1995, as a rare opportunity to expand their cross-border strategizing.

The UN's Beijing conference also provided an important opportunity to call world attention to the hypocrisy of the governments and corporations doing business in China. Numerous athletic shoe companies had followed Nike in setting up factories in China, factories in which workers' independent organizing is suppressed. They included Reebok — a company claiming its share of responsibility for ridding the world of "injustice, poverty, and other ills that gnaw away at the social fabric," according to a statement of corporate principles.

Since 1988, Reebok has been giving out annual human rights awards to pro-democracy dissidents from around the world. But it was not until 1992 that the company adopted its own "human rights production standards" — after labor advocates made it known that the quality of life in factories run by its Korean, Taiwanese, and Hong Kong Chinese male subcontractors was just as dismal as that at most other athletic shoe suppliers in Asia. Reebok's code of conduct, for example, includes a pledge to "seek" those subcontractors who respect workers' rights to organize. The only problem is that independent trade unions are banned in China. Reebok has chosen to ignore that fact, even though Chinese dissidents have been the recipients of the company's own human rights award. As for working conditions, Reebok says it sends its own inspectors to production sites a couple of times a year. But they have easily "missed" what subcontractors are trying to hide — like 400 young women workers locked at night into an overcrowded dormitory near a Reebokcontracted factory in the town of Zhuhai, as reported in August 1994 in the *Asian Wall Street Journal Weekly*.

. . .

Nike's cofounder and CEO Philip Knight has said that he would like the world to think of Nike as "a company with a soul that recognizes the value of human beings." Nike, like Reebok, says it sends in inspectors from time to time to check up on work conditions at its factories; in Indonesia, those factories are run largely by South Korean subcontractors. But according to Donald Katz in a recent book on the company, Nike spokesman Dave Taylor told an in-house newsletter that the factories are "[the subcontractors'] business to run."[2] For the most part, the company relies on regular reports from subcontractors regarding its "Memorandum of Understanding," which managers must sign, promising to impose "local government standards" for wages, working conditions, treatment of workers, and benefits.

By April 1995 the minimum wage in the Indonesian capital of Jakarta was expected to be $1.89 *a day* — among the highest in a country where the minimum wage still varies by region. And managers were required to pay only 75 percent of the wage directly; the remainder could be withheld for "benefits." Nike has a well-honed response to growing criticism of its low-cost labor strategy. Such wages should not be seen as exploitative, says Nike, but rather as the first rung on the ladder of economic opportunity that Nike has extended to workers with few options. Otherwise, they would be out "harvesting coconut meat in the tropical sun," wrote Nike spokesman Dusty Kidd in a 1994 letter to the *Utne Reader*. The corporate executives' "all-is-relative" response craftily shifts attention away from a grittier political reality: Nike didn't move to Indonesia in the 1980s to help Indo-nesians; it moved to ensure that, despite some Asian women workers' success in organizing, its profit margin would continue to grow. And that is more likely to happen in a country where "local standards" for wages rarely take a worker over the poverty line. A 1991 survey by the International Labor Organization (ILO) found that 88 percent of women working at the Jakarta minimum wage at the time — slightly less than a dollar a day — were malnourished.

A woman named Riyanti might have been among the workers surveyed by the ILO. Interviewed by the *Boston Globe* in 1991, she told the reporter who had asked about her long hours and low pay: "I'm happy working here. . . . I can make money and I can make friends."[3] But in fact, the reporter discovered that Riyanti had already joined her coworkers in two strikes, the first to force one of Nike's Korean subcontractors to accept a new women's union and the second to compel managers to pay at least the government's legal minimum wage. That Riyanti appeared less than forthcoming in talking to the American reporter about her activities isn't surprising. During the early 1990s, when Indonesia's government was dominated by military officers, many Indonesian factories had military men posted in their front offices, men who found no fault with managers who taped women's mouths shut to keep them from talking among them-selves. They and their superiors had a political reach that ex-tended far beyond the barracks. By 1998 Indonesia had all the makings for a political explosion, especially since the gap be-tween rich and poor was widening into a chasm. It was in this set-ting that the government tried to crack down on any independ-ent labor organizing — a policy that Nike profited from and indirectly helped to implement. Referring to an employees' strike in a Nike-contracted factory, Tony Nava, Nike representative in Indonesia, told the *Chicago Tribune* in November 1994 that the "troublemakers" had been fired. When asked by the same reporter about Nike policy on the issue, spokesman Keith Peters struck a conciliatory note: "If the government were to allow and encourage independent labor organizing, we would be happy to support it."[4]

Indonesian workers' efforts to create unions independent of governmental control were a surprise to shoe companies. Although their moves from South Korea were immensely profitable (see chart, page 54), the corporate executives do not have the sort of immunity from activism that they had expected. In May 1993 the murder of a female labor activist outside Surabaya set off a storm of local and international protest. Even the U.S. State Department was forced to take note in its 1993 worldwide human rights report, describing an Indonesian system of labor repression under then-military rule similar to that which generated South Korea's boom twenty years earlier: severely restricted union organizing, security forces used to break up strikes, low wages for men, lower wages for women — complete with government rhetoric celebrating women's contribution to national development.

Yet when President Bill Clinton visited Indonesia in November 1994, he made only a token effort to address the country's human rights problem. Instead, he touted the benefits of free trade, sounding indeed more enlightened, more in tune with the spirit of the post–Cold War era than do those defenders of protectionist trading policies who coat their rhetoric with "America first" chauvinism. But "free trade" as it is actually being practiced

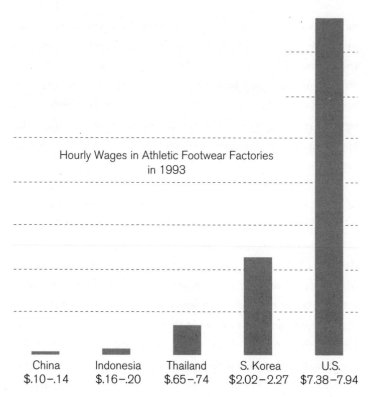

Hourly Wages in Athletic Footwear Factories
in 1993

China	Indonesia	Thailand	S. Korea	U.S.
$.10–.14	$.16–.20	$.65–.74	$2.02–2.27	$7.38–7.94

Figures are estimates based on 1993 data from the International Textile, Garment, and Leather Workers Federation; International Labor Organization; and the U.S. Bureau of Labor Statistics.

today is hardly *free* for any workers—in the United States or abroad—who have to accept the American corporate-fostered Indonesian, Chinese, or Korean workplace model as the price of keeping their jobs.

The not-so-new plot of the international trade story has been "divide and rule." If women workers and their government in one country can see that a sneaker company will pick up and

What do these young Chinese women factory workers think about "the politics of daughterhood"? Reacting in part to Indonesia's late 1990s pro-democracy movement, which mobilized thousands of Indonesian women factory workers, sneaker companies started moving their factories from Indonesia to China. Executives of Nike, Reebok, Adidas, and New Balance and their male factory-owning contractors were still pursuing in China what they had sought earlier in Korea and Indonesia: young women's labor that could be made cheap. (Photo by Erik Eckholm, © *The New York Times*, reprinted with permission)

leave if their labor demands prove more costly than those in a neighboring country, then women workers will tend to see their neighbors not as regional sisters, but as competitors who can "steal" their precarious livelihoods. Playing women off against each other is, of course, old hat. Yet the promotion of women-versus-women distrust remains as essential to international trade policies as the fine print in WTO agreements.

Women workers allied through networks like the Hong Kong–based Committee for Asian Women, however, sought to craft their own post–Cold War foreign policy, one that could address women's own needs: for instance, their need to convince fathers and husbands that a woman going out to organizing meetings at night is not sexually promiscuous; their need to develop workplace agendas that respond to family needs; their need to work with male unionists who trivialize women's demands; their need to build a global movement of women workers based on mutual trust; their need to convince women consumers in the United States, Europe, Japan, and Russia that when they see an expensive row of Reeboks or Nikes on the store shelves, there is more to weigh than merely the price listed on the tag.

CHAPTER 4

Daughters and Generals in the Politics of the Globalized Sneaker

Many of us are trying to chart the basic dynamics of contemporary globalization: the specific processes, the complexities of those processes, the resistance to those processes. What can asking feminist questions reveal?[1] Try to imagine what a feminist set of questions yields in terms of making sense of globalization — what it is, who benefits, who loses, and what the prospects are for it. Pursuing these questions successfully requires wielding a feminist curiosity. After being a political scientist for about fifteen or twenty years (I was a little slow), I began to realize that I was missing a lot. I was missing politics; I was not asking enough questions about where power is and how it operates. By not asking feminist questions, I had underestimated power.

We are carrying on this conversation in East Lansing. So let's start locally, with Michigan State University. With whom does Michigan State have its sporting goods logo franchise?

Audience: Reebok.

Is that because Nike has the University of Michigan's clothing and shoe contract?

The competition among not just university football rivals, but sporting goods corporations today is fierce — and it is global. Due to how this franchise system works, American universities are now deeply involved in the international politics of clothing and the international politics of sneakers.

How many of you have ever seen the fine print of Michigan State University's franchise agreement with Reebok? In its contract with the University of Wisconsin, Reebok's fine print initially stated that no members — no student, no member of any sports team — of the university could remove or in any way deface the company logo. If you did not want to have the telltale Reebok symbol on your sneaker or on your sports outfit when you were playing in front of the television cameras and so tried to take out the stitching or painted it a different color, you could be charged with violating the legal contract signed by Reebok and the University of Wisconsin.

I raise this to reveal the connection between American university politics in an era of shrinking public funding and the globalization of sporting goods manufacturing. It is this connection that links Michigan State University student athletes, administrators, and fans to both the Asian women who stitch sneakers and the investment-hungry Asian governments that try to control these young women.

One-third of all athletic shoes produced in the world at the end of the 1990s came from China. The other principal sources of sneakers were Indonesia and Vietnam. If we were having this discussion about the international politics of sneakers in 1980, it would be South Korea that would be demanding our analytical attention. That is, the particular dynamics between American universities, American state officials, Asian factory women, Asian state officials, and executives of companies such as Reebok and Nike must be historicized. Globalizing sneakers is not a political process that began yesterday. The end of the 1990s stood at a very particular moment in the long-developing and ongoing gendered globalization of sneakers.

The offshore manufacture of sneakers really began in 1970s South Korea and to some extent Taiwan, and it was infused with the politics of the Cold War.[2] Nike, Reebok, Adidas, Puma, and other sneaker companies began moving offshore. Nike's executives based in Oregon closed their last U.S. factory in Saco, Maine (one of America's poorest states), in 1975. They chose for their new factory sites two countries whose states were very closely allied to the U.S. state in the Cold War. This is not insignificant. Go home and line up your oldest and newest sneakers chronologically. I am suggesting that those sneakers that you could date back to the 1970s and 1980s, no matter what color they are, are khaki. That is, those pairs are militarized. Those sneakers were militarized by the kinds of agreements between three sets of political actors: American national security officials, South Korean generals then in control of South Korea's government, and corporate executives of the major American and European sneaker companies.

The politics of women in the globalization of sneakers is not understood by looking at simply the impact of globalization *on* women. Rather, women at several points have shaped globalization. Insofar as the sneaker industry — like the garment industry, like the tea industry, like the textile industry — depends for its bottom-line profits on the ability to make labor cheap and keep it cheap, those corporations' global strategizing is dependent upon local constructions of femininity. That is, in the 1970s and 1980s Nike's people in Beaverton, Oregon, were not just having an impact on women in South Korea. Those Korean women who became the assembly workers were crafting their own conceptions of femininity, and Nike became dependent on those women's constructions. What Nike executives, U.S. government Cold War strategists, Korean male factory managers, and the militarized officials of the 1970s to 1980s Seoul regime each — and together — thus sought to do was to exert pressure on those women so that their constructions of femininity would make their labor cheap.

Cheap labor. It's an analytically dreadful phrase. It hides politics. To casually (lazily) say that "cheap labor" was what lured Nike to South Korea is to tempt us to imagine that the labor of a Korean woman stitching a sneaker in 1975 was automatically ("naturally") cheap — as if it took no political effort to cheapen her labor. A more politically accurate phrase is "cheapened labor."

How? By whom? To answer these questions, one has to investigate the gendering of politics in a highly militarized South Korean society in the 1970s. Such a feminist exploration reveals that during the 1970s a lot of young women on small farms were being encouraged by the central government in Seoul to migrate from their small towns to cities in order to participate in the industrialization of their nation. South Korea's then highly militarized state encouraged young women migrants to see themselves as patriots, contributing to the nation by leaving their parents' homes to work in factories far from their parents' supervision.

Simultaneously, government officials sought to persuade parents to redefine daughterhood, specifically to radically reimagine what was a "respectable daughter," a "marriageable daughter." That is, an otherwise thoroughly patriarchal regime pursued its statist, nationalist goal of internationally funded industrialization by launching a campaign to redefine the meaning of the "respectable woman."

Insofar as a Korean woman depends for her long-term financial security on a good marriage (Jane Austen would have felt pretty much at home in 1970s South Korea), her parents must adopt a strategy to protect their daughter's reputation as respectable. If she loses her respectability, she may be doomed to a life of poverty. So it is not to be taken lightly when a government presses parents to redefine daughterly respectability in a way that persuades them to allow their daughters to live in the city without parental supervision, there to work in new factories — electronics factories, garment factories, textile factories, and athletic shoe factories. Thus, inside every computer chip, inside every elaborately stitched sneaker produced in the 1970s and 1980s, is a complex web of Cold War militarized, feminized respectability and daughterly patriotism.

Yet young Korean women were not mere pawns in this Cold War chess game. Women's studies scholar Seung-kyung Kim worked on the assembly line with those young women who answered the Korean regime's call to work for long hours at low wages in the name of patriotism.[3] Most of these women, Kim found, understood that the pay they were getting from various multinational corporations was inadequate to meet their multiple responsibilities. For while the South Korean women who served as the backbone of the "South Korean miracle" by assembling

electronics and garments and sneakers were not mere pawns, neither were they fully autonomous female citizens. They were
daughters. They saw themselves as daughters. You are a "daughter" insofar as, when you get your paycheck, you feel as though
part of your paycheck has to go home to your farming parents
who need some of your salary to make ends meet and to pay for
your brother's continued schooling. So let's take another look at
a pair of Nikes produced in South Korea during the 1970s and
1980s. We can now make out the khaki coloring. In addition,
now we can see the threads of daughterly loyalty: support for
farming parents in a time of government-favored industrialization and for school fees for sons, in whom parents have invested
such hope. When these factory women talked to Kim, all of
them, despite the differences among them, also described a strategy of saving money for their dowries. A good daughter, after all,
was a daughter who took steps to ensure a good marriage. In
South Korea by the 1970s young women were expected to bring
their own money into a marriage. They couldn't count on their
poor rural parents.

Now, at this point, let me indulge in an autobiographical
aside. When I was at Berkeley in the 1960s studying political science, nobody — nobody — told me that I should be interested in
dowries. Nobody said, "If you really want to be a keen observer
of the international political economy and the militarization of
the state you should spend a little time thinking about dowries."
What I believe now — belatedly — is that I have to be curious
about, learn about, things for which I really have few skills. I have
belatedly begun to see that the companies now producing sneakers and electronics for export have *depended* on these women
thinking of themselves as daughters and as potential fiancées.

It is with this insight in mind that we need to analyze South Korean factory women's likelihood of unionizing. We need to look afresh also at what was at stake when, in the early 1980s, activist university women such as Insook Kwon were urging factory women to join them in their public demands for democracy. It would have been perfectly logical for a young woman sewing sneakers for Nike or Reebok in South Korea in the 1980s to have hesitated. She would have strategically calculated that she needed to continue to send money home to her parents in order to maintain her reputation as a "good daughter" and to continue to put some money weekly into a savings account in order to accumulate enough to offer a suitable young man a dowry. For most of the women working in the factories around Seoul and Pusan, suitable husbands were men a little farther up the redesigned class hierarchy than they were — for instance, young men who worked for Hyundai shipbuilding or in low-level government civil service jobs. To work in the sneaker factory was many young women's strategy to rise a rung on the Korean class ladder. But it entailed their constantly thinking about what young urban men desired in a marriage. Those men wanted fiancées who would bring decent dowries into a marriage.[4]

Sneaker company executives depended on these Korean women's marriage strategies. The South Korean government depended on this. These elite men knew that women who were focused on their daughterly responsibilities and on marriage dowries were women who were not likely to strike for decent pay, for the right to unionize, or for democratic reforms. Thus when we think about globalization — and resistance to its more exploitative dynamics — we need to take women factory workers' own priorities and strategies seriously. We need to employ a new analytical curiosity, a curiosity that seeks to unravel the Gordian knot tying together sneaker design, sneaker company labor calculations, local regime's ideologies of femininity, working-class men's marital expectations, middle-class pro-democracy alliance-building efforts, and factory women's complex — and evolving — strategies.

South Korea is one of the success stories of democratization. To explain that success we must consider what it took in the mid-1980s for a Korean factory woman to reimagine herself so that she could, for instance, see it as reasonable to take the risk of attending a union rally. The democratization of labor unions came to be seen by many Koreans as integral to the democratization of the whole political system.

What do these insights imply for how we investigate the state, the foreign corporation, and its local capitalist subcontracting factory owner? Should we imagine that Nike executives in Oregon, generals and finance ministry economists in Seoul, and factory managers in Pusan each write formal memos about "the good daughter" and dowry practices? Perhaps not. We should, however, devise research approaches that make these masculinized elite calculations visible when they *do* exist.

Korean feminist activists and researchers, for example, have found that a number of factory owners set up dating services in the 1970s and 1980s. Why did they do that? Regularly replacing newly married women with unmarried novices ensured worker turnover. Turnover undercuts seniority. Thus regular departures of current women employees due to marriage help a factory owner cheapen labor. Sometimes, of course, employers have a great stake in fostering seniority. It depends on what skills are deemed necessary to produce the product for the profit level de-

sired. Sometimes high labor turnover worries capitalist employers because they need workers who will stay on and become more
and more skilled, ensuring the production of high-quality products. But in other industries, sneakers for instance, turnover enhances the bottom line because it means that managers are constantly taking in new workers, employees who can be paid at the
so-called "training" pay rate. Promoting the myth and practice of
the "good marriage" had an advantage for these capitalist allies of
their own government's Cold Warrior officials and of foreign executives relying on their factories to produce exported goods at
minimal cost. Promoting their women workers' dating prospects
would, managers hoped, keep assembly-line women focused on
themselves as daughters and "respectable," well-dowered wives.
That is, promoting dating would prevent these young women
from seeing themselves as *citizens,* as autonomous individuals
with public voices, with rights.

Nonetheless, in the mid-1980s thousands of Korean factory
women began to take themselves seriously as citizens. It was then
that the sneaker executives began to shut down their factories in
Pusan. They began to look instead toward Indonesia, to Indonesian women as still-daughterly, potentially cheapened labor.[5] It
may not be coincidental that it also was in the mid-1980s that
South Korea's masculinized state elite decided that the time had
come in the process of industrialization to shift the state's economic incentives: hereafter, the government would press Korean
entrepreneurs to eschew light industry — feminized industry —
and, instead, put their capitalist eggs in the basket marked
heavy — read masculinized — industry. Called "restructuring,"
this policy, when combined with the sneaker corporations'
flight — from democratization — translated into factory women

losing their jobs in South Korea. At the time, officials in Seoul tried to persuade those newly jobless women that giving up their paid employment was good for the Korean nation; resigning themselves to return to an earlier vision of womanhood as unpaid dependent was an act of feminized "patriotism." As Korean feminist Choi Soung-ai has explained, this massive loss of women's employment in the name of the state-designed "restructuring" was deemed good for the nation; it was only when the economic collapse of late 1997–98 compelled many *men* to lose their jobs that the South Korean elite (now democratically elected) deemed job loss a "national crisis."[6]

The sneakers produced today in Indonesia are, like their older counterparts, tinted khaki. Until the 1998 popular uprising against the generals in power, Indonesia was a militarized state. Global sneaker factories and local military rule appeared compatible.[7] Thus our understanding of women's participation in industrializing processes, so central to globalization, should generate more questions about the process of militarization. Indonesian researchers have noted that it was not uncommon for Indonesian factory owners producing for export in the early 1990s to bring retired generals on to their boards of directors. To any of us who have studied Thailand, this phenomenon is not new. We have learned that one cannot make sense of Thai banking unless one explores the retired generals' syndrome. Similarly, in the 1980s and 1990s, some overseas manufacturing factory owners setting up shop in Indonesia made explicit alliances with particular members of the Indonesian armed forces as a way of building the sorts of political networks then presumed valuable for doing profitable business under the militarized Suharto regime. It is not clear whether the pro-democracy movement's success in pushing Indonesian generals out of power in 1998 also has pushed senior military men out of their corporate offices and boardrooms. Combining women-as-daughters sewing the sneakers with generals-as-board-members opening the right doors proved to be a winning strategy for certain sneaker companies in Indonesia in the 1980s and 1990s. Yet a lot of analyses about local Indonesian resistance to the Suharto regime were surprisingly ungendered.[8] Who did the marching? Who walked out of factories to protest unlivable wages and denial of the right to independent union organizing? If one took a close look at photographs, one did see that oftentimes those demonstrations were composed of women. These were women who, according to researcher Diane Wolf, were recruited into factories here too as daughterly women workers so they could serve to cheapen labor enough to maximize profits in the making of athletic shoes.[9] Here too, just as in 1970s South Korea, a masculinized, militarized state officialdom made the rhetoric of "patriotic" daughterly womanhood a building block of its industrializing strategy. Here too, statist nationalism, structural militarism, and selective local and foreign capitalist entrepreneurship were deemed an insufficient tripod on which to rest a globally competitive industrial project. What the Indonesian elite decided, just as had the South Korean elite before them, was that a fourth leg had to be constructed — and maintained. That fourth leg was an updated form of patriarchy. Making visible that state-maintained fourth leg and revealing the reliance of the other three legs of nationalist industrialism on that patriarchal fourth leg have been central efforts of both South Korean and Indonesian feminists.

Reebok or Nike can only permeate the international market if local societies do not change their ideas about what a "respectable young woman" is. Nike has a global advertising and marketing strategy that calls for the world to be one big homogenized market. But Nike executives do *not* want the world in practice to lose its heterogeneity of constructions of "respectable" femininity. Insofar as women in Indonesia or South Korea — or Vietnam or China — challenge on their own terms what it means to be a "respectable daughter," what it means to be a "good wife," they become women who are harder to manage and whose labor becomes harder to *keep* cheap. So, on the one hand, Nike is perhaps one of the best-known symbols of globalization; on the other, however, Nike and other sneaker companies depend on the impenetrability of alternative notions of women-as-citizen into those societies where these companies produce products. Sneaker company executives share this dependence with local authoritarian state elites who rely on patriarchal order. Consequently, while Nike, Reebok, and other sneaker giants may celebrate the globalized girl athlete in their advertisements, they simultaneously rely on regimes to undermine the legitimacy of local feminists' challenging critiques with claims that those women activists are mere dupes of Western neo-imperialism.

CHAPTER 5

Whom Do You Take Seriously?

As a teacher, one thinks about silence. There is nothing quite so deafening as the silence that can greet a teacher who has just asked a group of students an unexpected question. People in university teaching talk with each other a great deal about their own current research and about the research of their colleagues. They talk much less often about what goes on between them and a classroom full of students. Still, when they do, one of the most persistent topics of conversation, often laced with considerable worry, is "how to get students to talk in class." The concern is not merely about getting some students to join in the class discussion — there is usually a handful of students who feel confident enough to participate. The puzzle is how to get those students who "never say anything" to lend their voices.

I start from this seemingly mundane site, the classroom, first, because it is where I have spent many of my waking hours, and second, because what goes on there every day may shed some light on two political questions: first, whose voices are heard in today's public realm; second, whose voices are heard in a manner that ensures that those speakers' experiences and ideas will be taken seriously when societal choices are weighed?

Returning to a teacher's worries, she or he knows that those students who are reluctant to speak may be motivated by a host of reasons: one woman simply may think that listening is more intellectually enriching than speaking; another woman may be so deeply engaged in the topic at hand that she pulls back from publicly voicing her thoughts for fear that her personal comments will be subjected to public criticism — or, worse, to casual inattention; still other women students (and usually they are being quite realistic) withhold their comments because they have learned from past experiences that many teachers only genuinely pay attention to male students when the subject is politics or world affairs.[1] Then there is the young man in the back row, the one with his baseball cap's visor pulled down so low that it casts a shadow over his face; he may be taking this course merely because it is a "requirement" and thus feels no obligation to help create a collective conversation. Yet another male student may be just learning this university's dominant language and so feel uncertain about whether his ideas will be understood by the teacher or his fellow students if he does try to express them out loud.

Not all silences come from a sense of being *silenced*. But many do.

Regardless of the cause, silences rob the public of ideas, of the chance to create bonds of understanding and mutual trust. It was for this reason that Hannah Arendt placed such importance on public speech — humans speaking to each other about public concerns in public spaces. Having delved into the deterioration of political life in France, Germany, Russia, and the United

States, Arendt became convinced that it was only by speaking to each other as citizens — not just as workmates or friends, not just as relatives or lovers, but as fellow *citizens* — that we could create and (this is the hardest part) sustain an authentic political life.[2] The necessary corollary, we are just beginning to appreciate, is that citizenship entails active *listening*, taking seriously what one's fellow citizens (and noncitizen neighbors) have to say.[3]

In the classroom, a potential microcosm of public/political space in the Arendtian sense, therefore, it becomes crucial that one find ways to reverse those dynamics that serve to silence, starting with those dynamics that silence by oppressing. Most of us who teach don't do this very well, or not as well as we would like. The consequences of our failures, I fear, can ripple into the future.

Perhaps the most common denominator of the recently mobilized Asian and Pacific democratization movements — several successful, more as yet unsuccessful — is their dedication to allowing more voices to be effectively heard — listened to — in the public arenas of their respective societies. "More." "Effectively." "Public." Each qualifier is politically loaded. The meanings and weight attached to each are shaping today's electoral reforms, internal party reforms, demands for labor union recognition, proposals for revising rules on immigration, and new legislation to control the internet. In New Caledonia, Fiji, South Korea, the Philippines, Burma, China, Thailand, Indonesia, Taiwan, Vietnam, Tonga, New Zealand, Malaysia — in each of these and other societies of the Asia-Pacific, the efforts and the movements organized to support these efforts have defined and prioritized these ideas about participation and public voice rather differently, affecting not only political strategies, but also determining

(1) who feels empowered by these movements, (2) who feels marginalized within these movements, and (3) who is left out altogether. A teacher who thinks of herself or himself as genuinely devoted to encouraging all students to have a voice may nonetheless practice the art of teaching in ways that stifle certain students' voices. In the same way, activist leaders of a movement or political party may imagine themselves to be promoters of democracy but nonetheless think and behave in ways that suppress some people's effective public speech — that is, public speech that is taken seriously.

Here I would like to discuss several particular modes of silencing, each of which relates to violence against Asian-Pacific women.

Hannah Arendt would be quite disapproving of taking seriously women's speaking out about domesticated power and sexuality. She had her own reasons for knowing that these topics did indeed demand thought, a lot of thought. Yet she was not convinced that they were properly defined as "political" subjects, matters for public speech among women and men when they were relating to each other as citizens. Arendt, perhaps the twentieth-century female political thinker taken most seriously by male political thinkers, has been the focus of growing feminist political theoretical attention precisely because of her troublesome two-legged stance. She insisted that authentic voice and public speech together be seen as the core of any meaningful polity, but dismissed, as appropriate only for "private" discourse, those matters that contemporary feminists, from Boston to Suva and Manila, contend must be debated in the public arena if the profoundly masculinist culture of political life is ever to be dismantled.[4]

One of the most potent mechanisms for political silencing is dichotomizing "public" and "private." In apparently adopting this dichotomy herself, Hannah Arendt has had plenty of company. Moreover, in that company have been those who were very uncomfortable with Arendt herself, with a woman who presumed that femaleness did not disqualify a person from speaking authoritatively about the origins of fascism and the corruption of democratic states. One of the longest and fiercest struggles that advocates for women's rights have had to wage has been against those — women as well as men — who have presumed that not only women's concerns but women themselves were most "naturally" kept within the allegedly private sphere. New Zealand's suffragists, the world's first to win national voting rights for women, had to confront and at least partially dismantle this deeply entrenched assumption. In fact, women's suffragist politics continue to be an essential topic of investigation for anyone interested in democratization precisely because suffragists everywhere — from New Zealand in the 1890s to Brazil and Japan in the 1920s to Kuwait in the early 2000s — have theorized so cogently about the silencing intentions of those who celebrate private/public dichotomies and those dichotomies' reliance on myths of femininity.[5]

Violence against women almost everywhere has been a topic kept out of the public arena or only sporadically and very selectively allowed into it in the form of a "scandal." This, in turn, has not only delayed for generations public officials tackling such abuse, but also entrenched the silencing of many of those women who have been the targets of that violence. Together, these two silencings have set back genuine democratization as much as has any military coup or distortive electoral system. The fact that violence against women—in its myriad forms—has recently been challenged in public by so many women in Asia and the Pacific should be seen as a significant development in the progress of democratization throughout the region. Of course, this also means that insofar as rape or sexual harassment or forced prostitution or domestic violence is anywhere denied or trivialized, real democratization is likely to be subverted.

Thus we need to become more curious about the processes of trivialization. How exactly do regimes, opposition parties, judges, popular movements, and the press go about *making* any incident of violence against women appear trivial? The gendered violence can be explained as inevitable—that is, not worth the expenditure of political capital. Or it can be treated by the trivializers as numerically inconsequential, so rare that it would seem wasteful of scarce political will or state resources to try to prevent it. Third, trivialization can be accomplished by engaging in comparisons: how can one spend limited political attention on, say, domestic violence or forced prostitution when there are market forces like global competition, structural adjustment, or nuclear testing to deal with—as if, that is, none of those had any relationship to the incidence of violence against women? Finally, trivialization may take the form of undermining the credibility of the messenger. As early as the 1800s, trivializers already were labeling women who spoke out publicly against violence against women as "loose," "prudish," or "disappointed" (it would be the trivializers' twentieth-century successors who would think to add "lesbian").

I think we all need to do the opposite, that is, to pay close attention to the implications for current political life in Asia and the Pacific of the activities of the Women's Crisis Center in Fiji, of the Okinawan women who organized in the wake of the September 1995 and January 1997 rapes of two local girls by American marines, and of those Australian feminists who critiqued the inadequate implementation of the state of Victoria's 1987 domestic violence law.[6] All three have been sites for exploring the ways in which gendered silencing occurs and in which such silencing can be challenged.

I spent many years — too many — being quite naive about what processes could silence women. Back then I had imagined that I was studying "real" politics. It wasn't that I was paying attention just to the formal processes of the state: my mentors and colleagues in Berkeley and Kuala Lumpur in the 1960s wouldn't have let me get away with that sort of shrunken definition of politics. Thanks to their nudging, I was pressed to look at landholding systems, at school textbooks, and at the racialized justifications for colonial rule. Yet, it was only later, in the early 1980s, that students, colleagues, and friends who already had become feminists showed me how to dig deeper, how to become more realistic when I investigated the processes that exclude women from political life.

It was at this point, for instance, that I became curious — curious as a political scientist, as well as a citizen — about "respectability." It was, I belatedly discovered, one of the most potent tools for keeping women silenced. It has been likewise one of the most prevalent means for keeping violence against women from being taken seriously as a *political* issue. In many societies in many eras it has been deemed improper for any "respectable" woman to speak at a public meeting. To speak out among strangers was, for a woman, to risk her "respectability." In the histories of Japan, the Philippines, the United States, and

France there have been "firsts" — the first woman to speak at a public meeting. Such an event did not mark the first time a woman spoke about public affairs. Women had written pamphlets under masculine pseudonyms; they had argued among friends and relatives; if they were more privileged, they might even have held salons. But this was speech within privatized spaces or without a public appearance. It was the publicness of speaking that marked a breakthrough — not just for the women who spoke, but, perhaps as radically, for the men and women who listened. So when one looks at a photo of a Japanese woman speaking from a stage at an outdoor labor rally in the 1920s, it is worth looking closely at the men (and smattering of women) in the crowd, to inquire about their reimagining of citizenship and political space.

Women speaking in public challenged the authority of the gender-policing concept, respectability. Some European and Latin American women who were breaking these exclusionary barriers wore hats. One looks at a photo of the first Brazilian woman to speak at a constitutional assembly, and then at a photo of the British women who organized their fellow textile workers for the right to vote, and one is struck by their broad-brimmed hats. As if, perhaps, wearing a hat, such a visible sign of feminized respectability, would protect them when they faced patriarchal ridicule.

In the Asia-Pacific in the late 1990s some of the most important assertions of democratic rights came from women and men working in factories — some wholly owned, as in New Zealand and South Korea, by local entrepreneurs; some created as joint local and foreign ventures; some wholly owned by foreign businesses but producing goods as subcontractors for even larger multinational firms; and some branches of factories owned by large foreign corporations. At times factory workers are not even certain just who owns their companies, that is, where the bread-crumbs of accountability should lead. Sexual harassment by male supervisors has been one of the chief complaints lodged by women factory workers. Yet to hold accountable a harassing supervisor, women workers need to know who owns their factory and what multinational corporation is that factory owner's chief customer. Being sexually harassed at work is an experience that until recently was imagined to be an inevitable hazard of the job. Thus women workers coped with it by using private stratagems — by avoidance, bawdy jokes, quitting. Making sexual harassment an "issue" has taken, however, not just a reimagining of what is inevitable and what is unacceptable. Converting it into a publicly acknowledged issue has required women factory workers to risk their own status as "respectable" young women.

Ever since the beginning of the industrial revolution, male factory owners have tried to accomplish two things simultane-ously: first, to recruit a feminized workforce in order to lower labor costs, and second, to persuade parents and local notables that a woman — especially a young, unmarried woman, working in a factory — would be able to retain her respectability so that she would neither bring dishonor on her family nor jeopardize her chances for future marriage. Thus it was that the politics of feminine respectability was woven into the industrial products of Manchester and Lowell.[7] In this effort the industrialists were not always successful. Mill "girls" could prove to be "unruly." The in-dustrialists' preoccupation with utilizing young single women for their own institutional purposes without triggering the mar-riageable-daughter anxieties of their mothers and fathers is strikingly similar to that of military recruitment officials past and present.[8]

Today the much-heralded economic success of what American policy-makers and investors routinely refer to as the "Pacific Rim" has been built to a significant extent precisely on this same gendered formula: feminizing certain industrial assembly processes while simultaneously assuring parents and other local opinion-makers that young factory women would keep their respectability — and thus their future marriageability. Nevertheless, despite official assurances, many of the potential factory recruits have worried about maintaining their status as "respectable women." In Australian-owned garment factories in Fiji, in Japanese-owned electronic factories in Malaysia, in American-owned toy factories in the Philippines, and in Korean-owned sneaker factories in Indonesia, there are women at this very moment making elaborate calculations about wage rates, daughterly obligations, consumerist tastes, marriageability, democratic aspirations, and political organizing.[9] These six considerations are intimately related in the lives of contemporary Asia-Pacific factory women. Just how the six are balanced and prioritized will determine whether any given woman in any particular factory will deem it worthwhile to speak out publicly about experiences of sexual harassment.

If speaking in public has been thought to be beyond the pale of feminine respectability, then imagine what risks might flow from speaking out publicly — that is, to strangers — about abusive sexualized experiences. As feminists have had to explain over and over again to uncomprehending managers, police officers, deans, judges, and legislators, most women who report sexual abuse find that it is they, not their alleged abusers, who are likely to suffer damage to their precarious social reputations. That damage is caused chiefly by their listeners' presumption that any woman who has undergone such a humiliating experience is *thereby* somehow less "pure" in her femininity than she was before that experience and before she spoke of it to strangers, even if those strangers were fellow factory workers, union organizers, human rights advocates, police officials, or pro-democracy activists. Furthermore, it is often some of these very co-citizen strangers who participate in the silencing politics of feminine respectability.

It is no wonder, then, that those groups of women devoted to mobilizing women factory workers have had to devise creative organizing strategies to ensure, first, that women employees can speak out in public realistically about their complexly interwoven concerns and, second, that they can speak publicly about sexual abuse on the job when it is among those concerns. Conventional forms of union and party organizing usually have failed to achieve both of these goals because those forms have been informed by presumptions about *masculinized* respectability, presumptions that speaking out is the manly thing to do, that sexualized experience enhances one's public masculine repute, and that politics itself is a proper pursuit for manly men.

One of the most energetic Asian women's groups doing innovative organizing work region-wide has been the Hong Kong–based Committee for Asian Women. Through its women worker exchanges (for instance, South Korean factory women traveling to Indonesia) and its publication, *Asian Women Workers News-letter*, CAW has acted as a facilitator among women employees who have sought fresh forms of organizing. CAW activists have tried to transfer skills from one Asian country to another, skills that would enable women workers to convert personal concerns into public issues and to speak about those concerns in public arenas. CAW activists have simultaneously tried to redefine sexual harassment so that it could be seen as less a matter of sexuality and more a question of power. In both strands of its work, CAW activists and the women who have participated in their activities have challenged the very notion of feminized respectability and thus too the masculinist presumptions that have narrowed the public arena.[10]

Violence against women has held such a problematic place in most pro-democracy movements. In Europe and North America, as well as in the Asia-Pacific, there have been celebrated instances of sexual abuse (especially rape, occasionally prostitution, but rarely domestic violence) being turned into fuel for a broad democratic mobilization when that democratic mobilization has been informed by nationalism. Under these circumstances, the pressure to expand citizen participation has increased when men and women have interpreted a given incidence of violence against women as evidence of the current regime's inability or unwillingness to protect the most vulnerable members of the putative nation. On occasion, as in China in the 1930s and 1940s, South Korea in the 1980s, and Okinawa in the 1980s and 1990s, it may look as though violence against women were about to be promoted to the rank of a seriously recognized issue within male-led anti-authoritarian movements.[11]

Yet too often what has actually happened has been that the violence perpetrated against one woman has been imagined by still-masculinized movement leaders to be an insult to or humiliation of the entire nation. While this may appear to infuse the issue with greater saliency, in practice it marginalizes women's own voices, their own political interpretations of that violence.

Women's experiences of violence then have become politically acceptable only if those events could be converted into the dishonoring of the "nation." By contrast, a woman who has suffered abuse at the hands of a coworker, or a political activist, or a husband — a fellow member of the nation — is not encouraged to tell her story in public; she is not held up as a model for the newly energized citizenry. In fact, if allowed to tell her story, and even more so if she is permitted to assign to it her own political meaning, this woman could be deemed a threat to both the movement and the fragile nation. Her speaking out could rob each of its legitimacy. She should keep quiet for the sake of the "nation."[12]

In the hands of nationalist, yet masculinist state policymakers, sovereignty also can be wielded as a silencer. As feminists have discovered when they have pressed for rape in war and domestic violence to be explicitly classified as violations of international codes of human rights, particular regimes have adamantly opposed such an expansion of international legal doctrine on the grounds that it would violate their states' hard-won postcolonial sovereignty. It is because the idea of sovereignty has been deployed as a silencer of women's public voices that so many international feminist activists, first at the United Nations' Vienna Conference on Human Rights and then again at the UN's Beijing Conference on Women, made a critique of sovereignty a plank in their platform.[13]

Therefore, while violence against women might in particular circumstances win public recognition, that in itself is not, I think, a sufficient test of whether recognition of violence against women is growing in a way that promotes genuine, nonpatriarchal democratization. A more complete — more realistic and reliable — test might include the following:

Are *all* forms of violence against women — not just a particular rape, but the daily incidents of domestic violence by male citizens on female citizens and other residents who happen to share these precarious spaces called "homes" — deemed appropriate for political deliberation?

Are women who dare to speak out publicly about violence at risk of losing some measure of their status as respectable — that is, credible, serious — persons?

Does sexual harassment rank as high on the agendas of trade union movements as, say, wages or bargaining rights?

How dependent is the ongoing creation of any national community on women's silence about the intimidation and violence in their daily lives?

There are undoubtedly other questions that need to be added to this brief list. Creating such a list and then using it to redirect and reinform participatory movements in the Asia-Pacific and in North America are, I believe, actions that will ensure that democratization is less superficial, more authentic.

CHAPTER 6

Feminist Theorizing
from *Bananas* to *Maneuvers*

*A Conversation between Cynthia Enloe
and Marysia Zalewski*

Marysia Zalewski (MZ): Let's begin with your book *Bananas, Beaches and Bases.* Many people identify this book as primarily posing the question: "Where are the women?" What I've noticed time and time again is how this question gets so easily disassociated from feminism. Have you noticed this? Why do you think this is the case? And what do you think it says about feminism?

Cynthia Enloe (CE): The reason I posed the question was because I thought it was actually quite a simple way of engaging people in trying to reimagine who is significant to analyze. That's really the question. "Where are the women?" says if you asked where are the women, you might see the men for the first time as men. One of the reasons that feminism is a movement rather than just an intellectual enterprise is because it does take pres-

83

sure. I mean, most people in the world would rather not ask the question. So if they're then asked the question, the strategy for not changing your analytical framework is to treat it just as that question, and you fill in the blanks and you don't ask what are really the important next questions, which are: why are they there, who got them there, and what happens to your understanding of the people you have already painted in once you see them there? Those are the follow-up questions. And those are the ones that are hardest to get people to take seriously.

MZ: Yes, as soon as you ask "Where are the women?" it does make you say: Well, why haven't we noticed that they aren't there? Or that we don't notice that they're there, which is where the feminism seems to come in to me. But does it say anything about feminism within the subject of international relations?

CE: I think within international relations, it has the effect of sometimes changing the dynamics of the class in ways the faculty member never intended. Sometimes women and men in the class react to the whole topic in a way that they hadn't in the weeks prior. One of the things that I'm most delighted about is that people who have read the book as students — as undergraduate students or graduate students — come up to me and tell me that it's the book they take home to their mothers, which is a great pleasure. I can't remember as a student ever thinking there was a book I'd take home to my mother. [*laugh*] But their mothers are lawyers and their mothers are full-time volunteers in organizations or their mothers are really good newspaper readers. And sometimes their mothers are diplomatic wives or CIA wives.

Sometimes when *Bananas* is used in courses it has an effect that the faculty member didn't intend. Sometimes it affects the way that person does their future teaching. That is not simply a credit to that book. I think it's much more what's in the air. It's a credit to students. Students really have these ideas, and they didn't know they could raise them in this class called an international relations class. Students — men and women but especially women — think these questions are legitimate throughout the course. That actually is the thing that is the most hopeful.

MZ: That's reminded me of some of the other things I've heard said about *Bananas*. Most of my students just love it. It is something that you'd take home to your mother or your teenage daughter. I even saw someone reading it on an airplane.

CE: Not just John Grisham! [*laugh*]

MZ: [*laugh*]And that's great! But a lot of people find it easy to dismiss because it has pictures in it. It is also accessible, which makes some think it is easy to trivialize.

CE: That's, I think, a desire to trivialize. I'm so opposed politically to the notion that nonaccessibility is the equivalent of seriousness. I've had to learn to write this way. I've always tried to be somewhat accessible . . . I was always determined if anything I wrote was good enough it should be understandable by people who are simply thoughtful, people who are simply willing to concentrate on a sentence. I never thought I was writing for the monkhood. Even before I became a feminist, I never thought that. Maybe it's my Berkeley days. I don't know. A lot of my Berkeley friends didn't . . . but when I wrote *Does Khaki Become You?* it was very clearly going to be published by Pluto Press in Britain and so I was very determined from the start that that would be understood by really smart women who were engaged in anti-militarist work, who I thought were a lot smarter than a lot of my academic colleagues, who in fact weren't thinking about anti-militarism at all. I was determined I would write in a way that had theoretical implications — in the sense that if I got it wrong, it mattered (if you don't have any theoretical implications, then it doesn't matter if you get wrong very much, right?). It would also be usable in academia if people wanted to use it. And because I was also a U.S.-based American writing for a British publisher, I had to do two things at the same time. I had to change my notion of the politics of the relationship between the writer and readers — and that means a multiplicity of readers — and I also had to change my notion of where I stood as an American-based analyst vis-à-vis other people in the world.

Also, I think it's very funny to think that putting photographs in a book could trivialize it since nowadays so much of intellectual life is about the meaning of images. We're afraid of putting images in because that will trivialize ideas, but in fact we gain a lot of our intellectual cachet from being the supposed authoritative interpreters of images. I find that nineteen-year-olds may not be able to write a good analytical sentence, but, boy, are they good at imagery. I think that really works in a book because they have authority with the professor because they can do a better job on the picture.

MZ: You really worked hard thinking about how to write differently.

CE: Oh my gosh, yes. I think it was one of the biggest things for me becoming a feminist. Because I had to change my notion of what it meant to be an academic. And I had to change my notion of whom did I take seriously. I think the hardest things for any of us to do are to admit whom we want to be taken seriously by and then change our ideas of whom we want to be taken seriously by.

MZ: So when you were a young student, who did you want to take you seriously?

CE: Well, I think when I was writing my dissertation (on ethnic and educational politics in Malaysia), I wanted to be taken seriously by my dissertation committee. And I think what happens to a lot of us is we keep the ghost of our dissertation committee in the back of every teaching room — which is disastrous for us — and we keep them in our heads when we sit down and turn on the computer. This is deadly because it is a killing kind of process to write [and teach] for the ghosts of one's dissertation committee, and I think it is anti-feminist.

MZ: Because?

CE: Because it is very elitist, because it doesn't admit the possibility that in fact lots of people theorize. Paid academics are not the only people who theorize. People who theorize are in fact the people who are constantly trying to figure out the everyday. I take seriously that the people who don't have a chance to put their ideas into writing are also theorists. I see them as my crucial judges. It is a feminist politics to . . .

MZ: . . . to move on from your dissertation committee or from your supervisor.

CE: That's right. And it also often feels quite risky to do.

MZ: It's quite a patriarchal relationship then?

CE: It's intended to be a patriarchal relationship.

MZ: Yes, and there is a real sort of holding on to that — certainly in the American system much more — a holding on to your student and their ideas almost. That is quite scary. Hmm, the theory point is very interesting because another criticism — and I don't mean to talk about just criticisms . . . [*laugh*]

CE: No, no, these are interesting . . . [*laugh*]

MZ: . . . is that *Bananas* isn't a theoretical book . . .

CE: Yes, right.

MZ: . . . which is to me an incredible statement to make. Perhaps you could give your view of that. You have a little bit already, but perhaps you could say more about your perception of theory.

CE: Theory is a level of explanatory generalization that is above the particular. It is risky to theorize because you should be able to be tested more widely. To theorize means you are going to be tested in reality. So that means you better be able to write in ways so that somebody else can put into words what you are theorizing. Theory is explanation, and if one gets explanations wrong, it has very serious consequences. My kind of theorizing constantly goes back and forth between general and particular because I want to actually test my theories on the page with the reader.

MZ: So, for example, if we look at diplomatic wives, how do you work that through?

CE: That was a really risky thing to do. I mean, nobody in the radical 1960s ever said to me as a serious political scientist I should ever utter the word "wife." That felt like the most risky chapter [in *Bananas*]. The only reason I felt I could be brave enough to do that is because I had done it in *Khaki*. *Khaki* was the first time I'd ever gotten up the courage to write an entire chapter as a serious political scientist about wives. That was military wives. What I found there was I learned something I had never learned about the state before.

My theorizing started by simply taking seriously my own proposition. In *Khaki* it was: states are more dependent on women and on particular ideas of femininity than they admit. If I could show that the state is so dependent on these people called military wives, who are never thought of as serious political actors, I could show two things: one, that states were more fragile than was presumed because, look, they were dependent upon a whole group of actors that people didn't give the time of day to; and two, the state is conscious of that dependence and expends scarce resources to try to control those women.

Doing that chapter on military wives most strongly confirmed for me my theoretical hunch. So the chapter in *Bananas* was to say: so that was true when I took this one sphere of state action, but I wonder if it will be true when I investigate this other group of trivialized women. Does the state really get nervous about foreign service wives?

MZ: And the answer is yes. [*laugh*]

CE: [*laugh*] Oh, you should have heard them.

MZ: You use the word "hunch." This seems to stem from your feminism . . . but one of the things my students often ask me is: "What sort of feminist is Cynthia Enloe?" If my students were to ask you, "So what kind of feminist are you?" how would you approach this?

CE: Well, first of all I'm an evolving feminist. I mean I get quite worried about boxes because boxes say I've stopped thinking. I guess one of the things I most certainly am not is an essentialist. I'm very nervous about essentialism because I don't think it is accurate. I am a constructionist, and I learned to be a constructionist out of my studies of ethnicity. I guess the second thing about my feminism is that it is very nonuniversalist in the sense that universalism is uncurious about differences in terms of sociopolitical location. But I never put woman in quotes. I'm not a constructionist who can so thoroughly deconstruct something that it doesn't exist at all. That may be very playful and it may be very intellectually pleasing, but you have to watch us people in the intellectual trades because there are some things that we do that are just intellectually pleasing, but that doesn't mean . . .

MZ: . . . it is of any use . . .

CE: That's right. We have to be held accountable. I think that if the theorizing we do matters, it means that other people are going to live their lives and strategize on the basis of it. If they're not, then what's the point of the theorizing?

MZ: So are you sort of saying that the more "extreme" postmodernism underestimates the stakes involved and the power involved?

CE: If there is one thing that people who consider themselves to be "international relations specialists" don't want to believe is that they are naive. I think virtually every international relations specialist who doesn't on a regular basis ask in a serious fashion "Where is the gendering of power here?" is at risk of being naive. They are constantly underestimating the power it takes the state to get the kind of international system each of them thinks they need. It is the underestimation of power that is the most telling attribute of nonfeminist international relations specialists. They constantly underestimate power.

MZ: That's certainly another thing that comes up with *Bananas* — the underestimation of power.

CE: Yes, it is. . . .

MZ: How much did your thinking change, in the almost ten years between *Bananas* and *Maneuvers*, about feminism and international relations and those really important things — "where are the women?," power, and the international is personal?

CE: In *Maneuvers*, I'm trying to understand the kind of theorizing about the state, violence, and the international politics of militarization by feminists who are situated in different theoretical sites. *Maneuvers* is more self-conscious about that.

In *Maneuvers* I've tried to capture the strands of feminist thinking that have been developing in the post–Gulf War and the post-Bosnia and post-Rwanda war years. The core theme is the subtle and blatant forms that processes of militarization can take. I've made lists of what can get militarized (refugee camps, gay and lesbian rights movements, humanitarian aid, AIDS prevention, hometowns, peace movements) — each militarizing process being dependent on specific attempts to maneuver both women as people and femininity as an idea. More than in any earlier book, I've tried to explore here how and why feminists in different locations can come to think about militarization quite differently. Thus I've tried to compare Belgrade feminists', Okinawan feminists', and South African feminists' analyses and strategizings (about war crimes tribunals, about nationalism, about sexual violence, about state access) because they are so central to making sense of the working of international political life. . . .

MZ: So what joins the feminisms together? Is there something that defines the feminisms?

CE: First, they all take women's experiences seriously because women matter as human beings: they are citizens of different states and of the world and what happens to women should be taken seriously in political discourse. And second, they are all feminists because they have all developed a hunch — a tentative theory — that in any kind of distribution of political power there is probably a gendering going on: masculinity probably matters causally and femininity probably matters causally.

MZ: The first thing you said there was "taking women's experiences seriously." And that is a sort of underpinning — a starting point if you like — for feminism wherever you are.

CE: Yes, that's right. This comes back to academia. Since academia is so careerist, academics are constantly being socialized to care most about being taken seriously by those people who control their careers. What if, as a feminist, you decide instead what should be taken seriously are the experiences of women so that you can be a better explanatory analyst? And what if the people who control your career don't take them seriously?

MZ: You're in trouble. [*laugh*]

CE: That's right. What you then find you have to do is take a deep breath and say, "Wives matter." I'm going to have to educate my dissertation committee. I'm also going to have to build other networks. I'm going to have to figure out other ways to change the career system. But what I'm not going to do as a feminist — and I know this is easy enough for me to say because I have tenure — is analytically trivialize women's lives and thus go silent. If we take that trivializing path, we are going to become politically naive. We'll get the promotion but do so by spinning out conventional ideas about politics that in fact nobody should rely on in their lives because those ideas underestimate power.

MZ: That's a really important issue: what is taken seriously. Has it changed since the 1980s? In the teaching of international relations, in the writing of international relations — what students do when they study international relations?

CE: Yes, I see a lot of change. For instance, most people who teach international politics now — even if they have no interest themselves — are pressed either by the expectations of their colleagues or by the expectations of their students to make at least a gesture toward a gendered curiosity, even if they can't hold on to it very long. And that's progress. One of the reasons it's progress is that it says to the next generation of thinkers "this is critical." At least those students and younger faculty don't get silenced in international relations. I think that is the first thing. The second thing is that today it is recognized that there is so much international politics of women to be studied. I mean, what is the feminist analysis of the World Trade Organization? There is one. What is a feminist analysis of NATO? There is one. What is a feminist analysis of the 1997 Asian economic crisis? There obviously is one. So there is now more and more of a sense that this work needs to be done, that it is work that will shed light more broadly, and that there are more and more men as well as women who think they have to think about this. I really do believe that. Part of it is because I'm an enthusiast.[*laugh*] Part of it is because I actually do see it out there on the ground. Slippage is always possible, though.

MZ: You mean like going backwards?

CE: Yes, that's always possible. That's true of any politics. But my hope is that the people who are now doing graduate work and the people who are now in the first years of academic work will hold on to this. They don't have to all be gender specialists, but what they have to do is say that leaving out the serious asking of the gender question probably will mean that their theorizing about international politics will be not just incomplete. It will be unreliable.

MZ: If more and more people include gender and take seriously the point that their work is going to be naive without it, that's really going to change what international politics looks like.

CE: I hope so. That's one of the things that gives me great pleasure: going to the ISA [International Studies Association]. I mean there are papers being given there that nobody even thought about ten years ago. And they are not trivial. The study of international politics is no longer just the study of "international relations." It used to be that the study of international politics was done only by researchers in one political science subdiscipline — international relations, but now . . .

MZ: So the walls are breaking down?

CE: We hope so, because the new curiosity is enticing people. Disciplines may be comfortable homes, but they don't matter if they block our ability to develop the most explanatory analyses. That for me is what I most want to do. And if political science is constructed in a way that it stymies the development of the most reliable explanatory analyses, then it is political science that has to go. What I hope is that since we are the ones who build political science and what it studies, we can change it. It doesn't have to become obsolete.

PART TWO

Wars Are Never "Over There"

CHAPTER 7

All the Men Are in the Militias, All the Women Are Victims

The Politics of Masculinity and Femininity in Nationalist Wars

Borislav Herak was an ordinary man.[1] He had not yet married and so lived with his parents in Sarajevo. Although ethnically a Serb, he, like so many Sarajevans, lived within an ethnically mixed family. His sister had married a Sarajevan Muslim Bosnian man. Borislav himself didn't have much luck with girlfriends, and maybe that is why he read pornographic magazines up in his room. This disturbed his father, a welder. Nor could his son's work life have been called a success. He had done poorly in school and had an undistinguished career as a conscript in the Yugoslav navy. In the early 1990s he was employed pushing a cart in one of the city's textile factories. Yet Borislav didn't seem to be a violent man. In his twenty-one years there were no records of his having vented his personal frustrations with assaults on women. And politics did not appear to provide an alternative outlet. He scarcely knew anything about either Yugoslav or Serbian history. Perhaps the political debates that had grown steadily more intense since the outbreak of controversy over control of Kosovo just seemed to this twenty-one-year-old less immediately relevant than the centerfolds of the magazines he stored in his bedroom.

All this changed in 1991. War came to Sarajevo. Like many of the besieged city's residents, Borislav fled to its surrounding mountains. He was taken into one of the scores of semi-autonomous militias formed with the intent of pursuing ethnic Serbian territorial control. One could, however, scarcely describe Borislav Herak as having "joined" or been enlisted into this militia. The process was a far cry from the formal routines by which young men were conscripted into the now-disintegrating Yugoslav state army. From his own rather vague account, he seemed, rather, to have fallen into the company of these Serbian militiamen. They offered shelter and protection in the midst of an increasingly chaotic social environment. Gradually, his new comrades would also provide this unfocused and listless young man with a purpose larger than himself.

We know these details about Borislav Herak because he had nothing to do in prison but talk. Speaking to French and American journalists broke the boredom during the days he waited for his trial. By late 1992 he had been captured by the Bosnian forces he had come to see as his militia comrades' and his own enemy. He was to be tried on charges not only of murder, but of rape. Mass rape. He was prepared to confess. Borislav Herak, a man who merely a year before had been one of history's nonentities, now had his photograph on the front pages of major newspapers. He would forever after be among the most widely recognized human faces behind that abstracted horror that had come to be called "the Bosnian rapes."[2]

It is clear that a student of ethnicity and nationalism has much to explain before the story of Borislav Herak makes sense. Why did he come to sexually assault Bosnian Muslim women when a person of the same religion and ethnicity was the object of familial affections? How had such an apparently unpoliticized individual come to take risks in the name of Serbian nationalism? But these questions expose only the tip of the analytical iceberg.

Buried in the story of this once unexceptional person are important puzzles — and potential revelations — about how ethnicity gets converted into nationalist consciousness, how consciousness becomes organized, and how organized nationalism becomes militarized. None of these transformations is automatic. Nor is their sequence from one to the next. Each calls for explanation. But exploring these questions, melting down the analytical iceberg, requires taking a close look at gender.

For Borislav Herak was more than simply (or not so simply) a Serbian working-class Sarajevan who grew to young adulthood under the post–World War II Yugoslav multiethnic Communist state. He was a man. More to the point, he was a man raised in the 1960s, '70s, and '80s to think of himself as masculine. Or perhaps it is more useful to say that Borislav was a man raised to think of himself as *needing* to be masculine. If we leave this process out of his story, if we treat this process as unproblematic, then we leave out an exploration of the gendered politics of nationalism. With such a gaping omission, we will have a hard time arriving at a satisfactory explanation of why a factory worker became a militarized rapist.

There has been a burgeoning literature in recent years on the gendering of nationalist identities and — quite distinct — the gendering of nationalist ideologies and organizations. Most of this revealing research has been done by feminist scholars. They have found the existing literature on ethnicity and nationalism incapable of fully describing, much less explaining, how it is that women have experienced either ethnic communalism or nationalist politics so differently from men, differently even from those men who have shared common ethnic, generational, and class conditions with them.[3] These feminist researchers have, quite wisely, focused their primary attention on women's experiences of ethnicity and of nationalism precisely because so much of the previous attention — particularly that concerning nationalism — privileged men's experiences.

Written between the lines of many of the most influential ungendered investigations of politicized ethnicity or of nationalist movements were several assumptions. First was the frequent assumption that men's experiences of both politicized ethnicity and nationalism deserved to be featured because it had been men (in Ireland or Algeria or Kenya or Quebec) whose ideas and actions had been the crucial shapers of those processes, leaving women to be spectators on the side of the collective road. Second, there was the common unspoken belief that men and women in any given community had roughly the same experiences, and since the experiences of men were the easiest to research — they left the most evidence in their wake — the investigator need not look further. Third, while few imagined that women and men actually cooked, negotiated, shot, or gave birth equally, it seemed convenient for some observers to assume that uneven task distribution had little impact on individuals' senses of belonging or on the strategies selected for collective mobilization.

New feminist research starts from the conviction that assumptions this sweeping are worthy of explicit testing. The result has been evidence that all three assumptions not only are seriously flawed, but that they yield an imperfect understanding of how both ethnic and nationalist processes actually operate.[4]

The research that takes women's experiences of nationalism seriously reveals that many more decisions are made that determine the course of any ethnic transformation or nationalist mobilization than most of us could ever imagine. Decisions about what to cook, decisions about who would drop out of school, decisions about what to wear, decisions about whether to use contraceptives, decisions about who should go to meetings at night—decisions that frequently have been treated as merely "personal" or "trivial"—suddenly were shown to be significant. They also were found to be contested.

Decisions involve power. Many observers of nationalism, by ignoring women's experiences and by trivializing relationships between women and men, have underestimated the number of decisions it has taken to construct nationalism. Those who have underestimated the number of decisions it actually has required to develop ethnic consciousness, to politicize it, to transform it into nationalism, and—on occasion—to turn it into a violent force, in turn, have vastly underestimated the flows of power.

Furthermore, paying attention to women's experiences of nationalism not only made women visible, it also made it possible for researchers to see men. Where once there were militiamen, workers, and political elites, now there were women workers, men workers, women refugees, men refugees, militia*men*. That is, as soon as we start making the experiences of Bosnians problematically gendered, we no longer can subsume all women under the sprawling canopy of "victims" nor all men under the category of "militia fighters." In fact, we may hesitate before we even use the easy term "militiamen" unthinkingly. Instead, we try to determine if there were some men in Bosnia or the other regions of the former Yugoslavia who perhaps were more likely to have been marginalized, silenced, or injured — to have been victimized — than at least some women. We have to ask which women exactly have been the most likely targets of assault, which women by contrast have been best situated to speak out publicly for themselves, which women have developed antiviolent interpretations of nationalism, which women have theorized in ways that led them to reject nationalist political identities altogether. To engage in this analytical activity is not designed to push women's vulnerability back into the shadows; rather, it is to roll back the canopy that discourages observers from taking a close look at women's varied experiences of nationalist conflict and thereby to specify the conditions and decisions that have turned some women into victims. Accepting a priori the assumption that women are best thought of as victims in any nationalist mobilization that has turned violent dulls analytical curiosity. Ultimately, this dulled curiosity produces explanations that are naive in their descriptions of power and camouflage men in the garb of ungendered actors.

Thus it would be a mistake to file Borislav Herak's experiences solely under "militia fighter" or "factory worker" or "Sarajevan Serb." He is also a man. We don't know at the start if his maleness is significant in making sense of how and why ethnicity becomes nationalist and how nationalist consciousness feeds violent conflict. Did all Sarajevan men join militias? Was there something in the 1990s gendered urban labor force that pushed more male factory workers than female factory workers to resort to arms? Having put on our gender goggles, we are compelled to inquire whether Borislav's being male has mattered and, if so, why. The answers may reveal something about the gendered ethnic and nationalist processes that shaped the actions of Borislav Herak. Pursuing gendered lines of inquiry also may expose more about the path of intercommunal violence in the 1990s, which could help us to make fuller sense of how and why nationalisms develop so differently in Flanders, Burundi, Scotland, Armenia, Quebec, and Slovenia.

Borislav Herak, from the little we know, did not seem motivated by nationalist conviction to join the Serbian militia in the hills above Sarajevo. From his recounting, it would appear that the sequence was the reverse: he began to see his Serb identity as justifying military action only after he joined the militia. Although there are reports of some Serbian and Croatian women having joined militia forces, the particular militia Borislav joined in 1991 was an all-male company composed of men who self-consciously thought of themselves as Serbs.[5] The micro-culture these men were developing was simultaneously masculinized, militarized, and ethnically politicized. From the older men in the militia, Borislav first learned that Muslims, ancestors of his urban neighbors and his extended family, had oppressed his own ancestors. According to his new militia tutors, it was Muslims, from the Ottoman imperialists in the past to Islamic believers in the present, who were largely to blame for his own personal lack of success. Borislav Herak, he now learned, was a man oppressed. A *man* oppressed. Maybe that was why he was pushing a textile cart to earn a living. Maybe that was why girls didn't find him attractive. Maybe that was why he had to find solace in pornographic centerfolds.

While the young man's entrance into the evolving world of Serbian militias apparently was not politically premeditated or deliberate, there still are decisions here to explore. First, some Serbian men made the decision to form armed all-male militarized groups rather than to trust their destiny to civilian parties or to the state's own shrunken but still potent and largely Serb military. What calculations prompted their decision? Perhaps a number of these male militia founders already had done their tours as military conscripts in the Yugoslav army and had learned there that the manly thing to do when faced with a perceived threat was to take up arms in company with other men. Perhaps as conscripts in the Yugoslav army they had mixed with Slovene, Muslim, and Croatian male conscripts, but had been socialized by their Serb officers to think of military activity as the special calling of men who identify themselves as Serbs. We don't have the answers yet, but we need them if we are going to make adequate sense of the Yugoslav conflict and if we are going to use that conflict in any comparative analysis of post–Cold War nationalism. Have the British, Russian, Canadian, and Indian armies, for example, had the same impacts on the masculinization of ethnic identities of their respective male enlistees?

There is evidence that the warrior is a central element in the modern cultural construction of the Serbian ideal of masculinity. Researchers are also demonstrating that the ideals of Serbian femininity have been constructed in ways deliberately intended to bolster the militarization of masculinity. Constructing ideals of masculine behavior in any culture cannot be accomplished without constructing ideals of femininity that are supportive and complementary. Thus, many feminist analysts search for the decisions and actors that have the greatest stake in controlling notions of feminine respectability, feminine patriotism, and feminine attractiveness. For it is these ideas that need to be shaped and monitored if standards of manliness are to remain persuasive and legitimate. For instance, cultural constructions of masculinity in many societies have been dependent not simply on celebrating men as soldiers, but on simultaneously elevating women as mothers-of-soldiering-sons, valuing women chiefly for their maternal sacrifices for the nation. Consequently, pro-natalist policies by government officials espouse a militarized nationalism. This means that to make full sense of what has been happening to Borislav, we need to be curious about his mother and his sister as well. Journalists who tried to understand the Serb militiaman spoke only to his father. That is a start, but it is not enough.

Paying attention to cultural ideals of femininity and masculinity and the processes by which they are propagated and made mutually reinforcing, however, should not be the end of the investigation of the gendering of nationalism. Cultural ideals under certain circumstances can be challenged — they can become confused, contradictory; even widely accepted ideas about what it means to be manly or to be a good woman can become the objects of social controversy rather than veneration. Thus, for example, the notion of communally legitimated maternalized femininity has been contradicted by the occasional promotion of women as fighters for the Serbian nation, though the contradiction has been partially contained by assigning far more importance to the patriotic mother than to the patriotic woman soldier. Such norms, even when bolstered by potent historical myths, as in Serbian communal lore, do not, however, automatically lead all men to take up arms all the time. Borislav's father didn't. Nor apparently did his brother. Thus, the existence of such norms and legends is not a sufficient explanation for the rapid multiplication of mostly male militias in the early 1990s.

When war with Croatia broke out in 1990, many young Serbian men, often with the explicit assistance of their mothers — women whom Serbian nationalist propagandists were urging to meet the standards of the Serbian "patriot mother" — in fact fled the country to escape the increasingly dangerous and politically controversial military service.[6] We do not yet have a gender-curious analysis of the pre-1990 Yugoslav military, so we do not yet even know how successful or unsuccessful cultural elites and public authorities were in masculinizing soldiering and militarizing manliness. We do know, however, that in the decades prior to the recent conflict some Yugoslav women activists had complained that by so thoroughly masculinizing the idea of national service, the central federal government was diminishing women's contribution to the creation of the post–World War II nation. By raising this as a public issue, these women were not only attempting to pry military service apart from masculinity; they were also attempting to problematize the gendered historical memory of nation-building.[7]

Militarization of ethnic nationalism often depends on persuading individual men that their own manhood will be fully validated only if they perform as soldiers, either in the state's military or in insurgent autonomous or quasi-autonomous forces. But although the most persuasive socialization strategies succeed because they manage to portray soldiering as a "naturally" manly activity, in reality socialization requires explicit and artificial construction, sometimes backed by coercion. Large advertising budgets allocated to defense ministries in countries that rely on volunteer militaries, and harsh penalties assigned by the state to draft-dodgers in countries dependent on conscription, both signal a degree of deliberateness in sustaining militarized notions of masculinity. One of the most interesting studies on the artificiality of the connection between manhood and soldiering comes from South Africa. Zulu men have been deliberately encouraged by leaders of the Inkatha movement to imagine their ethnicized manhood as rooted in the performance of warrior roles. Not all Zulu men have been persuaded. Furthermore, as in contemporary Serbia, the contradictions within the nationalist rhetoric over whether the ideal woman should be herself a fighter for the nation or merely a maternal supporter of the nation's male fighters have served to undermine the militarizing process.[8]

Thus the process by which the Serbian men in Borislav's militia initially decided to form an armed group and the process by which they recruited other men are not at all obvious. Each of these social processes calls for detailed descriptions and subtle analyses. If Borislav Herak's story is at all representative, it may well be that many Serbian men were very incompletely militarized in their manhood by their experiences as lowly conscripts in the Yugoslav state military, so they fell into militias in the early 1990s rather than self-consciously seeking them out, and that they were militarized in their own ethnicized masculinity only after they experienced physical and emotional dependence on these deeply masculinized groups.

There are yet other decisions that need investigation. What

were the decisions — and by whom were they made — that led Borislav Herak to rape sixteen Muslim Bosnian women, some of whom were murdered afterward? An ethnicized, masculinized man, even one enrolled in a group that wields violent weaponry, does not *inevitably* commit atrocities.

A blueprint for conducting this investigation may be found in another study of men who committed war atrocities. Historian Christopher Browning's curiosity was provoked by a group of working-class men from the city of Hamburg, who in the early 1940s had been conscripted by the Nazi government into a special police unit that took part in several mass murders of Polish Jewish civilians in the later years of World War II.[9] How should one think about these men? Is it enough to assume that they were anti-Semitic in their German identities before joining Reserve Police Battalion 101? Maybe some of these men sought service in a police unit because they hoped it would save them from performing more militarized duties that would involve killing other people. Were their own notions of themselves as manly — as longshoremen or as fathers or as heterosexuals — deliberately manipulated by their police superiors in an effort to ensure that they would kill Jewish civilians? Was that manipulation totally successful? All of these questions are relevant to our making sense of Borislav Herak's behavior in 1991–92 Bosnia.

Each question suggests that the location of a man — or woman — in an organized group such as an autonomous militia or a state police force has to be understood if the processes of militarized nationalism are to be accurately portrayed.

Christopher Browning used archival documents, postwar trial testimonies, and more recent interviews with the men of Reserve Police Battalion 101 and their bureaucratic superiors to answer the question: What would make ordinary German men shoot defenseless Jewish children, women, and men between June 1942 and early 1943? Browning's intent was not to relieve these middle-aged policemen of responsibility. Rather, he was curious to know what exactly it took to turn these men into mass killers.

According to Browning's account, these shootings were not preceded by rapes. Why not? Were the men's sexual frustrations less intense before they joined the armed unit? Was their anti-Semitism less dependent on misogyny? Did their officers construct their male subordinates' ethnic militarism with less reliance on sexuality? Browning didn't inquire. Perhaps if he or another historian looked at these policemen's killing activities in light of the puzzle surrounding Borislav Herak, these questions would be pursued.

What Browning did discover was that most of the German men in Battalion 101 had not been actively involved in politics before the war, although some had joined Nazi youth groups. He also found that, while several of their commanders were committed Nazi careerists and self-conscious anti-Semites, and while anti-Semitic messages were part of the battalion's training manuals, an anti-Semitic form of German nationalism was not deeply embedded in the personal identities of most of the men who eventually followed orders to shoot unarmed Polish Jews. What Browning uncovered instead were conflicting messages coming to these men from their officers — their immediate superior tried to give his men a nonkilling option. On the other hand, these men were socialized to kill by a steady stream of assignments devised in Berlin over several months, assignments that gradually escalated in their levels of dehumanizing harshness.

These male police troops' male superiors, however, did not assume that either the troops' preconscription notions of their masculinity or their personal commitments to German nationalism would in themselves be sufficient to guarantee that they would follow orders to shoot on command. Documents reveal that steps were taken by male superiors to lower the "psychological stress" they believed would be experienced by the men on killing assignments.[10] An effective commander does not leave morale to chance. Yet morale is thoroughly gendered in the minds of most military commanders. Dignity as fathers, reassurance as boyfriends, pride as sons, comradeship as fictive brothers-in-arms, satisfaction as masculinized heterosexuals — each has been weighed and employed by commanders in male military forces as different from each other as the American army in 1960s Vietnam and the German police in 1940s Poland.

From his interviews, Browning learned that the men who chose their commander's nonshooting option worried especially that they risked being ostracized by fellow policemen: "The nonshooter was potentially indicating that he was 'too good' to do such things." Rather than risk losing his comrades' valued masculine friendship, nonshooters appealed to their fellow policemen to excuse their failures of masculine toughness: "They pleaded not that they were 'too good' but rather that they were 'too weak' to kill."[11] But Browning is not a feminist investigator. Thus it is only toward the conclusion of his otherwise richly detailed account that he confronts directly the role played by the social construction of masculinity. Considering the pressures to shoot on command that came from within the group rather than simply from above or outside, Browning observes, "Insidiously, therefore, most of those who did not shoot only reaffirmed the 'macho' values of the majority — according to which it was a positive quality to be 'tough' enough to kill unarmed, noncombatant men, women and children — and tried not to rupture the bonds of comradeship that constituted their social world."[12]

Browning's study of these particular Nazi male police conscripts suggests that ungendered nationalist propaganda alone is not sufficient to transform a male recruit into a committer of atrocities. Nor did he find that mere maleness or even simply a culture of masculinity was adequate. Instead, it took a complex set of bureaucratic relationships among officers at different ranks who had not always held harmonious ideas about what policing or soldiering might rightly justify. It also took the sometimes confusing relationships between male officers and male troops. And it required the evolution of a particular brand of masculinized comradeship among peers. Each factor was infused with deliberateness.

Another study of military men that might shed light on the making of Borislav Herak is the U.S. Defense Department's 1993 "Tailhook Report."[13] While it does not portray violence at the extreme levels found in 1940s Poland or 1990s Bosnia, this report's authors also seek to explain what caused an all-male military unit to engage in assaults and the harassment of women. Like Browning, the Defense Department investigators looking into the Tailhook convention of 1991 concluded that a potent mixture of bureaucratic decisions and masculinized social pressure to turn men in military units into assailants was at fault. The American aircraft carrier pilots, according to this highly critical report, only adopted misogynist practices at their annual Las Vegas meeting after their hospitality suites were no longer sponsored by weapons manufacturers but instead were sponsored by different pilots' units, which had been encouraged by their commanders to look at one another as fierce competitors. Competition in fighter-raid targeting hits off aircraft carriers translated, it seems, into competition in stripping women of their clothes in hotel corridors. These pilots' naval superiors explained that they had come to believe that aircraft carrier pilots — "tailhookers" — were a particular breed of men, that they were especially brash, immature males who needed to have the opportunity to drink in excess and chase after women if they were going to perform successfully as fighter pilots. The Pentagon investigators, unfortunately, did not devote any attention to nationalism. But they did note in passing that the 1991 convention — the gathering that first attracted public criticism when one naval woman officer went to the press after her own superior officer brushed aside her charges of abuse — was held in the heady atmosphere of victory of United States military forces against Iraq in the 1991 Gulf War, an atmosphere that may have intensified the male pilots' peculiar form of masculine behavior.

The following excerpt is from an interview with Borislav Herak conducted by *Dallas Morning News* reporter George Rodriguez.[14]

> Borislav: We had an order to go to restaurant Sonja in Vogosca. We were told that we were going to rape girls there.[15]
>
> Journalist: Who told you this?
>
> B: My captain. The commander of our unit. So as to increase the morale of our fighters. . . .
>
> J: You had never raped a woman before this?
>
> B: No, I had not.
>
> J: And if the women had been Serbian, would you have thought it OK to rape them?

Borislav Herak went on trial in 1993, accused of raping and killing Bosnian Muslim women. Not shown here, however, are the older men in the Serbian militias who manipulated Herak's anxieties and insecurities. Systematic wartime rape is fueled by men's relations to each other. (AP Photo/Michael Stravato, courtesy AP/Wide World Photos)

B: The order was to rape them. . . .

J: What would have happened to you if you had not?

B: They would have sent me to the worst front line in Trebinje, in Herzegovina, or sent me to jail.

J: They would not have killed you?

B: I cannot say that. But I know they would have taken away the house that they had given me. . . .

J: They picked out one girl for the four of you?

B: Yes.

J: You were all in the room when she was raped?

B: Yes.

J: Didn't this seem strange to you?

B: Just a little bit.

J: Why did you do it?

B: Because I had those guys with me. I had to listen to the order, or I would have consequences if I did not. . . . We told her to take off her clothes. . . . She didn't want to. And that guy Damjanovic Mish started to beat her. . . .

J: Did he beat her with his rifle butt or his hands?

B: With his hands. And then she took her clothes off and we raped her. And she put her clothes back on, and we took her away.

J: Did you feel good about this, or guilty?

B: I felt guilty. But I didn't want to say anything or to show it to the others. . . .

J: I do not want to sound anti-Serb, because I am not. But how could you stand to fight for such people?

B: I could not return to Sarajevo to join the Bosnian army. . . .

J: What happened on the drive back after you had killed this woman? Was anything said? Did anyone laugh, or say they felt bad?

B: We never talked about that.

J: Was this good for your morale?

B: Not at all. And before that and after that I had to go to the front lines, so it was the same for me. . . .

J: Was there anything good about fighting with the Serbs? A feeling of togetherness or being part of a team? A feeling of being important?

B: The only good time was when we found schnapps, and we could drink together. Or when we had barbecues. Then we could be together and drink and eat.

J: But I think that in the same way your bosses gave you the drink and food, they gave you the women. As a way to show you were important. Is that right?

B: Yes. For me and for all the soldiers. They wanted to keep us together.

Reports of the number of women raped by male combatants during the 1991–93 war in the former Yugoslavia vary between three thousand and thirty thousand. Muslim women residing in Bosnia appear to comprise the majority of women raped by male soldiers, but human rights monitors have documented rapes of ethnic Croat and Serb women as well. Rapist men include soldiers both in the Yugoslav army and in the militias, and Serbs as well as Croats and Muslims. Yet the incidence of rape by Serbian men serving in autonomous militias fighting in Bosnia appears to be the highest.[16]

Even a skeletal outline of one male militia fighter's thinking about his participation in wartime rape leaves more puzzles than certainties. Borislav Herak, the twenty-one-year-old former navy conscript, a lonely textile worker from an ethnically mixed family, fought with fellow Serbs. But he seemed to weigh the possibilities of returning to Sarajevo to join their Bosnian adversaries. He did not object to raping Muslim women when commanded to do so, but he appears to have felt that male bonding was most authentic over barbecues and schnapps. He was accepted as a Serb man among Serb men, but what he cared most about was avoiding the front and holding on to the once Muslim-owned house given to him. He acted violently on numerous occasions but expressed no warrior's joy in his actions.

The gendered politics of militarized ethnic rape in Bosnia will not end when the leaders of each faction finally call a halt to the war. There will be thousands of men who will be left to make sense of their militarized or nonmilitarized actions, including figuring out—with help from cultural elites in their own communities—whether they should have been able to protect "their" women from male opponents' assaults and, if they could not, what this means for their own ideas about manliness and the future relations of men toward women in their ethnic groups. These women will not be mere victims, real or symbolic. There will be thousands of women who will attempt to reimagine what it means to be feminine in a postwar society, who will actively respond to pressures to restore the community's purity or replenish their community's pool of male fighters, who will devise ways to come to terms with having been raped or with having lived in fear of being raped.

Out of these efforts at social construction—imagining, policy-making, persuasion, and response—will come postwar societies. Borislav Herak, now convicted of murder and rape, may not be alive to take part in this process. But there will be other ordinary men and ordinary women. And their notions about masculinity and femininity will call for just as much serious attention as did that of the youth who pushed a cart by day and read pornographic magazines by night when life was peaceful in Sarajevo.

CHAPTER 8

Spoils of War

In September 1995, on the Japanese island of Okinawa, a twelve-year-old girl was assaulted and raped. Three U.S. Marines were charged. In the wake of the rape, the commander in chief of the U.S. Pacific Command, Admiral Richard Macke, told reporters: "I think it was absolutely stupid, as I've said several times. For the price they paid to rent the car, they could have had a girl." While the comment forced the four-star admiral into early retirement, it also gave us a glimpse of the patriarchal assumptions that encourage U.S. men in uniform to see women as warriors' booty.

There is a widespread belief that soldiers' sexuality is determined by uncontrollable "drives." Any military's fighting effectiveness, this theory holds, is jeopardized if those soldierly sex drives are not accommodated. U.S. base commanders have often worked closely with local and national officials to provide their male troops with "safe" commercialized sex — even, as in Japan, where prostitution is illegal. Rape causes public outrage and political embarrassment. But prostitution? It can be zoned and policed in a way that serves to release the male soldiers' "natural" urges, while at the same time providing business opportunities for local entrepreneurs and allegedly protecting the "respectable" women living near the bases.

The conventional wisdom is, therefore, that a woman who is raped by a U.S. soldier is deserving of headlines and, if necessary, official apologies. By contrast, the woman paid to dance nude at the bar outside the base or to have sex in a bar's "dark corner" is considered unworthy, not only of our sympathy, but of our attention.

There are two fallacies in this accepted military thinking. The first is that rape is discouraged, when in fact it is facilitated by an officially condoned industry that serves up women's sexuality as if it were fast food. Such organized prostitution is often laced with racism, as it is around so many U.S. military bases, turning local women into exoticized game.

The second fallacy is that women in prostitution and women outside prostitution are on opposite sides of the political chasm, when, in fact, feminists have long argued against pitting women in prostitution against so-called respectable women. Both are often working to support their children and both are often trying to develop nonviolent relationships with men.

There's a further danger: the 1995 Okinawa rape, like those committed by other military men, will be converted into mere fodder for a larger, "more serious" political contest. The soldiers and the girl will thereby be turned into mere symbols in a debate over the long-term consequences of Japan's adherence to the U.S.-Japan Security Treaty.

Korean, Bosnian, and other feminists have warned us about this sort of political exploitation of militarized violence against women: left to their own devices, men will take seriously sexual assaults on women only when those assaults can be used to make some other point that those men hold dear — the need for nationalist mobilization, the opposition to an unequal bilateral treaty.

Okinawan and other Japanese feminists, fresh from the UN Conference on Women, which was held in Beijing in fall 1995, drew links between this assault and Second World War and postwar prostitution politics. Then they chastised the Okinawan governor for not using the rape case as a lever for launching a wider investigation of violence against women in Okinawa at the hands of the U.S. military.

Our current attention may have shifted to focus on U.S. soldiers in other war zones, but we need, most importantly, to continue to insist that the U.S. military's entire policy regarding sexuality be subject to public scrutiny: military rape and military prostitution are not separate. They're connected. In addition, we need to shoehorn feminists' voices — Okinawan, Bosnian, and others — into the U.S. media. Reports about soldiers' abuses of women are not enough. What these abuses mean for women is the real story.

CHAPTER 9

Masculinity as a Foreign Policy Issue

The militarization of any country's foreign policy can be measured by monitoring the extent to which its policy:

 · is influenced by the views of Defense Department decision-makers and/or senior military officers,

flows from civilian officials' own presumption that the military needs to carry exceptional weight,

assigns the military a leading role in implementing the nation's foreign policy, and

treats military security and national security as if they were synonymous.

Employing these criteria, one has to conclude that U.S. foreign policy today is militarized.

A feminist analysis can help reveal why U.S. foreign policy has become so militarized — and at what costs. Since 1980, due to the growth of the women's movement, it has become almost commonplace in many domestic U.S. policy circles to ask: "Will this proposed solution have disproportionately negative impacts on girls and women?" and "Does this policy option derive from unspoken assumptions about men's employment, men's health, or men's supposed abilities?" Notable strides have been made in domestic policy arenas, even if there is still a long way to go before such intelligent questioning produces equally smart policy outcomes.

By contrast, in foreign policy, progress toward a more sophisticated — realistic — understanding of the causes and costs of policy options has been sluggish. In the 1970s and 1980s women activists and feminist analysis did help drive popular protests against U.S. wars in Southeast Asia and Central America. Yet, generally, U.S. foreign policy has been tightly controlled by the president and Congress, limiting a genuinely public debate. Stalling progress toward bringing feminist analyses into foreign policy decision-making processes has been the conventionally naive belief that international affairs — trade, immigration, high-tech weapons sales — have nothing to do with gender. They do.

Feminist foreign policy analysis is not naive. It derives from a systematic, eyes-wide-open curiosity, posing questions that non-feminists too often imagine are irrelevant or find awkward to ask. For starters:

Are any of the key actors motivated in part by a desire to appear "manly" in the eyes of their own principal allies or adversaries?

What are the consequences?

Which policy's option will bring women to the negotiating table?

Does the alleged reasonableness of any foreign policy choice rest on the unexamined assumption that women's issues in the target country can be addressed "later," that it is men's anxieties that must be dealt with immediately?

American feminist analysts and strategists have had the strongest impact on international political debates in recent years when they have worked in concert with women's advocates from both developed and developing countries, and when the U.S. military and its congressional allies have not felt that they had a stake in the outcome. Feminist networks have had success, for example, in putting trafficking in women on the agenda of international agencies, making systematic wartime rape a distinct prosecutable charge in the Yugoslavian and Rwandan international war crime tribunals, making women refugees' interests administratively visible, and defining women's control over their reproductive processes as warranting the status of an internationally recognized human right.

However, when Defense Department officials have weighed in on a given policy question, Congress and the administration have shied away from feminist analyses. Consequently, the U.S. government either has invested energy in watering down new international treaties designed to roll back militarism, or has refused outright to ratify such agreements as, for instance, the treaty to ban land mines, the UN convention acknowledging the rights of children in war, and the treaty establishing the International Criminal Court (the first permanent international war crimes tribunal).[1]

In each instance, it has been the Pentagon's ability to persuade civilian officials that the military's own goals would be compromised — its desire to maintain land mines in South Korea, its desire to recruit those under age eighteen, and its prioritizing the protection of American soldiers stationed abroad when they are charged with criminal acts — that has carried the day in Washington. Civilian representatives' repeated privileging of military concerns over other important U.S. international goals is due in part to the nervousness that many male civilian executive and congressional officeholders feel when confronted with military resistance. This is not about hormones. It is about the male politician's angst over not appearing "manly." This, in turn, is about American political culture.

PROBLEMS WITH CURRENT U.S. POLICY

Many observers have remarked on the peculiar American contemporary political culture that equates military experience and / or military expertise with political leadership. It is this cultural inclination that has made it very risky for any American public figure to appear less "manly" than a uniformed senior military male officer. It is a culture — too often unchallenged by ordinary voters — that has given individuals with alleged military knowledge a disproportionate advantage in foreign policy debates.

Such a masculinized and militarized culture pressures nervous civilian candidates into appearing "tough" on military issues. The thought of not embracing a parade of militarized policy positions — to launch preemptive war, increase the defense budget, make NATO the primary institution for building a new European security, expand junior officer training programs in high schools, ensure American male soldiers' access to prostitutes overseas, invest in destabilizing anti-missile technology, justify past crippling but politically ineffectual economic sanctions and bombing raids against Iraq, accept the Pentagon's flawed policy of "don't ask, don't tell, don't pursue," and finance a military-driven anti-drug policy — would leave most American public officials (women and men) feeling uncomfortably vulnerable in the political culture that assigns high value to masculinized toughness. The result: a political competition to appear "tough" has produced U.S. foreign policies that severely limit the American capacity to play a useful role in creating a more genuinely secure international community. That is, America's conventional, masculinized political culture makes it unlikely that Washington policy-makers will either come to grips with a realistic analysis of potential global threats or act to strengthen those multilateral institutions most effective in preventing and ending conflicts.

A feminist analysis turns the political spotlight on the conventional notion of manliness as a major factor shaping U.S. foreign policy choices. It demonstrates that popular gender presumptions are not just the stuff of sociology texts. Every official who has tried not to appear "soft" knows this. For example, early in his administration, Bill Clinton made known his abhorrence of land mines and his determination to ban them. But by 1998, he had caved in to military pressure and stated, instead, that the United States would not sign the widely endorsed international land mines treaty until the Defense Department came up with an "alternative."

Feminist questioning also produces a more realistic accounting of the consequences of "macho" policies. Despite slight increases in the number of women in policy positions, U.S. militarized policies in the post–Cold War era have served to strengthen the privileged positions of men in decision-making, both in the United States and in other countries. For instance, the U.S. government has promoted NATO as the central bastion of Western security, at least when the United States can be sure of its position as the "first among equals" within NATO. Although it is true that there are now women soldiers in all NATO governments' armed forces (the Italians were the most recent to enlist women), NATO remains a masculinized political organization. The alliance's policies are hammered out by a virtually all-male elite in which the roles of masculinity are silently accepted, when they should be openly questioned. Thus, to the extent that the United States succeeds in pressing NATO to wield more political influence than the European Parliament (where women have won an increasing proportion of seats), not only American women but also European women will be shunted to the wings of the political stage.

Consider what feminist analysis reveals about the consequences of militarizing anti-drug policy. In 2000 the American government's billion-dollar-plus aid package to the Colombian military promised, as its critics noted,[2] to further intensify the civil war and human rights abuses. But less discussed was the fact that this policy will serve to marginalize women of all classes in Colombia's political life. This — the obsession of America's elected officials and senior appointees with not appearing "soft" on drugs — militarizes drug prevention efforts and, in so doing, disempowers women both in the United States and in the drug-producing countries. Women — both as grassroots urban activists in American cities and as mobilizers of a broad, cross-class peace movement in Colombia — have offered alternative analyses and solutions to the problems of drug addiction and drug trade.

Its own masculinized culture helped make the U.S. Congress remarkably passive in the face of the Bush administration's post-9/11 militarized foreign policy. Senator Patty Murray, pictured here among her male colleagues, challenged this masculinized culture by joining a small group of congressional women to override the Bush administration's 2003 decision to totally omit programming for women from the $87 billion appropriation it proposed for reconstructing Afghanistan and Iraq. (Photo: Melina Mara/AURORA)

However, their valuable ideas are being drowned out by the sounds of helicopter engines and M16 rifles.

This example illustrates a more general phenomenon. When any policy approach is militarized, one of the first things that happens is that women's voices are silenced. We find that when the United States touts any military institution as the best hope for stability, security, and development, the result is deeply gendered: the politics of masculinity are made to seem "natural," the male grasp on political influence is tightened, and most women's access to real political influence shrinks dramatically.

TOWARD A NEW FOREIGN POLICY

Asking feminist questions openly, making them an explicit part of serious foreign policy discussion, is likely to produce a much more clear-eyed understanding of what is driving any given issue debate and what are the probable outcomes of one policy choice over another. Precisely because the United States currently has such an impact on the internal political workings of so many other countries, we need to start taking a hard look at American political culture. If this globalizing culture continues to elevate a masculinized "toughness" to the status of an enshrined good, military needs will continue to be assigned top political priority, and it will be impossible for the United States to create a more imaginative, more internationally useful foreign policy.

Cultures are not immutable. Americans, in fact, are forever lecturing other societies — Iraq, Afghanistan, Indonesia, Russia, Mexico, France — on how they should remake their cultures. U.S. citizens, however, have been loath to lift up the rock of cultural convention to peer underneath at the masculinized presumptions and worries that shape American foreign policies.

What would be the most immediate steps toward unraveling the masculinized U.S. foreign policy knot? A first step would be for both congressional and presidential policymakers to stop equating "security" with military superiority. A second step would be to muster the political will for Congress to ratify the International Criminal Court treaty, the land mines treaty, and the Convention on the Rights of the Child. A third step would be for Democrats and Republicans to halt their reckless game of "chicken" regarding both the anti-missile defense system and increases in U.S. military spending. A fourth step would be to shelve U.S. efforts to remilitarize Europe and Japan. Together, these four policy steps would amount to a realistic strategy for crafting a less militarized, less distortedly masculinized foreign policy.

A feminist-informed analyst always asks: "Which notions of manliness are shaping this policy discussion?" and "Will the gap between women's and men's access to economic and political influence be widened or narrowed by this particular policy option?" By deploying feminist analytical tools, U.S. citizens can clarify decisions about whether to foster militarization as the centerpiece of the post–Cold War international system. Moreover, by deploying feminist analysis, Americans are much more likely to craft a U.S. foreign policy that will provide the foundation for a long-lasting global structure of genuine security, one that ensures women, both in the United States and abroad, an effective public voice.

CHAPTER 10

"What If They Gave a War . . ."

A Conversation between Cynthia Enloe,
Vivian Stromberg, and the Editors of Ms. Magazine

In March of 1999, the latest in the twentieth century's scores of armed conflicts was raging — this time in the former Yugoslavia, with NATO bombs falling on Belgrade and thousands of refugees driven by Yugoslavia's army over the border of Kosovo into Albania and Macedonia. The editors of Ms. asked Vivian Stromberg, executive director of MADRE, an international human rights organization that works with women in communities in crisis, and Cynthia Enloe, author of Bananas, Beaches and Bases: Making Feminist Sense of International Politics *and an authority on militarism, to talk with Ms. editors about the patriarchal roots of war and to envision a world in which war is not the ultimate problem-solver. Shortly after their conversation, a fragile Kosovo "peace" was negotiated.*

Ms.: Those of us who have been around for more than ten minutes are only too aware of the fact that a habit of war has become the subtext of our contemporary history. As feminists, we need to talk about the alternatives when differences escalate to the point of collective violence. But is there any situation in which violence is justified?

VS: I would take any peaceful means until I hit a brick wall, such as Somoza's regime in Nicaragua or apartheid in 1960s–80s South Africa. I'm also suspicious of premature conflict resolution that attempts to negotiate rights. When rights are on the line, what's to negotiate?

CE: All of us in the second and third waves of the women's movement have come to our feminism in the midst of wars — in Algeria, Vietnam, Namibia, Cuba, Nicaragua, Rwanda, Yugoslavia. These wars have taught us to be much more nuanced in assessing any given insurgency's implication for women's genuine empowerment. Fighting an oppressive regime doesn't make a group of armed insurgent men immune from patriarchal beliefs. So I wonder what you think of the Kosovo Liberation Army [KLA], formed in the late 1990s.

VS: I'm not a supporter of the KLA. We missed the boat when we in the U.S. didn't lend support to the democratic opposition in Kosovo, a movement that had been developing since the late 1980s in opposition to the Milosevic regime's police state and its attempts to exclude ethnic Albanians from public life in Kosovo. Kosovar women played a role in this democratic movement, and they had close working relations with Serbian feminists. The KLA is a nationalist force that does not look kindly on people who have visions of a society different from theirs.

CE: The KLA also looks pretty masculinist?

VS: I think violence is fundamentally masculinist, but I'm not prepared to say that only men act violently or think in masculinist ways about conflict. Just look at Madeleine Albright [then U.S. secretary of state and a principal advocate of using NATO bombing raids to halt the Serbian regime's aggression in Kosovo].

CE: Most feminists have never said that women can't be militaristic. What feminists have revealed, though, is that it's masculinity as an idea and most (not all) men as individuals that garner the longest-lasting benefits from militarization. Still, the idea that war is a liberating time for women can be seductive. A lot of U.S. women today, for instance, wear their "We can do it!" Rosie the Riveter T-shirts with pride, as if World War II actually advanced women's liberation. A close cousin to the Rosie the Riveter myth is the idea that women gain first-class citizenship by enlisting in the U.S. military. Both ideas depend on our ignoring women's experiences of war all over the world. U.S. feminists need to listen closely to women in war zones as they try to make sense of war.

VS: We've been getting e-mails from Serbian, Kosovar, Croat, and Bosnian Muslim women. They're working against tremendous odds to stay in touch with each other, as well as with North American and other European women. They identify as feminists and are nonnationalist. They aren't members of a massive organization like the Federation of Cuban Women, but they're very mighty, especially the feminists in Belgrade, working in groups such as Women in Black.

CE: Talk about bravery and guts!

VS: Right now they're trying to keep their chins above water. The activist nonnationalist Serbian women I'm in touch with are very clear that bombing isn't going to help anything. One feminist in Belgrade, a psychotherapist, tells me that twenty-four hours a day she's just trying to respond to people who feel desperate and hopeless.

CE: And what does this sort of war-generated terror do to families? Journalists without a feminist curiosity talk about "refugee families" or "Yugoslavian families" as if there weren't dynamics *inside* families that are severely altered by the Milosevic regime turning the screws while NATO bombs. Families under these pressures are still made up of individuals with their own notions of what's "feminine" and what's "manly."

VS: I've learned that during war, the resulting social disintegration often gets played out in increased family violence.

CE: The people who set up refugee camps think in security terms. But whose security is being prioritized? Women trying to escape militarization, it seems to me, often find their lives remilitarized once they've arrived in a refugee camp. The host government will insist to the UN or NATO or the Red Cross that there be more military presence around the refugees so they won't filter out into the local society. I worry that refugee camps can become like prisons, making women inside feel as oppressed by their male camp "protectors" as they do by some of the more nefarious men inside the camp or by the men from whom they escaped.

VS: People are totally disempowered in that kind of situation. One of the really beautiful parts of a project that we funded in Yugoslavia in '93 — if there is anything beautiful about that situation — was giving mothers in a refugee camp small items for their children. We learned from these women that it felt terrible not to be able to respond to their kids' simplest requests; they had to direct their children to the international relief agency that ran the camp. So MADRE gave mothers candies and other modest things, so they could respond directly to their kids.

CE: It's hard to keep one's eye on the big picture and the little picture simultaneously. Nonfeminists will often say to feminists, "You have to look at the bigger picture." And the bigger picture is always one in which gender is not important. Even some feminists seem more comfortable talking about this ungendered "big picture." And when addressing Kosovo, some nonfeminist progressive commentators have seemed devoid of any curiosity about how sexism has been manipulated to fuel a militarized kind of nationalism. They try to explain the power of Milosevic [then the authoritarian head of Serbia's government] without exploring the politics of motherhood, or they try to analyze the political relationships between Blair, Clinton, Albright, Chirac, and Schröeder as if those relationships — which shape this thing called NATO — were free of gender issues. So I get a little nervous when some of our good friends urge us to focus on the "bigger picture," which is one where they don't have to be made uncomfortable by feminist ideas.

VS: But I do think, Cynthia, that you need to look at each piece in the context of the bigger picture.

CE: Yes, but a bigger picture has to be one informed by feminism, because sometimes the bigger picture is patriarchy. Do you find that with nonfeminist groups, you have to say, "Hold on now, you can't just count on us as your good allies here, you've got to incorporate some of our understanding"? Or is that hard to do?

VS: Well, MADRE's chosen as its partners community-based women's groups that share our perspective. They're feminists who do understand the role of the military, the economic violence of the World Bank and the IMF [International Monetary Fund], and the opportunism of the Global North and of some solidarity groups.

CE: Has MADRE changed as a result of doing this work?

VS: Yes, I think we've learned a lot, and the challenges that we're up against have changed.

CE: How?

VS: Well, it used to be you turned on the TV, you saw marines, it was a war. Now it's not always that easy. When I was growing up, if there was a labor dispute, you were on the side of the union no matter what. Now, even trying to build a union has to be thought of in different ways. How do you support women in another country who are having atrocious violence at work but who desperately need the jobs? Community-based women's groups — in close conjunction with labor unions — may be useful to those women workers because the women's groups are concerned with a broader spectrum of their needs than a labor union alone would be.

CE: In recent years, we've watched peace negotiations and attempts to create more long-term reconciliations — in Northern Ireland, Palestine/Israel, Bosnia, Rwanda, South Africa, El Salvador, Haiti. Women-based community groups have sought a seat at the negotiating table. But in each place, only the "chief protagonists" are deemed eligible to take a seat at the table. Northern Ireland stands out as an exception, and even there, the Northern Ireland Women's Coalition was marginalized. Have you seen signs of success in this area among the groups MADRE has worked with?

VS: On one hand, women are better positioned to increase their participation in public life as the violence winds down, precisely because they started with nothing. On the other hand, many formal peace negotiations have avoided justice issues. What sort of peace can one build if justice issues are left off the agenda?

CE: Justice is expressed daily through the fair distribution of decent housing; granting women full inheritance and landowning rights; and the guarantees of access to public resources for women as well as men, and for people of all sexual orientations. It's these issues that so often slip off the negotiating table, as if they were irrelevant to creating peace and preventing war.

VS: Yes, then there's the risk that any women who are invited to the negotiating table will be co-opted. There's a consciousness that there needs to be an appearance of participation by women, but if that consciousness is only skin-deep, then the participation will be in appearance only. We don't want the negotiations to go on without women.

CE: One thing to do is to prevent peace negotiations from being so shrouded in secrecy. Even a woman with feminist political awareness who's developed her consciousness in community-based activism can succumb to diplomatic pressure during long negotiating sessions if she is cut off from her community. This happens to women in the diplomatic corps, in UN agencies, in nonfeminist humanitarian relief groups.

Ms.: Sometimes we in the U.S. don't pay enough attention to what's going on in other countries to spot the chance for authentic peace making with women who are in the thick of it.

CE: Yes, this is one of the fallouts of the government using aerial bombing — it dulls Americans' political attentiveness. Bombing lures us into thinking only of "hits" and "collateral damage." For instance, we didn't pay attention to the Serbs' pro-democracy demonstrations against the Milosevic regime in the fall and winter of 1996–97.

VS: And, again, in Kosovo's earlier organizing of a genuine peaceful democratic opposition. In both instances — in Belgrade and in Kosovo — Americans and Europeans didn't treat those mid-1990s pro-democracy efforts as worthy of support.

CE: Serbian women have struggled nonviolently against Milosevic since 1991 to build an alternative that incorporates sexual equality in a multiethnic democratic Yugoslavia. And today they feel most betrayed by the European Union and the U.S., and their reliance on NATO and on bombing to try and create lasting solutions.

VS: They're just bereft.

CE: So, we Americans need to recognize effective democratic movements when they're staring us in the face. Sometimes they don't look like political parties; sometimes they aren't armed insurgents.

VS: We must also look at what we call democracy and the way language is used in this country. Most of the time when Americans talk about democracy, they're talking about political parties and voting. For me, that's not the most important part. In the U.S., we don't have a democratic model. If we have such a good democracy, how come so many people don't have decent jobs, and so many kids don't know where they're going, and so many people don't vote? Everyday acts of racism and homophobia disenfranchise Americans. Privatized health care and education, building and maintaining privatized prisons — this is "democracy" in today's America.

CE: So we also need to pressure the media to consider a much wider range of people as political "experts." Vivian, we need you on *Nightline*.

Ms.: Had you been on *Nightline*, what would you have said about NATO's bombing in Yugoslavia and about the Kosovar refugees?

VS: That NATO should withdraw, and that the UN needs to do its job. That's why we have it. However, I do think armed peacekeeping forces are needed on the ground. But the UN, not NATO, and certainly not the U.S., should be making these decisions.

CE: We can't allow a carbon copy of the 1995 Dayton peace process [which brokered the peace agreement between Serbia, Croatia, and Bosnia and Herzegovina], even though that's the only way most governments can even imagine resolving conflicts — rival male negotiators holed up together, bonding over scotch at 2:00 in the morning and thinking they're solving the world's problems.

VS: There also needs to be a permanent International Criminal Court [ICC] that allows entities other than states to bring violators of international law to trial. In 1998 the U.S. government, together with the Vatican, led the opposition to an international treaty that could create the world's first-ever permanent International Criminal Court.

CE: This means each of us can vote in November 2000 against any U.S. senator who threatens to vote against the ICC treaty, which is up for ratification. As you said, voting is not all of democracy, but it does matter. [The U.S. Senate still has not ratified the ICC treaty.]

VS: Taking steps to prevent war can happen in areas that don't look anything like the UN or international courts. A greater emphasis has to be put on the kinds of things that influence young children. I agree with people in the U.S. who worry about the amount of violence kids see on TV. But I don't think those programs that they think are the violent ones are the dangerous ones. When kids see news programs that treat the aerial bombing of people in another country as normal, even admirable, those kids are absorbing the idea that military solutions are normal solutions.

CE: Schools are a place where feminist ideas could roll back a militarized culture. Think about the U.S. Army Junior ROTC program. Lots of local boards of education and parents' groups around the U.S. have now adopted Junior ROTC for their high schools, accepting ROTC's argument that militaristic programs — overseen by non-state-certified teachers, mostly male veterans — inculcates in American children the skills for coping with contemporary American life.

Ms.: But people often seem at a loss as to how to squelch militaristic ideology.

CE: Daily conversation can become a political act. When an acquaintance casually refers to the "ancient hostilities in the Balkans" or to the "centuries-old hatreds" between Rwanda's Hutus and Tutsis, it's a throwaway line that one usually just lets pass. But these phrases are meant to persuade you that there's no decision-maker to be held accountable. So nowadays, when I hear anyone refer to "ancient hostilities," I try to summon up the energy to challenge them.

Ms.: And what about practical ways to help people who are actually in conflict areas?

VS: Donations, volunteering, spreading the word about women's organizations that are working in these places — all are helpful. The major aid organizations are more equipped than small community-based organizations to provide water, sanitation facilities, food, shelter, fuel, medical care, transportation, and tents. But some of them are ill-equipped to deal with the human anguish and the sexual trauma. A UN report released at the end of April 1999 said that there had been a "significant upsurge" in sexual violence that corresponded with the first week of NATO's bombings. So I think that we need to provide support to those women's organizations that are working with rape victims, and the U.S. government needs to stop thinking that bombing is an acceptable form of violence because it's not "hands-on" like ground warfare.

Ms.: Can we step back a minute, though, because there seems to be an enormous number of people who think the U.S. government has gone into the Yugoslav conflict for humanitarian reasons. They genuinely see analogies between Milosevic and his Serbian nationalist supporters, on the one hand, and Hitler and the Nazis, on the other, and they believe therefore that we must not repeat the 1930s.

CE: People of very good will can often find themselves supporting things they feel are quite horrifying. You may not normally be in favor of military solutions, but you get stuck. For instance, I sometimes just go silent, because I'm horrified by events in Kosovo, but I can't think of what to do about them. Therefore, I'll just let the people who think they do know what to do go ahead. And it's that kind of silence that's often taken for popular support of a militarized solution. I should have been paying more attention in 1995, '96, and '97, when there were nonmilitary possibilities for resolving the Serbian-Kosovo conflict. I shouldn't let myself get to the point where I imagine there are only two possible stances: being passive in the face of Milosevic's injustices or supporting the NATO bombing.

VS: If we're serious about wanting to stop the phenomenon, we should start talking about ethnic cleansing throughout history. In 1948, for example, three-quarters of the Palestinian people were forced off their land. And American Indians in the eighteenth and nineteenth centuries and the indigenous Mayan population in Guatemala from 1970 through the '80s are other examples.

Ms.: But U.S. officials and media try to persuade us that the problem in each new instance is just one man whom we can demonize. If we just get rid of this guy, the problem will go away. Which ignores the other elements at play. On the other hand, we've got to de-link leadership, manliness (even if aspired to by a Margaret Thatcher), and military prowess.

CE: Americans just don't know enough about other countries to imagine that there can be a male-dominated leadership that doesn't necessarily lead to institutionalized militarization — as in Canada or contemporary Ireland, for example.

VS: And when there is a war, people underestimate the actual costs. They talk in terms of dollars spent and maybe lives lost, but they don't mention the rivers polluted when a chemical factory is bombed, or the farmland made inaccessible when an army plants it with invisible land mines.

CE: And they don't tally up the less visible costs — the social trust destroyed, the definitions of "heroism" shrunken.

Ms.: Vivian, MADRE now has projects all over the world?

VS: In Mexico, Guatemala, Nicaragua, Haiti, Cuba, Palestine, Rwanda, Yugoslavia. Each project is in partnership with local women's groups. MADRE's mandate is to work in places where the crises women and their families face are caused directly or indirectly by the U.S. The lives of the people we work with are in the balance. One of the things we do is bring local women into more formal settings like the UN, so they can speak for themselves.

Ms.: Are there some places that give you more hope than others?

VS: When women are organized, there's hope. Southern Mexico inspires hope because there's tremendous participation from citizens in lots of communities, and they have a vision of what they want to build. And the participation in civil society in Chiapas — especially women's participation — is palpable.

Ms.: Speaking of hope, what elements would have to be in place for the world community to even imagine a century without war?

CE: I don't buy the smug argument that wars are inevitable. Feminist activists in lots of countries have been outlining actions we can take to bring such a world into being. We can challenge, for example, anyone who says that the only real patriots are people, typically men, who've been soldiers, and that the best way for the U.S. to earn international respect is to wield military power. We can vote out of office people who refuse to sign on to such international antiwar treaties as those outlawing land mines and creating a permanent International Criminal Court. I don't think that it's mere fantasizing to envision a world without war.

VS: To imagine a world without war, we must imagine and work for a world with justice. A world in which young people of all nations can dream about the future and picture themselves in it. A world in which we do not merely tolerate differences but are enriched by them. A world where people are valued, and exploitation and greed are phenomena that we only read about in history books.

CHAPTER 11

Sneak Attack

The Militarization of U.S. Culture

Things start to become militarized when their legitimacy depends on their associations with military goals. When something becomes militarized, it appears to rise in value. Militarization is seductive.

But it is really a process of loss. Even though something seems to gain value by adopting an association with military goals, it actually surrenders control and gives up the claim to its own worthiness.

Militarization is a sneaky sort of transformative process. Sometimes it is only in the pursuit of *de*militarization that we become aware of just how far down the road of complete militarization we've gone. In the fall of 2001, Representative Barbara Lee (D.-Calif.) pulled back the curtain in the aftermath of the September 11 attacks when she cast the lone congressional vote against giving George W. Bush carte blanche to wage war. The loneliness of her vote suggested how far the militarization of

Congress — and its voters back home — has advanced. In fact, since September 11, publicly criticizing militarization has been widely viewed as an "unpatriotic" act, as an act of disloyalty.

Whole cultures can be militarized. It is a militarized U.S. culture that made it easier for President George W. Bush to wage war without most Americans finding that militarized foreign policy itself a threat to democracy. Our cultural militarization makes war-waging too often seem like a comforting reconfirmation of our collective security, identity, and pride.

Other sectors of U.S. culture have also been increasingly militarized:

Education: School board members accept Junior ROTC programs for their teenagers, and social studies teachers play it safe by avoiding discussions of past sexual misconduct by U.S. soldiers overseas. Many university scientists pursue lucrative Defense Department weapons research contracts.

Soldiers' girlfriends and wives: They've been persuaded that they are "good citizens" if they keep silent about problems in their relationships with male soldiers for the sake of their fighting effectiveness.

Beauty: In 2001 the Miss America Pageant organizers selected judges with military credentials, including a former secretary of the navy and an air force captain.

Cars: The Humvee ranks among the more oversized cars to clog U.S. highways, yet civilians think they will be feared and admired if they drive this vehicle, which is inspired by the armored vehicles designed for American war-waging in the Middle East.

Then there is the conundrum of the American flag. People who reject militarization may don a flag pin, unaware that doing so may convince those with a militarized view of the U.S. flag that their bias is universally shared, thus deepening the militarization of U.S. culture.

The events since September 11 have also shown that many Americans today may be militarizing non-U.S. women's lives. It was only after George W. Bush declared "war on terrorists and those countries that harbor them" that the violation of Afghan women's human rights took center stage in American political discourse. Here's the test of whether Afghan women are being militarized: if their well-being is worthy of our concern only because their lack of well-being justifies the U.S. military occupation of Afghanistan, then we are militarizing Afghan women — as well as our own compassion. We are thereby complicit in the notion that something has worth only if it allows militaries to achieve their missions.

It's important to remember that militarization has its rewards, such as newfound popular support for measures formerly contested. For example, will many Americans be newly persuaded that drilling for oil in the Alaskan wilderness is acceptable because it will be framed in terms of "national security"? Will most U.S. citizens newly accept government budgetary raids on the Social Security trust fund in the name of paying for the "war on terrorism"?

Women's rights in the United States and Afghanistan are in danger if they become mere by-products of some other cause. Militarization, in all its seductiveness and subtlety, deserves to be bedecked with flags wherever it thrives — fluorescent flags of warning.

CHAPTER 12

War Planners Rely on Women

Thoughts from Tokyo

In Tokyo, early in 2003, I counted six of these photographs in the Japanese English-language daily papers: pictures of American and Australian wives and girlfriends of soldiers, sailors, and pilots teary as they kiss and wave good-bye to their military husbands and boyfriends, off to deployments in the Middle East. My Japanese feminist friends tell me that a month earlier there were strikingly similar photographs of Japanese military wives standing on the shore, waving to their Self-Defense Force husbands as they sailed on the *Kirishima*, off to support the same Bush administration buildup to an invasion of Iraq.

Each photo had merely a brief caption. This was not "hard news." Implicit in the editors' layout choices was their shared assumption that photos of women waving and weeping just speak for themselves: no serious story there; women just doing what women always do, supporting their men.

But it isn't so simple. It never is. Feminist scholars in Japan, the United States, Canada, Israel, France, Britain, Korea, and

South Africa have revealed that war-waging — and the preparations for war-waging — relies on women. Women as mothers of potential recruits, women as girlfriends and wives of soldiers, women as patriots, women as voters, women as entertainers and prostitutes, women as workers in defense industries ("the women who wire"), and at least a few women to serve inside the military (today women make up 4 percent of the Japanese Self-Defense Force, 6 percent of the British forces, 15 percent of the U.S. military, and 12 percent each of the militaries of Australia, Canada, South Africa, and Russia).

These women aren't identical. Feminist researchers never lump all women together. They realize, and so too do the military planners whom feminists are critiquing, that the military wives, the women who wire high-tech weaponry, the military prostitutes, the mothers of recruit sons, differ by class, often by race, usually by age, and frequently by nationality. But each of these groups of women is typically slotted into a particular supporting role in the wishful scenarios devised by officials preparing a government's war plan.

Many of these women are willing to play the military role expected of them for the sake of a paycheck, a sense of pride and belonging, educational benefits, or a stable marriage. Other women play their assigned militarized part because they don't have much choice: they have a child to support, they have had no access to education, they are trapped in debt bondage. If the editors assigned reporters, not just photographers, to these waving women on the docks — and to the other women rarely deemed even worth a picture — they might hear a more complicated political story of what it takes to prepare for war. If these journalists followed clues back up the chain of command, into the offices of the senior politicians, they might eavesdrop on male officials expressing worries about AIDS, about declining birthrates, about rising divorce rates, about domestic violence inside soldiers' families, about worrisome electoral "gender gaps," and about male soldiers' wobbly morale.

The fact that today all of this political worrying and decision-making rarely is deemed newsworthy, that feminist researchers' revealing findings are ignored by international commentators, means that the full politics of the buildup for the invasion of Iraq has been woefully underreported.

There is more. Not all women today are willing to play these roles thought by military planners to be so essential to their operations. Women married to soldiers, for instance, are not mere weeping icons. They are thinking adults. Being often isolated on military bases, and depending on their husbands' promotions for their own economic security, military wives' discontent and outright critiques of their government's foreign policy are usually camouflaged. Yet the fact that the divorce rate in the U.S. military is rising might be thought of as military wives "voting with their feet."

Then there is many women's unwillingness to accept their political elite's gendered notions of what constitutes "national security" and "patriotism." Public opinion polls conducted in the months leading up to the U.S.-led invasion of Iraq suggested that governments' efforts to persuade all women — but especially women as "maternal citizens" — that an open-ended and preemptive international war on terrorism is in their womanly best interests have been less than successful. In the United States, a June 2002 *Wall Street Journal*/NBC poll showed 20 percent more men than women approved of the Bush government deploying ground troops to Iraq. Five months later, an ABC polling analyst noted, "Men and Republicans are much more apt to support U.S. action against Iraq; women and Democrats, much less so."

That same month, November 2002, a survey of Australians by the national daily *The Age* exposed a similar gender gap: while 52 percent of the Australian men surveyed said that they opposed a military attack on Iraq, even more Australian women, 62 percent, did. In Britain, the Blair government seemed to have had an especially hard time persuading its female citizens that going to war made sense: opinion pollsters commissioned by the daily *Guardian* found in late January 2003 that, although women were significantly more anxious about a terrorist threat in Britain, they were slightly more likely than male Britons (52 percent compared to 49 percent) to oppose British participation in a war.

Feminist analysis is subtle and sophisticated. Its users do not assume women anywhere are "naturally peaceful." Instead, they take women — in all their complexity — seriously. Using a gender curiosity, they listen carefully to women; they watch government officials' sometimes confused efforts to maneuver women of different classes, ages, and ethnicities into positions that will serve their war-preparing objectives, and they pay close attention to varieties of women assessing and responding to those maneuvers. If we are to realistically understand the drive toward war with Iraq — and its alternatives — we need far deeper analyses of women's lives than supplied in the photos of women weeping on the dock.

CHAPTER 13

Feminists Keep Their Eyes on Militarized Masculinity

*Wondering How Americans See
Their Male Presidents*

Masculinity. It's always there just below the political surface. Propping up authority. Causing anxiety. This prime minister's wavy hair. That dictator's khaki fatigues. A president's cowboy belt buckle.

Feminists notice these things. Feminists all over the world — in Turkey, South Korea, the United States, Japan, and France — use gender tools to investigate things that more conventional foreign policy "experts" find uncomfortable: the ways in which manipulations of manliness often shape foreign policy decision-making.

As an American feminist, therefore, I find strange, worth investigating, George W. Bush's seeming ability to so thoroughly infuse his presidential authority with militarized masculinity. George W. Bush never served even close to a wartime battlefield. During the Vietnam War young George W. Bush sought safety from danger by enlisting in the Texas Air National Guard. There were five hundred men ahead of him on the waiting list. But, perhaps with some help from his well-connected family friends, he got in. For the last months of his National Guard service, records reveal, young George W. Bush didn't even bother to show up for his tame, bloodless duties. Nor was he ever penalized for those absences. Yet during most of his presidency he has been able to convince a sizable portion of American citizens (more men than women) that his presidential authority is a natural fit with militarized manliness.[1] Odd.

Feminists everywhere have learned to be wary of using military service or military support as a criterion for any public official's fitness for power. That sort of basis for political eligibility always privileges masculinity and thereby marginalizes most women. So when I puzzle over George W. Bush's early use of class privilege to avoid wartime service, I am *not* suggesting that his lack of battlefield experience made him unfit for the U.S. presidency. Instead — and this is very different — I am questioning how a man who apparently wielded family connections to escape being sent to Vietnam in the 1970s managed thirty years later to deepen even further the masculinized militarization of a legally gender-neutral, civilian democratic institution, the American presidency. Only a feminist-informed gender analysis can unravel this important puzzle.

The solution, I think, lies in a peculiarly American phenomenon. American political culture during the last century increasingly imagined the job description for the presidency as prioritizing just one part of its myriad complex responsibilities: commander in chief of the uniformed armed services. This imagining is a serious political distortion. It amounts to the militarization of what is constitutionally designed to be a multidimensional civilian post. Imagining that "commander in chief" is the *essence* of the U.S. presidency is a profoundly gendered distortion that shrinks the meaning of governance and gives any presidential officeholder and "his" strategists a constant incentive to feature military solutions above more subtle, prolonged, complex sorts of solutions. Militarism legitimizes masculinized men as protectors, as actors, as rational strategists, while it places feminized people in the role of the emotionally informed, physically weak, only parochially aware protected. Thus militarization of the U.S. presidency generates dangerous consequences for both women and men. Their voting, their running for and holding office, and even their access to participation in political debates are distorted by the militarization of the presidency. For if — in order to be seen by the electorate, journalists, and members of Congress as a credible candidate for, a holder of, or just an ordinary critic of the U.S. presidency — one must above all prove one can act like and think like a person who can command the deference of military professionals, many men and most women will be shoved to the periphery of political life.

Many commentators have noted that the attacks of September 11, 2001, have made more Americans feel vulnerable. To exploit that sense of vulnerability in ways that entrench further the distorted militarization of the office of president is irresponsible and risky. In the short term it might have camouflaged George W. Bush's precarious purchase on his own militarized manliness. But in the longer term, a feminist analysis reveals, this distortion is certain to undermine international stability and to shrink political life by marginalizing women as full citizens and by privileging the narrowest version of masculinity.

CHAPTER 14

Becoming a Feminist

Cynthia Enloe in Conversation with
Three British International Relations Scholars

If I can just ask you about some of the formative influences upon you.
You mention, at the beginning of your book Maneuvers, *your relation-*
ship with your mother.[1] *You write that your "mother's life kept beckon-*
ing me to ask fresh questions."

My mother and I almost never talked politics. She actually voted
Republican most of her life, but she didn't vote Republican with
as much emotion behind it as did my father when he voted
Republican. My mother was never worried about my becoming
increasingly feminist. She died in 1983, and by that time I had
been doing feminist work one way or another for, oh, maybe five
years. In her later years if one of her friends had asked her, "Do
you think Cynthia is becoming a feminist?" I think my mother
would have said, "Oh yes," and I don't think it would have worried her. So it's in a broader sense that my mother has had a political influence on me. She really met and dealt with the world in

such a different way than my father did. I'm in many ways my father's daughter except for the fact that I'm my mother's daughter, and that is, for me, a saving grace. My father was very argumentative. I was the oldest child and my brother wasn't very interested in engaging in that kind of argument at supper. For her part, my mother enjoyed a more genuine, easy kind of conversation. So from early on, I was the one who was supposed to rise to the occasion and engage with my father politically at mealtime. I learned a lot of skills that way, not necessarily skills that one wants to learn. I think now that my mother's way of engaging with the world is more meaningful, less competitive. She was a facilitator, somebody who wanted people to feel comfortable. My own efforts to reunderstand my mother came out of my becoming a feminist. In the late 1970s and 1980s it was my feminist friends who really encouraged me to take my mother's life seriously. So when I went back and looked at those diaries she kept — this was just as I was starting to write the final draft of *Does Khaki Become You?* — diaries she began when she was fifteen and continued 'til the day she died when she was seventy-five, I looked at them through new eyes. My mother never wrote anything indiscreetly. There is nothing in her diaries that's "juicy." But in the 1970s and 1980s feminist friends were pushing me to redefine what's "political," to break out of my narrow political science box. So I gradually began to reappreciate my mother's experiences as being something that could tell me about international relations.

When your mother used the term "feminist" in respect of your work, would she have used it positively or negatively? In the past, and still today, many women reject the term and give it negative connotations.

I should think she was very proud of what I was doing. There was a kind of trust. She might have been a little nervous on my behalf, but I don't ever remember her, in any way, being negative about my becoming a feminist. I mean, I wasn't living the life she'd lived, but I was living the life that a lot of her own college friends had chosen to live. My mother went to college in the mid-1920s in California; she went to the all-women's Mills College. She had a lot of friends who either didn't marry or married late and who had careers. She met a lot of women when she and my father were living in Germany during the rise of Hitler. My father, who was from Missouri, was going to medical school there at the time. My mother married him and lived in Germany from 1933 to 1936. The whole expatriate community there included, I now realize, a number of women who were studying medicine or having their own careers, and my mother was always very positive about those friends of hers. To tell you the truth, I think that once my father divorced her after twenty-five years of marriage (my mother had left her own waged job when she got married), she became even more convinced that young women of my generation should gain their own economic security. So she would never have encouraged me to stop working.

So the presumption with which you grew up was that you would have a career — you would be a wage-earner and you would, in all ways, pursue an independent path?
Well, that would have been my mother's hope. I graduated from university in 1960, after having gone to high school in my suburban New York town. I went to a women's college, Connecticut College, which was very good. Yet in 1960 it had the reputation among all the elite women's colleges in the American Northeast

of having the highest percentage of girls who got married! [*laugh*] Huh! I don't know if that's the kind of rep the school desired. So most of my classmates — many of whom were genuinely more scholarly that I was — got married quite soon after college. I was in one wedding after the other, with all those dresses having shoes and bags dyed to match. On the other hand, I knew friends of my mother who'd never married. I had women teachers in high school and at college who had never married. I was taught politics by two women who hadn't married, and they seemed to have been living very jolly, interesting lives.

What led you to choose the study of politics as a student?
I loved politics. I think that is being my father's daughter in a way. I'm really a suburban kid! I grew up in Manhasset, Long Island. Every morning we got the New York *Herald-Tribune* and the *New York Times* on our front doorstep. My mother and father both presumed that if you read two daily New York papers, you were sort of up on things. I remember when Roosevelt died. I was six (there, now that's dating me). The next morning, my father coached me so I'd be able at school — when Miss Erikson would ask, "Now children, who's the new president?" — to pipe up and say, "Harry Truman." I always thought politics — in the conventional sense of "politics" — was interesting. And that is my father's doing.

So, was your early engagement with politics as a field of study an extension of your sense of what it meant to be a "citizen"? And then, you just kept pursuing it after your degree?
Yes. I mean I don't think there was anything else that I would have liked to do. It's kind of boring, isn't it? I don't ever remember wondering, oh, should I choose biology or classics or English

lit? Studying politics was really something that felt very natural to me. What did change was what I imagined the study of "politics" to be.

And what produced the big change? Was it life experience, or was it the result of scholarly reflection — the outcome of reading books?

My first academic job after getting my Ph.D. at Berkeley was at a big state university in Ohio called Miami University. This was 1967. They'd never had a woman in the political science department before, and they actually called up Bob Scalapino, the senior Japanese politics specialist at Berkeley, and asked, "Will she make trouble?" And he, this is terrible, do you know what he said to them? "No. Don't worry." When they told me his responses, I thought: Oh, that's too bad! Friends of mine were beginning in the late 1960s to discover that there was this thing called the Women's Movement, but I wasn't part of the early Women's Movement. I'm afraid I wasn't in on the movement's ground floor. I was just on its fringes by the early 1970s. I subscribed to *Ms.* magazine when it first appeared as just an insert in *New York* magazine. But feminism — and I scarcely knew then what that word meant — didn't affect any of my teaching or any of my writing in those years. I don't think I ever even used the word "woman" in my dissertation, which was on the ethnic politics of education in Malaysia. I realize now that it was a very gendered politics, but back then, in the midst of the allegedly radical '60s, I didn't notice it. I don't think any of the first four books I published had the "W" word in it. *Ethnic Politics and Political Development*, my first post-dissertation book, didn't. Nor did *Comparative Politics of Pollution*, which was a very early book looking at the politics of the environment in Japan, the Soviet Union, the United States, and Britain.[2] So I was a little slow. When, in the late 1970s and early 1980s, I did start paying serious attention to women's lives in my academic work, it was due to friends and then students nudging me, alerting me to all that I was missing. Feminist questions crept first into my teaching (by the mid-1970s I was at Clark University) and then into my writing. Teaching before writing.

Can I go back to your time at Berkeley? You credit your experiences at Berkeley with having molded your work and career. How did that happen?

Berkeley in the 1960s was a very exciting place to be, especially with the launching of what became the Free Speech Movement on campus, a movement that began one day as a protest against bureaucratization of university life. The IBM card symbolized the villain. Of course, hundreds of us had already become politicized by civil rights activism and by participation in protests against growing U.S. government military involvement in Vietnam. But it was more than this overt politics that made Berkeley such an exciting place for me in those years. There were poetry readings, foreign-language films, classical concerts, theater. You really could stumble upon Joan Baez singing out on the Sproul Hall steps at lunchtime and go to hear the great poet Denise Levertov later that night. On top of this, one of my best graduate student pals was a Vietnamese friend, who raised my consciousness even before I went to Southeast Asia. Then, when I was in Malaysia in 1965–66, I became even more aware of and critical of U.S. intervention in Asia. Berkeley's Free Speech Movement only erupted after I returned to campus in 1966.

There was blatant gender politics in every department at Berkeley in the 1960s, but none of us thought to challenge — or even to be curious about — that. I was the first woman ever to be a head TA [teaching assistant] for Aaron Wildavsky, then a "rising star" in the field of American politics. He was a fast-talking, street-fighter sort of intellectual. There were six hundred students and twenty-five TAs in his "Intro to American Politics" course. So the head TA was handed a big operation to run. The Berkeley political science department then had fifty tenured faculty and not a single one was a woman (Hannah Pitkin, the political theorist, wasn't given a tenure track contract until later). So there were little gendered firsts along the way, but I wasn't smart enough to realize what that meant or why a first was a "first." Even though it had zero feminist consciousness, the 1966–67 Free Speech Movement did help change my notions of the relationship between my studies and social action. A young women's studies student asked me recently what I thought the sexual politics of Berkeley's radicalism was at that time. It was a superb question and has made me think. It was very masculinist (though I didn't have this concept back then) and it was quite heterosexist. Even though I was without the words to articulate any concerns about the student movement's internal culture then, I did distance myself a little from that culture. These were all my buddies who were involved, and I supported boycotts of classes and carried picket signs. Nonetheless, I sort of stood back from the social life inside the movement. Being a TA, I had to make daily decisions on what to do and what to resist doing. The decisions we all were making split the political science department wide open; Sheldon Wolin and Norman Jacobson, two political theorists, were very supportive of what became the agenda of the Free Speech Movement. On the other hand, professors such as Bob Scalapino were made very nervous by it; they thought it was a leftist version of McCarthyism, a political ideology they had fought against a decade earlier, in the 1950s.

You seemed almost to be sleepwalking into being a Southeast Asian specialist. Is this how you see it now?

Funny, isn't it? Today I never call myself a Southeast Asian specialist because that feels quite inaccurate. I am a member of the Asian Studies Association: I keep up with Malaysia in politics; I have taught the politics of Vietnam and the Philippines as a regular undergraduate course, as well as the politics of Japan. When I was an undergraduate at Connecticut College I went on a summer Washington internship and was assigned to the Department of Agriculture. Now, remember, I'm from New York suburbia; I could tell forsythia from azaleas and grass from weeds, but that was about it! Yet during that hot Washington summer, I was essentially a gofer for male agricultural technicians visiting from Ghana, Turkey, and Indonesia. I was twenty years old; I could have told you the difference between parliamentary and presidential systems, but I knew nothing about the political life in any of these countries. The nice fisheries fellow from Indonesia took me under his wing, and for that whole summer he sort of tutored me in Indonesian politics. He was appalled at how little I knew — this would have been the summer of 1959, soon after the Indonesian revolution that ended Dutch colonial rule. I didn't even know that Indonesia had had a revolution. I was pretty naive. I knew Russia had had one; I knew France had had one, and I knew something was going on in Algeria, though mostly from the vantage point of de Gaulle. So two years later, now in grad school at Berkeley, I signed up for a course on the politics of Southeast Asia taught by an Indonesia specialist, almost out of a sense of obligation to my fisheries friend, Gelar.

I didn't have an academic career mapped out for myself when I entered Berkeley. I thought vaguely I was going to get a master's in one year, and then I would go back East and teach in a private girl's school. Then David Apter, at that time a brand-new comparative politics professor, asked me to come to his office one day after class and said to me: "You are going on for a Ph.D." I said, "I am?" He said, "Of course." And so I did. I loved comparative politics, but instead of focusing on Indonesia, I moved over to Malaysia because nobody else then seemed interested in Malaysia. In the mid-1960s Indonesia was the "hot" academic topic in Southeast Asian studies because it had had an anticolonial revolution. But I didn't want to do what everybody else was doing. I thought, I'll take the country everyone else thinks is "boring," which was Malaysia. It turned out to be so fruitful because one couldn't understand Malaysian politics without trying to make sense of ethnic politics. By the time I got my first teaching post, I was thinking of myself as a "comparative ethnic politics" specialist.

You mention comparative politics, and in the past you have sometimes described what you do as comparative political analysis. Is this still how you would describe yourself today, if forced to give yourself an academic label?

I think today I would say that I do feminist comparative politics with — thanks to all of you — an explicit, even intense, curiosity about when and how international dynamics shape the internal gendered politics of societies. That's why I bring to bear on the investigation of international relations an explicit curiosity about intrasocietal political dynamics. I've never let go of that initial curiosity. At Clark University, we have a small political science department of nine: until recently, five Americanists, three comparativists, and just one whose post is officially labeled international relations. I have never been that international relations person. I've always been one of the three comparative politics faculty. For years I taught the intro to comparative politics in a rotating cycle. I've also taught the comparative politics of Japan; the comparative politics of race, ethnicity, and gender; the comparative politics of militarization; the comparative politics of women; the politics of Vietnam and the Philippines; and a seminar on women and the state. So I really am a comparativist, and I think that's stood me in good stead because the scholarship informed by feminist analysis emerged a lot earlier in comparative politics than it did in international relations. The very first little piece I ever wrote using a feminist set of questions — in 1980 — was on the sexual division of labor in a Levi's jeans factory in Manila. But I thought I was writing about Philippines gendered politics (under Marcos), not about international politics. The friends who read it at the time were feminist social historians tracking the history of women as textile and garment workers since the early nineteenth century. Their readings raised my cross-national historical consciousness about women, the state, and political economy.

One of the questions people always ask when they discuss your work is: How do you manage to do it all? You keep up with a wide range of countries and you have many interests; and of course, you write a great deal. Do you have research assistants, to keep you going?

No. I don't have research assistants and I've sought grants only now and then. I think I've taken one partial unpaid leave apart from my sabbaticals in thirty years. Sabbaticals themselves are a privilege in the workaday world. Maybe there are two things that have kept the generator fueled. One, I do love what I'm doing. People who are ambivalent about what they are doing have a much harder time. I hate to use the word "productive" because it sounds so capitalist, or state socialist, but it is harder to be productive if you really don't like what you're doing very much. The second thing is, I really like teaching. I like teaching a lot. My teaching and my research don't feel competitive to me. I often work out in courses ideas and puzzles that will then become themes for books. Whereas I think some people, because of their job description, or because they're not very comfortable with teaching, find teaching and scholarship pulling in opposite directions, and that tension is very draining. I've been very lucky that I haven't felt that tension.

In your book Maneuvers *you talk of the importance of having "non-American" readers in your mind's eye. You seem to have a "special relationship" with Britain. Your first feminist book,* Does Khaki Become You?, *was published in Britain in 1983 and you have often spoken of how important being conscious of a distinctive British perspective is to your work.[3] How did Britain come to shape your critical thinking?*

Bananas *was the fourth book of mine to be initially published in Britain.[4] The first of my books published in Britain was bought by the British editor Neil Middleton. In the late 1970s Neil Middleton was a deservedly well-known senior editor at Penguin. He published books by Susan George, Mary Kaldor, and Teresa Hayter — each an exceptionally smart critical analyst of

In the early 1980s, about the time when I was publishing *Ethnic Soldiers*, this Kurdish woman was coping with wartime displacement and her relationships to armed men. But at the time I didn't see her. I was naively imagining that "Kurdish politics" was comprised merely of the ideas and actions of ungendered Kurdish men. (Photo © Jacqueline Bottagisio)

the international political economy. It was 1978–79 and I was writing a book called *Ethnic Soldiers* — this would have been about my third or fourth book, I guess, and I was looking at the ways that racism and ethnicity work inside dozens of militaries (and police forces).[5] It wasn't a feminist investigation. I wasn't asking any feminist questions. I had my eyes just on race and ethnicity. I didn't see men as men. I had no curiosity about women. I did most of the research at the little Richardson Institution, located on North Gower Street in London. The Princeton University Press editor Sandy Thatcher, a wonderful guy, suggested I think about submitting *Ethnic Soldiers* to Penguin, London. So I sent it off. The manuscript just disappeared, you know, into the ether.

About a year later, though, I was in London again and I got a call at the Y (I used to stay at the Y on Great Russell Street — you shared rooms; you woke up some mornings never knowing who was going to be in the room's other bed: it was great). The voice at the other end of the Y's phone said, "This is Neil Middleton at Penguin. Would you come round and talk to me." I said, "Sure." I had never been invited to an editor's office before. When I arrived, Neil began apologizing: "Oh, I'm terribly embarrassed. I've had this manuscript for ages; I sent it out to a reviewer at Oxford and he really likes this book. Can we publish it?" It felt quite unreal, a Penguin editor asking me if they could publish something of mine! When I was in Malaysia, back in the 1960s, there was a remnant of a British colonial life, a department store called Robinson's. I used to go downtown in Kuala Lumpur to Robinson's every Saturday and treat myself to one or two new Penguin paperbacks. I can still feel the pleasure of seeing all those shelves lined with orange- and green-covered Penguins. Also, from my year right after college of working in New York at McGraw-Hill Publishers, I knew that if *Ethnic Soldiers* were published by Penguin it would come out as a "trade edition," unlike most academic books (and unlike my own first three books, which were published as what publishers call "text editions"), and that meant that ordinary bookshops could afford to carry it. That was the first time that I realized, there in Neil's office, that I wanted to be read by people who walked into bookstores.

I think since then, since 1980, all my books have come out in trade editions. It's one of the reasons I so enjoy my long relationship with University of California Press. UC Press has published *Bananas, Morning After,* and *Maneuvers,* each as a trade edition. None of us walking down the aisles at an ISA [International

Studies Association] or BISA [British International Studies Association] book exhibition would be able to tell the difference between a trade edition and a text edition. It's strictly a strategic discounting marketing decision made inside the publishing house. But a book assigned only a 20 percent seller's discount for bookshops — that's a "text edition" — is a book that most bookshops cannot afford to carry. Caring about a combined academic and nonacademic readership has become part of my politics.

So Neil took over *Ethnic Soldiers* and gave it a great cover. It didn't look like my earlier books; it looked like something a human might want to read. Soon after, in 1983, I published *Does Khaki Become You?* with another London publisher, Pluto Press. Then in 1989 *Bananas* came out with Pandora Press, another London-based press, a feminist press. Pandora then sold the U.S. rights to *Bananas* to the University of California Press, which agreed to publish it on their "trade" list.

The British — and especially London — publishing connection (three publishers beginning with "P") will perhaps not be suspected.

This British connection has both personal and intellectual/political dimensions. Both became important to me initially in 1975, when I worked on *Ethnic Soldiers* at the Richardson Institute. The political theorist Mike Nicholson was the director. Zoe Fairbairns was in the basement hatching what would become the Feminist Library. Nira Yuval-Davis, who's become a prominent feminist sociologist of ethnicity and nationalism, was there. Later I shared an office with then fresh-out-of-Cambridge CNDC [Campaign for Nuclear Disarmament] activist Dan Smith. It really affected me, trying out ideas with British colleagues. I always see writing for non-American readers as a sort of intellectually protective device. I think it's very dangerous intellectually to be an American writer because it's too easy to mentally stand in the United States and see the world from New York or Boston or Chicago. The American brand of parochialism (and arrogance) is so seductive and so risky.

We would like to shift attention now to the approach you adopt in your books, and a comment we have sometimes heard from students when they've read your best-known and best-loved book, Bananas, Beaches and Bases. *This view is that you provide the reader with a fascinating account of the effects of gender on the world of international politics, but you do not give an explanation of why and how it is the way it is. Would you agree with such a description of your approach?*

What I have been trying to do — not only in *Bananas*, but more particularly with the two books that have followed, *The Morning After* and *Maneuvers*, is to explore not only effects but also causalities.[6] In *Maneuvers* I'm more self-conscious than I have been in any book so far about political causality. It's a mistake, I think, to portray feminist analyses as merely about impacts — for example, revealing the effects of war on women or of international debt on women. That, in fact, is significant to reveal. But most feminist analyses reveal more than impacts. For instance, *Bananas* tries to show why the colonial project occurred the way it did. *Bananas* and *Maneuvers* both seek to show why states are so needful of ideas about masculinity and femininity. That's making a theoretical argument about causality.

There are two recent international relations books that have grown directly out of *Bananas*. One is by Christine Chin, *In Service and Servitude*.[7] In 2000 it won a prize awarded by the International Studies Association's Feminist Theory and Gender Section.

Christine explores the stake that the Malaysian state has developed in facilitating the international import of women to work as maids. She demonstrates that the Malaysian government under Mahatir designed a gendered manipulation of immigration and labor law as part of its state security strategy, in order to maintain the loyalties of the expanding Malaysian middle class. Suddenly Filipinas cleaning middle-class kitchens in Kuala Lumpur take on significance for anyone seeking to explain the constructions of state security in contemporary Southeast Asia. Another recent book that takes some of the hunches introduced in *Bananas* and then digs deeper is Katharine Moon's *Sex among Allies*.[8] Kathy has asked why elites of two states — the U.S. and South Korea — saw their respective state securities dependent upon their joint capacity to control the prostitution industry around the U.S. military bases. She found the minutes kept by the Nixon-era American negotiating team when it was conducting alliance negotiations with officials in Seoul. The minutes — and her follow-up interviews — clearly show that these two governments were attempting to reorganize prostitution so it would defuse racial conflict between black and white American soldiers stationed in Korea. Each state's diplomatic and military authorities, for their own masculinist reasons, had a stake in making sure that certain Korean women were sexually available to certain American men. Kathy Moon thus takes a hunch offered in *Bananas* and uses it to shed new explanatory light on the waging of the Cold War. Both Chin's book and Moon's reveal causality in international relations. That makes each of them theoretically significant.

Where does gender fit in your view of causality? Putting it at its most simple and basic, what makes the world of international politics go 'round? In particular, what makes "states" act the way they do?

Half the time, state officials (I like to think about particular people making decisions rather than monolithic states operating) are operating out of a desire to preserve state security; and that means that notions of state security drive their official attempts to manipulate ideas about masculinity and femininity. Under other conditions, though, it appears to be their worries about masculinity and the proper ordering of relationships between men and women that seem to fuel their state policy-making. I'm an empiricist insofar as I want scholars to go out there and see which of these two causal possibilities is at work in a given state at a particular time. I am not interested in asserting, "Oh, it's always a concern for male privilege that drives big officials," or "It's always concerns of state security that make a state official try to manipulate masculinity and femininity." What I do urge, though, is: "Always ask the question: under what conditions do state officials invest state resources in order to manipulate masculinity and femininity?" The necessary corollary question then to be asked is: "When do state officials try to manipulate women as people?" What worries me is that so few people, until recently, have asked these questions. This lack of questioning has produced a very naive understanding of how state power works and how interstate relations work.

One of the things that strikes me in your work, certainly in Maneuvers, *is the tension you describe between feminism and patriotism. Is it possible, in your view, to be a feminist and a patriot?*
Oh! Patriotism! Many women have a very ambivalent relationship to patriotism precisely because the conventional prescriptions for being recognized as woman-as-patriot are grounded in notions of feminine "respectability." In exposing this ambiva-

lence and its causes, feminists have made the very model of the patriot less tenable. Most militarizing states need women to seek to be patriots, yet need them to do so without stepping over the bounds of "proper" femininity, since that would then dispirit a lot of men, who would feel that their own masculine turf was being challenged. In a patriarchal state a woman can aspire to be a "patriotic mother" but not a "patriotic citizen." On the other hand, we now have increasing historical documentation of women who have challenged this orthodox, gendered idea of patriotism. These are women, for example, who have sought to be voters in the name of patriotism. I'm very interested in the development of the Kuwaiti women's suffrage movement before and after the 1991 Gulf War because it reveals exactly this sort of deliberate resistance by women to the standard feminized version of patriotism. Then, we have other women who challenge patriotism altogether. Take Virginia Woolf. Woolf's *Three Guineas*, published in 1938 as war clouds amassed over Europe, is, for me, one of the most exciting, difficult, and worthy-of-rereading books of political theorizing. I come back to *Three Guineas* at the conclusion of *Maneuvers*. I think I've now read *Three Guineas* maybe eight times. I've gone through two whole paperbacks; each is now falling apart, marked up with various colored inks. Woolf dug deep into the very idea of the patriot and found it so corrupted by its patriarchal foundations that, she argued, it was not worthy of either aspiration or reform. It's an astounding book, really.

Some of these ideas that you elaborate upon could be regarded as dangerous or subversive in many ways, and yet you raise issues in what might be described as a gentle way. Is there a tension between these very powerful arguments over the causes and effects of militarization and yet your reasoned approach? What inspires this approach?

What a great question. Yes, I want to be read. I want to be heard. I'm always writing for multiple audiences. This goes back to my being so excited about Neil Middleton taking the *Ethnic Soldiers* manuscript and publishing it as an ordinary trade paperback. I've really wanted to write so that multiple audiences, readers who are at different stages of their own political thinking, will find the book digestible. But "digestible" doesn't, for me, mean bland. I'm eager for readers to think their own thoughts about what I offer up; I hope they'll write in the margins, and tussle with ideas and information, maybe reject parts of it, yet be curious about other parts of it, even go on to then launch their own explorations to see if my hunches do hold water. This approach to writing comes out of being a teacher. When you're in a classroom, you know that some students are just going to latch on to your ideas. They're ready; they're there; that's the reason they chose this course. Then there will be other students — in the United States it's the kids in the back row with their baseball caps on backward, sliding so far down in their seats that you can barely see the tops of their heads — whose initial attitude seems to be, "I'm cool, I'm detached, you're not going to faze me." Well, I'm after that kid; I'm never going to let him or her go. And so I write so that at least those skeptics, those "Why the hell am I being asked to read a book about women?" readers, will be engaged despite themselves. I want to provide a basis for readers to get far enough into the feminist discussion that they can start making their own decisions about what is worthy of further thought. I don't come on like gangbusters for that reason. There can, of course, be times when you want to have an abrasive effect; it's just not usually my mode. On the other hand, I wouldn't have been pushed to develop the consciousness (it's still evolving)—the midlevel consciousness—I now have if there hadn't been a lot more outspoken radical people, particularly in Britain, Ireland, Canada, Chile, and in the United States, around me. If those people hadn't been out there, wielding that kind of beyond-the-pale language and launching respectability-be-damned actions, I probably wouldn't have been pushed to even my currently modest level of political consciousness.

Would you please identify who those important people were?
I've been deeply affected by the women activist-thinkers at Greenham Common, those British women who in 1981 set up tents outside the fence of the U.S. Air Force base in England to draw national attention to and protest the nuclear-headed Cruise missiles held there. When I was writing *Does Khaki Become You?* for Pluto Press, it was going to be published first in Britain, before it even had an American publisher. This was the early 1980s and I wanted *Khaki* to be written in a way that it would contribute to the intense intellectual conversation sparked by the "Greenham women" about what is the "political," about what notions of womanhood Cold War strategists relied upon. At the same time in Britain I was reading, listening to, being influenced by feminist social historians and journalists such as Dale Spender, Bea Campbell, Judy Lown, Sheila Rowbotham, and Hilary Wainwright. In both Britain and the U.S. I've been affected by people who aren't in the social sciences, who are activists, essayists, journalists, and artists—for instance, the American essayist and poet Adrienne Rich. They have had the curiosity and skills to reveal things about the nuances of gendered power that even so-

cial scientists too often miss. You can't talk about patriarchy, of course, unless you can figure out how racism and ethnicized nationalism rely on certain relations between women and men. So people like Barbara Smith, the American lesbian black feminist writer, and Kate Rushin, the black poet, have had a big effect on me, I think. And with virtually all of these intellectuals, I've always known I'm more tame than they are.[9]

Is there a problem or a tension for the discipline of international relations in the relationship between feminist theorizing and feminist activism?

I'm not sure if there is a problem. Certainly there are several explanatory enterprises going on at different levels simultaneously. I think we all are fortunate that we get to take part in a number of conversations at the same time. One of the reasons I talk about activists a lot in *Maneuvers* and my other recent writings is that I want us all to reimagine just where theorizing takes place. I've been made very nervous in recent years by an image of who does theorizing — and where — that has gotten so rarefied. It's an image that I think is naive. In reality, exploration of causality and building of explanation usually are happening in a lot of places. Thinkers not published by university presses or not seeking tenure are the intellectuals who created such profound concepts as "rape as an instrument of war." Intellectual/activist feminists in the Philippines, South Korea, Chile, and Serbia have taught me so much about, for example, the genderings of the state/regime/nation interactions.

Your central question in Bananas *is: "Where are the women?" But then, what do you do about their being where they are? What sorts of politics might that lead to?*

Trying to answer that core question changed my notion of how power works. That's because I was compelled to then ask the necessary follow-up questions: "How did those women get there?" and "Who has a stake in their being there?" When I began to see the necessity of asking all three of these questions, I started to realize that my writings and my teachings for the prior fifteen years had all underestimated how power works. Taking women's lives seriously made me see that the world, both in terms of societal and international relations, is nowhere near as "natural" as I previously had imagined it was. And that fresh understanding began to make me feel more responsible. I mean, as just an individual citizen, I find that (I know it sounds like an extreme case) it's unacceptable to learn that some Rwandan women, especially Tutsi women, in 1994 were forced to become "wives" of certain Hutu militiamen and then for me to treat that information merely as fodder for my own analysis. Making this form of sexual coercion analytically visible is important since most of the reporting about the genocide didn't talk about rape and forced marriage at all. Is this making sense? That is, my trying to understand the political lives of women whom I had never even bothered to notice before does change my relationship to them. Employing a feminist analysis in trying to make sense of international politics, therefore, has infused my academic life with a far greater sense of accountablity. Take another, seemingly very different, sort of example. I'm kind of a classic American breakfast diner. I eat bananas on top of my breakfast cereal, and I have high banana standards. This is a bit embarrassing. I actually do shop for the bananas that are a perfect yellow, with a touch of green. I buy bananas with Dole and Del Monte stickers on them, and I buy them in air-conditioned supermarkets. I haven't stopped eating bananas, but I'm now much more aware that, as an ordinary, humdrum consumer, I'm actually connected to a woman in Honduras or Costa Rica who is standing ankle-deep in pesticide to wash these bananas so that they look nice to me there in my Boston supermarket. And I'm aware now of the Central American and U.S. corporate and state wielders of power who put her there. If I do decide to boycott certain companies' bananas, I now will have to think about that Central American woman banana worker's own location and any little ripples my actions might set off in her life.

At the end of Maneuvers *you pose five of the puzzles that your recent work has uncovered. Do you have any answers to those puzzles? In particular, you raise a question about the incidence of rape in warfare and whether we can mobilize support for women raped by soldiers without allowing those women who have endured rape to be turned into new symbols of national humiliation. Do you have any answers for puzzles such as this one?*

Writing a concluding chapter — you probably find this too — is always tough. You feel you've already written eight chapters and the reader has gotten the message, and so, you think, "I just want to go off and have a cappuccino." Conclusions shouldn't sound too satisfied, all the edges rounded off. So I tried to come up with a format for the conclusion of *Maneuvers* that would energize me to write it and readers to read it. Out of all that's explored — I hope, revealed — in *Maneuvers*, I've pinpointed dilemmas that maybe other people haven't defined in quite the same way. One of those dilemmas, I realized, was how does one make visible mass rapes of women by men as a systematic weapon of war in a way that does not turn those raped women into new commodities: commodities for our angst; commodities for human rights activism; commodities, especially, for galvanizing the next generations of nationalists to seek revenge? Each one of these dilemmas posed at the end of *Maneuvers* has serious implications for both scholars and practitioners, people working for Oxfam, staff people for the UN High Commission for Refugees (UNHCR), UNIFEM (the UN Development Fund for Women), as well as independent activists and commentators. More and more, I find, feminist academics working on militarism — but also those researching the international politics of poverty and debt — are at the junctures where policy practitioners, activists, and scholars meet. Being there, trying to be useful in these interchanges, is energizing and very stretchy. I'm not a public policy practitioner; I've only made policy inside of my own university. But nowadays I'm trying to work out those dilemmas by posing them as sharply as possible and engaging with a broad range of other people in unraveling them — for instance, feminists working now in Kosovo, Liberia, and Sri Lanka. Not to see these as dilemmas is to miss the risks, to underestimate the negative consequences of a thoughtless decision. There's so much I've still got to learn. I've listened to people who are really smart out there. They are working with international agencies; they're doing a really difficult new kind of international activist work. The very intensity of the work they're doing can make them miss the dilemmas and thus the risks.

In terms of people listening to other people, do you think feminist scholars' efforts to promote "gender and international relations" as a recognized academic field are going anywhere? Are different groups of people seriously listening to each other?

Oh yeah! I'm not sanguine, but just listen to what's going on in the hallways or in the conference rooms at the International Studies Association meetings: a lot of new, younger scholars presenting fresh research findings framed by an explicit gender curiosity. I was on a panel, for instance, where a feminist economist from the University of Michigan described her gendered analysis of the World Bank's new development paradigm. She demonstrated how this new economic paradigm allows the World Bank's economists to feel comfortable with taking gender on board when they didn't previously. One of the striking things to me is how the "gender and international relations" scholars move easily back and forth between theory and empirical research — sometimes it's the same person doing both, sometimes it's theorists and empirical researchers on the same panels, in conversation.

Do you think this work is really doing anything on a significant scale to transform the way people think? Is it a dialogue of the deaf, between specialists in gender and those of a traditional political science international relations persuasion?

You'd have to talk about what's going on journal by journal, department by department, university by university: Who in each is not just embracing gender analysis, but rethinking what one needs to study (and to teach) to make sense of "politics"? My own political science department is as small in faculty numbers (and as large in student majors) as it was ten years ago, but our collective notion of what is "political" has expanded remarkably. The slowness, though, of intellectual change in political science as a whole is a bit frustrating. It's embarrassing if you listen to publishers and editors talk about which of the many academic conferences they'd most like to go to; they rarely put a political science meeting at the top of their wish list. They choose, say, the anthro meetings, and there's a reason: they don't seem to think the intellectual atmosphere among political scientists is as vibrant as it might be. It's the scholars doing gender and politics, gender and international relations work who are changing this. They're doing a lot to make the International Studies Association a much more lively place to be. For instance, it's the panels and plenaries sponsored by the Feminist Theory and Gender Section that are attracting people not only in political science, but also in anthropology, women's studies, history, economics, and sociology, because feminist analysis is so interdisciplinary in its approach and in the questions it asks about international politics.

Today, almost any political science department worth its salt will have somebody doing gender research and/or gender teaching. If you went into a political science or international politics department that didn't have any regular course offerings on gender, you'd think they were a kind of backwater department. In this sense, the people doing gender and international relations have had a genuine impact. But in many departments (and on many journals and assessment committees) there's still a tendency toward tokenism: for instance, thinking that hiring one gender scholar in a department of twelve or twenty passes for real intellectual commitment. It doesn't. In Britain it's the national assessment committees responsible for international relations and politics that form the arena to watch: for instance, is the *International Feminist Journal of Politics* on the assessment committee's list of serious scholarly publishing vehicles? Is *Signs*?

It is very interesting that the illustrations you give, such as the World Bank, rely on empirical research for their significance. There is a wide-

spread perception these days, in Britain at least, that the study of gen-
der and international relations is pretty much being taken over by peo-
ple who are postmodernist/poststructuralist in inspiration and do not do
traditional empirical research. Citing Foucault is deemed by these writ-
ers as more authoritative than citing a World Bank report. Is that your
view?

No. Actually, in gender and international relations circles today people doing theory and people doing empirical research are in constant communication: all talking to each other, on the same editorial boards, jointly organizing conferences. There isn't a divide. Ann Tickner reads — and shares conversations with — Kathy Moon. Jindy Pettman, Gillian Youngs, and Kathy Jones jointly edit the wonderful, lively *International Feminist Journal of Politics.* Jindy being more empirically inclined, Gillian and Kathy more oriented to theory. Similarly, Sandy Whitworth, whose earlier book was on a gender analysis of the ILO and whose new book is an empirical investigation of the struggles over masculinity and femininity inside of militarized peacekeeping forces, has been an intellectual ally for years of theorists Spike Peterson and Marysia Zalewski, working together to create the International Studies Association's Feminist Theory and Gender Section.[10]

When people are labeling various feminisms, where do you fit in: Would
you say your political stance is fundamentally liberal? Is the drive for
equality between people the way to resolve the political issues that your
work throws into relief?

Ah! "Fundamentally." Well, I think if one is born and raised in pretty mainstream America, which I was, it is very hard to escape the liberal culture (I mean liberal as in Locke, not liberal as in

Democrats versus Republicans); in many ways I'm very affected by that American culture. So I think it would be disingenuous of me to say that I wasn't, in some significant part, a liberal. In the narrower, more parochial, sense of liberal, the way it's used in contemporary America. Since I was raised in a Republican household, I have had to become what Americans today call a liberal. But in terms of what is meant by being a classical liberal — finding it easy to focus on individuals, finding equality an appealing aspiration, valuing limitations on state power essential for achieving human liberty — I do think I've internalized much of that worldview.

On the other hand, in researching and teaching politics, and especially learning from feminists, I've become wide awake to the flaws and limitations integral to that inherited liberalism. In my own work I've had to think through these critiques, particularly in order to figure out how to make sense of the debates over my writings about militarization. For instance, I have deliberately avoided putting women-in-the-military at the analytical center of my thinking because to have privileged that one aspect of militarization would have fallen into a naive form of liberal thinking — that is, slipping into assuming that the pursuit of equality with men everywhere, even in a state's military, is transformative. I've had conversations with women serving in lots of different militaries, however, and I've learned that one has to be able, in a respectful way, to respond to their often daring strategies designed to halt intramilitary sexism, while one still makes visible the deeper politics of militarism. Pursuing equality inside a military is not adequate because, too often, such a pursuit silences needed debates about militarism. I think it's a good thing that I've been constantly put in positions where I have had to make clear why I think that sexism —

and racism — inside any military should be made visible, should be resisted, should be overturned because, in countries such as the United States, Indonesia, Chile, and Britain, the military is a very powerful state institution. You can't allow any powerful state institution to normalize sexism. You can't.

You seem to talk completely unselfconsciously about women. Not all feminist scholars would. Do you ever put quotation marks around the word "woman"?

No. I am by no means essentialist in my thinking; I never have been. Very, very few feminist scholars are. Human actors identified as men and human actors identified as women are not essentially — that is asocially, aculturally, ahistorically — "feminine" or "masculine." If there are terms that need to be skeptically highlighted with quotation marks, at the top of that list would be "feminine" and "masculine." On the other hand, in virtually every society analyzed, women as a group are treated as if they were not just a distinct category but an ideologically loaded category.

Right! And you have said somewhere that you are a nonuniversalist.

Yes! I mean, I grew up as a suburban, white Anglo-American bourgeois girl. How could I imagine that that's typical of all women? I just couldn't. So one of the things I've learned always to ask when trying to make sense of the politics of Nike in Indonesia or the politics of NATO in Kosovo is: How is the broad category of the "feminine" wielded by those with power at the same time (usually) as categories of class and race/ethnicity are used to manipulate subgroups of women?

Might your work in future explore the effects of gender on men? That is, looking at men as victims of gendered constructions?

Men, in fact, increasingly, figure explicitly in my work. One can see this in *The Morning After* and particularly in *Maneuvers*. In both books I've tried to examine how multiple masculinities get manipulated, what the manipulators' motives are, and what the consequences are for international politics — in industrialization policy, in nationalist movements, in war-waging efforts, in trade negotiations, in the formulation of weapons policy. But I am very wary of any scholarly attempt to analyze the politics of masculinity that concentrates solely on the actions and experiences of men. Remember, I did that, four books' worth. I know now it is not analytically productive. I honestly think that when and where masculinity is politically wielded can be understood only if one takes women's lives seriously. Women and ideas about femininity are manipulated usually by political actors intent upon persuading men to behave in certain ways. Just think of all you learn about states' anxieties about masculinity from paying attention to military wives!

This is moving toward several policy-relevant questions. You're attacking militarism; it's a theme that has run through your work. Do you agree with the argument that militarized force can sometimes be used for good? Do you agree with such a view? If so — if force can be used for good — then we obviously need a military organization. How do you begin to square all this — the new lure of wielding violence in the name of humanitarianism and the historic threat of militarism?

Um! I don't think I have ever said outright that all states should not have militaries. What I've been more concerned about is the way in which the rationalization of the use of force has been used to justify militarism, which in turn normalizes and legitimizes secrecy, hierarchy, masculinism, and a culture of threat. In Haiti in the mid-1990s, when the military regime was being ousted largely with American military support, the American ambassador became the most powerful person in Haiti. When the newly installed Aristide regime proposed to do away with a military under the new government — following the Costa Rican model — the American ambassador reputedly warned, "You will not be recognized as a mature, respected state in the international community unless you have an army." That the very status of a "mature" state — a status bestowed by an international elite — should rest on a state having an institutionalized military does make me nervous; adopting such an international assumption militarizes not only the status of statehood, but the potent concept of "maturity."

But coming to grips with the use of state force isn't easy. In the midst of the 1991–95 war in Bosnia, among people of goodwill, a lot of them feminists, there were intense debates about what we should be pushing our respective governments to do. In the U.S. it was the Republicans in Congress who did not want the U.S. military to be sent into Bosnia in any alliance configuration. They opposed interventionist humanitarian operations; only direct U.S. national security, they argued, could justify deployment, and that deployment had to be under American command. No "blue-helmeted" American soldiers. I remember at the time being so frustrated with that Republican parochialness. It felt like a very masculinist form of protecting the U.S. military. So there I was in 1994, rooting for going to Bosnia with some kind of international force, some kind of military operation, yet still thinking of all the risks this would entail — not the sort of risks, though, that Colin Powell and his Republican congressional supporters had in mind! I admit that I was quite torn about that. Oddly, the post–Gulf War "Powell Doctrine" rests on the militarized notion that any U.S. foreign policy must make the protection of American soldiers its top priority. That doctrine makes a militarized criterion the determiner of U.S. civilian government foreign policy decisions. Thus, when an American administration does choose military intervention, it is likely to prefer overwhelming aerial and heavy-armored assault.

It sounds as though you were in support of NATO's later, 1999 bombing campaign against Serbia, bombing attacks launched in the name of protecting ethnic Kosovars, then under siege by the militarized nationalist Serbian regime of President Milosevic.

No. I actually do not think that the military interventions in Bosnia 1994–95, and in Serbia 1999, were politically identical. I did think that the U.S. and European initial embrace of the Kosovo Liberation Army in 1999 was disastrous. I was watching the emergence of the KLA and its masculinized, militarized politics just as I was writing *Maneuvers*. It was a politics that sidetracked 1990s ethnic Albanian local political efforts to develop a different kind of Kosovo nationalist masculine identity, one that allowed for a genuine inclusion of activist women. The NATO military/political strategy devised in 1999 was one that privileged not only aerial bombing of Serbia's civilians, but also support for a masculinist, militarized politics among Kosovar Albanians, a distorted politics that still today is being played out in violence.

You make it plain, though, that you have concerns about the U.S. global role and, specifically, its physical and ideological influences after the end of the Cold War.

I think the U.S. global role should not be what it is today. I have been exploring the current widespread American cultural anxiety about the United Nations. I'm pretty sure that that anxiety — and contempt for the UN — is gendered. It is being fueled in part by elite and popular uncertainty about American masculinity. Sovereignty and isolationism — they are obviously important to think about — but if we are uncurious about the politics of masculinity, we won't get to the bottom of this, the American fear of donning a blue helmet.

Why is that? Would it make them look too boyish, and not sufficiently fearsome? "Blue does not become them"?
One has to think historically and cross-nationally. For instance, what seems to be true of senior U.S. military commanders and civilian Republican senators today does not seem to be true of the Fijians. The popularly accepted proof of ethnic Fijian men's masculinity is to have been on a UN peacekeeping operation, wearing the telltale blue helmet. Not Indian Fijian masculinity, but ethnic Fijian masculinity. This, in turn, is not unconnected to the increasing militarization of Fijian domestic politics since the early 1990s. Generalizing off the American case is never a good idea.

Our question to you about the global role of the United States raises the old question about drawing a line between one's role as a scholar and one's role as a citizen. Does this old problem present you, given your explicitness about working as a feminist scholar, with a particular problem? Do you worry about it?
Most of the time it doesn't feel worrisome to me, so long as one is open to, and part of, a critical conversation. It would be more worrisome if — in one's academic life or in one's activism — one got closed off from an ongoing intellectual growth and the sort of open serious discussion that allows for criticism. Also, in fact, I'm just an ordinary academic, right? I mean, I'm not very often "on the barricades." That's nothing to be proud of either. Maybe the

reason oftentimes my work is taken to be somehow engaged with activism is because a lot of my stuff isn't read just by academics. So it's the readership that actually changes the perception of my work. I do, though, feel accountable to my students and my colleagues, but also to people who are outside of academia. So perhaps, in addition to the extra-academic readership, it's this sense of accountability that makes me feel as though I'm engaged with activists.

Bananas, Beaches and Bases draws the reader into wanting to do something. As you say there — more elegantly than this paraphrase — the personal is the (politically) international. Our students have asked us, so let us now put you on the spot: What would an Enloe-esque defense policy look like?

People feeling motivated to do something as a result of reading and article or a book — that's being a citizen: a citizen/student, a citizen/scholar, a citizen/teacher. Of course, it's both terribly rewarding, but also nervous-making to think that someone is going to do something with what you have taught or written!

As far as "a Cynthia Enloe defense policy" goes — thank God I'll never be a defense minister — but what I would hope is that in such a policy process there would be an open, unpatriarchical discussion of what the gendered stakes of each policy alternative are. I know that would be extremely hard to guarantee. But it seems to me it would make for a much more honest and productive foreign policy (the larger arena in which defense policy is crafted) if these things that are now left unsaid yet are so potent were placed up on the table for explicit assessment.

Finally, the question academics always ask each other: What are you working on now, and what do you plan to do next?

As many of us do, I've got several things on the burners simultaneously. They are on the two tracks of politics I've been following for some years — one in international political economy, the other in the international politics of militarization. The first is my ongoing interest in women working in export factories, specifically women in the international politics of sneakers. I don't wear Nikes, but I keep pretty close track of Nike — and Reebok and Adidas — in the politics of Indonesia, Korea, China, Taiwan, Vietnam, and the U.S. Probably the most reprinted article I've ever written is the one first published in *Ms.* magazine on the gendered global politics of sneakers [chapter 3, this volume]. Because the international political economy of any commercial product — copper, shipbuilding, diamonds, jeans, electronics, bananas — is patriarchally gendered and yet always in transition, I've made a feminist monitoring of international political economies one of the continuing efforts in both my teaching and my writing.

Then there's militarization. I'm especially curious these days about how humanitarian aid programs in conflict and postconflict societies can become subtly militarized. For instance, which departments of which NGOs or which government aid agencies are most likely to find themselves adopting the military's agenda and priorities? What I'm curious about is why this is so seductive and how this seduction privileges masculinity and marginalizes certain men and most women in democratizing efforts.

So — I have plenty to feed my curiosity and keep me on my toes!

PART THREE

Feminists after Wars— It's Not Over 'til It's Over

CHAPTER 15

Women after Wars

Puzzles and Warnings from Vietnam

Wars don't simply end. And wars don't end simply.

Most of us who have observed wars or experienced them firsthand know both of these things. Still, there is the temptation to give any process a too-neat starting date and too-neat ending date. To do so makes the world seem more manageable, more susceptible to human understanding. At no time is this temptation more potent than when we are analyzing a war. Then we are subject not only to our historian's urge to assign definitive dates; we are, in addition, inclined to put the hurtful past behind us, to look forward, to get on with our lives. But to give in to this combination of emotional and intellectual urges not only, I think, risks general analytical naiveté; it risks seriously underestimating the differences between women's and men's experiences of postwar social change.

"Gender awareness" is a phrase now being used by United

Nations women officials in order to describe an attitude, a way of seeing. Advocates of doing research equipped with "gender awareness" argue, I think very convincingly, that paying close attention to how ideas about womanhood and manhood shape individuals' behavior and institutions' policies will produce a much more realistic understanding of how this world operates. If, as scholars and activists, we don our "gender awareness" eyeglasses, we will be able to make better sense of how foreign investment affects a local community, we will be smarter in figuring out how family dynamics shape citizen participation, and we will be better able to explain why policy-makers forget to ask certain questions at all.

In this chapter I will try to use gender awareness, then, to spell out what seem to me to be some of the lessons about the often unequal postwar conditions that women's studies research has revealed. The research and the lessons it has generated come from countries as diverse as Zimbabwe, Japan, and France. But some of the most important analyses of the ways in which postwar social processes are gendered — that is, are fueled by informal and official presumptions about femininity and masculinity — have come from women's studies researchers in Vietnam, scholars who themselves have experienced not one, but four, wars that tripped over each other's heels in deadly succession from the late 1930s through to the late 1980s. Hopefully, the questions and tentative conclusions that follow, therefore, will shed light on Vietnamese women's complex experiences of postwar life. At the same time, what follows is partly inspired by the work already done by this pioneering generation of Vietnamese women's studies scholars.

MUSEUMS: INSTITUTIONALIZING POSTWAR
MEMORIES OF WARTIME WOMEN

The museum commemorating southern Vietnamese women's resistance to French colonialism and contributions to national liberation is situated, fittingly, in one of the stately colonial mansions that still line many of the streets of postwar Ho Chi Minh City. Its spacious front driveway and its high-ceilinged interior remind today's visitor of an earlier era, an era when men and women related to each other according not only to presumptions about regional cultures, class rankings, and ethnic backgrounds, but also according to notions of the globally maldistributed credits for being "civilized," "rational," and "modern." The earlier residents of this mansion most probably were French women and men — and later perhaps Americans — who imagined that Vietnamese women were born to serve. They were in for a surprise.

The South Vietnam Women's Museum is one of the few in the world today devoted entirely to the wartime risks, sacrifices, and achievements of women. It has been built with funds privately collected by southern Vietnamese women themselves. Its displays are comprised of objects collected by women from women. The captions interpreting each display have been written by women. The guides and the directors are women.[1]

Every war museum is in fact a postwar museum. It portrays wartime experiences, but its design is based on postwar memories, postwar worries. Not until the shooting stops, the forced migrations end, the dust — quite literally — settles, can anyone muster the time and resources to sort out trivial from significant memories and provide the latter with walls, a roof, and typed captions.

Most war museums are inspired not just by men's memories, but by masculinized memories. That is, it is not simply that most war museums are funded and designed by men, usually men of the elite; it is also that the assignments of significance or triviality — that is, visibility or invisibility — are typically based on the gendered presumption that what men did must have been more important than what women did in determining how the war was fought, how it ended, and what its impact is on postwar society. Men are on most war museums' center stage because war is imagined to be a masculinized process; women are the sideshow because femininity, it is erroneously thought, does not, cannot, shape the course and outcome of a war. Thus it is the male policymakers — inside rival governments and movements — who have their childhood photographs, their diaries, their declarations, their furniture, their pipes and uniforms featured in the standard war museum. Likewise in the masculinized war museum it is male soldiers of all sides who have their battles mapped, their weapons on display, their letters home under glass.

To underscore the presumptions informing a masculinized war museum and to start suggesting the impact of such museums on postwar women's ideas about themselves, about the men in their lives and in the public sphere generally, one might therefore compare the Ho Chi Minh City women's museum with any other museum in Vietnam. Or one might travel to London and visit Britain's famous Imperial War Museum. Responding to pressures from a new generation of British feminist war historians, its curators have tried to demasculinize somewhat its displays and its underlying messages. But thus far those efforts have made women barely visible. On a recent visit to the Imperial War Museum I tried to imagine what would happen to our postwar understanding of war if, instead of just two glass cases filled with women's ration books and "support your boys" posters, the museum's curators added a battlefront nursing station — and perhaps a brothel.[2]

The displays in the Vietnamese women's war museum cover the period beginning with the 1920s, a decade of lively Vietnamese debate over the prescribed roles for women in family life and public life according to Confucianist teachings, Vietnamese historical experience, and new ideas coming from France. It was also a time of autonomous women's organizing in Vietnam. But the museum curators' principal focus is the years 1945 to 1954, the time of the anticolonial war against the French, and 1960 to 1975, the years in which nationalists waged war against the Americans and their Saigon-based Vietnamese allies. More recent military conflicts, on the northern border with the Chinese and to the west in Cambodia, are not yet addressed by the museum. This makes women from non-Vietnamese ethnic groups almost invisible. The implications for women of the insurgent character of the anti-French and anti-American wars are made clear by displays showing photographs of and testimony from women arrested by the Saigon regime and subjected to torture and imprisonment. Rural women's participation is made visible by two statues. The first, carved out of a highly polished dark wood, depicts an elderly woman seemingly going about her ordinary routine of grinding betel nut with a mortar and pestle, a motion that in fact village women designed to alert resistance fighters that enemy troops were nearby. A second statue, carved out of a smooth cream-colored stone, depicts a younger woman stretched out on the ground, one arm around her infant, the other grasping a rifle. The guide explains to visitors that women such as the model for this statue gained a well-deserved reputation for being able to hit American helicopters overhead.

As in any museum, there are themes that float up to the surface because of particular choices made by the curators. Some of those themes are deliberately crafted. Others may be more subliminal. In this rare women's war museum, one theme is that the Vietnamese women who participated in the resistance and liberation movements never surrendered their femininity. A woman could wield a rifle and suckle a child; there was no need — and no desire — to choose between motherhood and nationalist combat. As all feminists know, this is an assertion fraught with political pitfalls insofar as it covers up not only ideological contradictions, but actual struggles that had to occur between fathers and daughters, perhaps between mothers and daughters too, over what it meant to be a woman *and* a nationalist. Any museum that leaves out contradictions and the processes by which they are resolved — or left unresolved — has to remain a museum as incomplete as it would be if the electrical outlets remained unwired.

One of the museum's glass cases, for instance, shows colorful, careful needlework done by women while they were in prison, needlework for which Vietnamese women are famous and which today is making its way into the rapidly spreading international market economy. The guide wants to be sure that visitors look at this impressive embroidery not only to admire the skills behind it, but to appreciate that wartime embroidery proves that a woman who engaged in anticolonial politics was a feminine woman all the while.

This curatorial theme — femininity's compatibility with otherwise disruptive nationalist wartime mobilization — is not unique to the Vietnamese women's war museum. It is a theme — often far more bluntly insisted upon — that runs through virtually every institutionalized remembrance of women's active war efforts in every society for which we thus far have accounts. And it is a theme with distinctly *postwar* significance. Especially in wars fought to preserve the existing social order — for example, World War II as waged by Americans — but even in wars fought to alter the existing social order — for example, the Rhodesian civil war as waged by Zimbabwean rebels — there has been anxiety expressed about femininity. If women are mobilized to wage the war, if they are pulled out of the kitchen, out of the farm field, will they lose their supposedly essential feminine qualities: domesticity, sexual reserve, emotional sensitivity, and maternalism? While this anxiety may be expressed during any war in ways that shape wartime decisions about military recruitment, personnel deployment, and political symbolism, it is a feeling that doesn't disappear when the war is over. It thus crops up in museums.

Some women are convinced during a war and immediately after the war that any unconventional roles they played were due only to extraordinary wartime exigencies. These are the women who will be most accepting of a postwar reimposition of prewar gendered "normalcy." They won't expect to run the postwar government; they won't expect to be promoted to the higher-paying jobs; they won't expect their husbands to take more responsibility for housework or for birth control. By contrast, those women who see their new wartime skills and responsibilities as challenging older notions about what is "natural" or "proper" for a woman may well be reluctant to squeeze themselves back into prewar gender conventions once the shooting has stopped. How any war museum — or schoolbook or popular movie or formal ceremony — engages with these competing interpretations of wartime femininity will affect postwar women's self-images and opportunities for generations to come.[3]

The women's museum in Ho Chi Minh City does not represent, nor is it meant to represent, the experiences of all southern Vietnamese women who lived through the colonial period and the war years. Rather, its designers intend to make visible the contributions to the nation of those southern women who refused to be co-opted by the foreigners and their local allies, and who became politically conscious in such a way that they joined the anti-French and then anti-American nationalist movements.

A comparison with a United States effort might be useful here to suggest how any women's museum involves choices not only about how to interpret femininity, but also about which women to include at all. Out of seven thousand museums in the United States in the mid-1990s, only three were devoted exclusively to women. One — the Women of the West Museum in Boulder, Colorado — was only in its conceptualizing and fund-raising stage (it has yet to be built). It was not formally called a war museum. But because conflict for control of that region, now referred to as "the American West," so often escalated into open warfare, one might think of this projected Women of the West Museum as at least in part a war museum. During the planning stages, this museum's designers, many of them feminists, asked each other hard questions, questions that probably would have a familiar ring to some of the southern Vietnam women's museum organizers: Which women should be represented in the museum? Which dimensions of those women's lives were important enough to be made visible? Perhaps they even asked each other, "What is the 'West'?"[4] Had their plans gone through, the particular answers they reached would have determined how "women" would be defined for future visitors. But those answers also would dictate what lessons visitors would derive from the displays, lessons about the range of behaviors that can be classified as "feminine," lessons about what events open up opportunities for women and what events close them down. Also, both the Vietnamese women's war museum and its planned Colorado counterpart might have generated lessons about women's relationships to men. These museums could suggest — by omission or commission — either that the very violence of interstate wars reduces the violence of men against women in their own families or that violence at the public level often exacerbates it at the private level. This is what an accurate Salvadoran or Serbian women's war museum display would show. Neither the Vietnamese nor any American women's museum curators have dared broach this politically delicate topic — yet.

A museum is made of brick and electrical cable, but it doesn't have to be any more fixed than a memory is. As women reimagine what happened to them during a war and what they contributed to that war, a women's war museum might be redesigned. A "postwar" era in any country lasts as long as its people have a stake in debating exactly what wartime experiences meant. Many of those debates are about what it meant during that war to be a woman or to be a man.

Thus it is possible that future southern Vietnamese women museum curators will add new rooms to include new ideas and new groups. For instance, a new wing might serve to make visible the lives of those Vietnamese women who during the 1940s or 1960s remained politically uncommitted, women who devoted their daily energies merely to coping with colonial humiliations and wartime dangers, even women who at least superficially cast their lots with the foreigners for reasons we may not yet fully fathom. Adding such a new wing would make the women's war museum less celebratory. It could indeed cause the visitor to question, even to scowl. But it would produce a museum that would suggest the full impact of gender on the waging of war. It would thereby help postwar lessons to be more fully informed by "gender awareness." Did the presumptions about femininity's relationship to transplanting rice or building irrigation dikes change during wartime? How were the relationships between mothers and fathers in the raising of children upset by military conscription and government arrests? This isn't the stuff of heroism, but making it visible, giving it material meaning and explicit labels, would reveal just how deeply any war is a series of surprisingly gendered events.

Such an expanded museum of women in wartime could throw new light on why prostitution became so integral to both the French and American wars in Vietnam. Why did women who fled villages become prostitutes servicing soldiers in the towns and around the foreign military bases? A reimagined women's war museum could help us understand, in other words, *all* of the ways a particular war becomes gendered. Such a museum could also help us to understand what the "nation" meant to women who chose to stay on the political sidelines in the midst of a dislocating war. It would throw into even sharper relief the processes by which ideas about "womanhood," "daughterly loyalty," "wifely support," and "motherly sacrifice" could inspire some women to cast off in boats on moonless nights, while they prompted other women to smuggle messages, endure prison, and shoot down helicopters.

Other Vietnamese women's studies researchers might direct

their attention northward, to the modern, well-financed, and handsome Ho Chi Minh Museum in Hanoi. There, amid the beautifully designed displays depicting the history of the Vietnamese nationalist struggle through the life of Ho himself, women are virtually invisible. It is clear that none of the curators of this impressive museum traveled from the capital down to Ho Chi Minh City to discuss their plans with the curators at the women's museum. Or perhaps those making the choices for the sparkling Ho Chi Minh Museum about what was serious, what trivial, concluded that precisely because the women's museum existed, they were licensed to design a conventionally masculinized museum. As Vietnamese women's studies researchers dig into the deeply gendered realities of the wars against the French and the Americans (and their Vietnamese allies), they will have the opportunity not only to subtly redesign the women's museum, but to intervene radically in the currently nationalist but still patriarchal flagship of Vietnamese war museums in Hanoi. The amount of resistance they encounter in either of these ventures will be a measure of the extent to which ideas about wartime femininity and masculinity remain politically charged decades after the end of the nationalist war.

War museums are powerful institutions. They bestow the mantle of "seriousness" on only some memories, but not others. They preserve some interpretations, but not others. By the very sequencing of displays — what is placed next to what, what comes after what — a museum can imply an explanation for why at least some people acted the way they did during the war. All of these choices, all of these selective inclusions and cause-and-effect sequencings, help shape *postwar* relationships between women and men and among various groups of women themselves. We, the postwar visitors, walk out of any war museum with ideas newly backed up by graphic images. We come away with stronger beliefs about how our society got to be the way it now is; we, the postwar museumgoers, come away from our hour among the statues, glass display cases, and mural paintings with firmer ideas about who deserves the credit or the blame for that. We also wander out into the sunlight with lasting notions about role models — negative as well as positive: the kind of men worth admiring, the kind of women to emulate, the sort of masculine behavior that is abhorrent, the sort of feminine behavior that deserves contempt — or maybe just forgetting.

MARRIAGE AND DIVORCE AFTER THE WAR

Most masculinized war museums, which is to say most war museums, don't have much to say about widows. They have even less to say about the wives of male soldiers who fought on the winning side and managed to survive the war. Banished from the murals and display cases altogether in these conventional war museums, these institutions designed to teach us what the war meant, are the wives of male soldiers who survived but had the misfortune to fight on the losing side. Yet many marriages go on after a war ends. And many of those marriages are forever changed because of the gendered dynamics of that war.

Wars have their endings inside families. Just as putting on one's "gender awareness" eyeglasses allows one to see a war museum in a new light, so donning those same lenses enables the keen observer to think about postwar marital relationships with a fresh understanding of what wartime gender dynamics do to relationships between women and men in the years after that war.

If the family is assigned that crucial status by nationalist officials, intellectuals, and organizers, then disruption of marital relationships is likely to be imagined by them not just as weakening a family, but as threatening the very fabric of the nation itself.[5] Such a belief imposes a burden on any woman or man who considers divorce. It might also make courts and other state institutions reluctant to facilitate divorce proceedings. At no time is nationalism more salient than during wartime. If the family is being described by wartime mobilizers and their supporters in the popular culture as a wartime resource, analogous to the agricultural harvest and a skilled workforce, then divorce will become especially hard for ordinary wives and husbands to legitimize during wartime. This will be true despite the fact that the war itself may generate new tensions in an already strained marriage. In fact, American feminist historians have found that U.S. divorce rates did decline during the 1940 to 1945 wartime period. French feminist historians have found the same trend in wartime France.[6] Women in both countries were expected to keep up morale on the home front. In practice, that meant staying in unhappy marriages and thus silencing themselves when writing to their husbands and lovers on the battlefronts. "Dear John" letters (in which a woman at home might tell her male soldier husband/lover of her own new romances or of ardor cooled) allegedly were written only by cruel women, women who cared little for their soldier and, by extension, for their nation.[7]

Post-wartime is not simply a time when weary soldiers come home to happy women and children. It can be a time of extremely difficult personal adjustments. These adjustments may — mistakenly — be trivialized as merely domestic or private because they take place outside the public arena, behind closed family doors. But in reality, every one of these adjustments — the successful and the unsuccessful — is a step taken to create or destabilize the postwar society. Many postwar governments in fact count on women to bear the brunt of these adjustments. Officials in many governments struggling with postwar economic dislocations need women to step aside when male veterans come home expecting to take over the paid jobs that women assumed during the war. They expect women who have become independent managers of households to at least feign dependency when their veteran-husbands return to the family expecting to find a masculinized role to fulfill. These same officials also often expect a woman to provide physical and emotional therapy if her husband returns damaged by the war, therapy that the strapped postwar government itself lacks the capability or will to provide for its returning soldiers. The postwar wife of the wounded soldier-husband is a woman to watch, to think about.

It is no wonder that, under these conditions, divorce rates in many postwar societies rise. Vietnamese women's studies researcher Thai Thi Ngoc Du, for instance, has found that divorce rates in Ho Chi Minh City rose markedly in the years following the end of the war in 1975. She also discovered that women were as likely as men to initiate those divorces. Many of these women noted that the long separations imposed by wartime conditions made their husbands strangers to them. Furthermore, many women married to men who were sent away after 1975 to re-education camps — camps that were established in a deliberate effort to re-create a postwar society — found the extended separations intolerable.[8] In postwar America, by contrast, divorce rates declined to levels lower than in the 1930s.[9] The marriages on which the nuclear family depended in these postwar years came to be seen as proof of U.S. superiority in the emerging Cold War rivalry with the Soviet Union.[10] But even this international scenario could not contain the impetus for divorce in America for a long time. By the late 1960s women and men were ending their marriages at an unprecedented rate.

SHRINKING MILITARIES
WITHOUT PRIVILEGING MEN

Thus marriages have both wartime and postwar careers. If divorce rates rise after a war has ended, then women's relationship to the paid labor force will change as well. It could well be that if women divorce, or are divorced by their husbands, they will need salaried work not only to support themselves, but to support their children. This newly urgent need for women to have access to decently paid jobs may come precisely at a time when the government wants to demobilize a mostly male military force. It is not inconceivable, therefore, that in many postwar societies the newly divorced woman and the newly demobilized male veteran will be competitors for the same postwar job.

If there were an American equivalent of the South Vietnam Women's Museum, certainly "Rosie the Riveter" — the 1940s welding-torch-wielding icon and the actual women who came closest to matching her — would have pride of place. And in fact many of the women portrayed in the Ho Chi Minh City museum do capture a similar spirit insofar as they are represented as having torn themselves away from conventional feminine roles and from personal routines and aspirations in order to carry ammunition, feed guerrillas, or relay secret messages. They were joined by thousands of women in the North who played similar wartime roles that were heralded at the time and for the years after 1975 as having been crucial for the communists' and nationalists' victory over the American forces and their local allies.

But postwar eras can last more than a generation. They can extend into future generations if their members believe they too have a stake in thinking about that war's implications for them, not just for their parents. Thus it is that young Vietnamese women visit the museum in the South to find models for themselves, though in the larger Hanoi museum they have to search much more diligently to spot a woman to model themselves after. Thus too it has been the American women who are the daughters, even the granddaughters, of World War II women industrial workers who have invested intellectual energy in learning more about Rosie the Riveter — again, both the symbol and the women she allegedly represented.[11]

Vietnamese women researchers still are in the early stages of this exploration. It may be too politically delicate, given that so many of the senior women intellectuals are themselves of the generation that was active in the war and given, too, that the same party and many of the same male officials who led the fight against the Americans — and Chinese and Cambodians — remain in power today. Finally, given that so much else of the past nationalist and socialist program is being thrown overboard for the sake of luring badly needed foreign capital, maintaining the halo around the war itself has become all the more strategically necessary for officials in Hanoi. In the United States, research tracing Rosie the Riveter's postwar journey from a paid job during World War II back into the kitchen or into a low-wage service job has been conducted recently in many cases by American feminist historians wanting to better understand their own mothers' not entirely voluntary postwar redomestication.[12] Perhaps younger Vietnamese researchers today will be prompted by a similar motivation to conduct their own fresh investigations into the journeys taken by their mothers before and after wartime.

Militaries, as well as defense factories, undergo major transformations after a war is over. But those transformations do not necessarily take the shape of mere military labor force reductions. Some governments don't shrink their militaries when wars end or enemies fade because of their gendered anxieties. Often it is the very shortage of jobs "fit for grown men" in the civilian economy that makes government officials reluctant to demobilize soldiers in a postwar era. The Nigerian government, for instance, was slow to cut its forces after winning the Biafran war in the 1960s. Similarly in the 1990s the Russian government reduced its military manpower at a snail's pace because it could not guarantee civilian employment for male veterans. Even the American administration of President Bill Clinton, an administration that came into office with relatively few emotional ties to the military, moved more slowly than many expected in the 1990s in cutting back U.S. military personnel. All of these governments dragged their feet in demobilizing soldiers for fear that veterans will join the unemployment lines, as so many did in the years following the end of the Vietnam War.

And "fear" is the operative word here. Many government officials responsible for cutting military manpower in a postwar era act out of fear. They are afraid of the disgruntled *male* veteran. Women veterans do not seem to inspire the same political fear. They are less organized. They do not control other influential public organizations. Few military manpower strategists in any country lie awake at night worrying about women veterans conspiring to perform a coup or creating dissident clubs that will foment discontent in the general public. The woman veteran becomes invisible in these officials' minds because they imagine her simply returning to what she does "naturally" — caring for her children, emotionally supporting her husband, taking most of her personal satisfaction (even if she had a paid job) out of unpaid domestic work. This official imagining is the flip side of the fear-of-the-unemployed-male-veteran coin. As is usually the case in any sphere of gendered public policy — policies about housing, about landownership, about population control — official decisions about male citizens rest upon official presumptions about female citizens. Conducting public policy research in a postwar era, therefore, calls for gender awareness precisely because (1) any policy choices make distinctions between women and men, and (2) most of the policies concerning men could not be rationalized without supporting arguments concerning women.

Thus a women's studies researcher needs to be curious about any postwar image of the unemployed male veteran that makes senior government officials nervous. That image, when made the basis of state policy, will have profound effects on that society's women. But this does not mean that officials' worries are totally unrealistic. In countries as different as 1930s Germany, 1950s Yugoslavia, 1980s France and the United States, and 1990s Zaire and South Africa, male veterans turned themselves into a potent political force. They mobilized out of their sense of patriotism and betrayal: they have sacrificed for their country, and now they come home and discover that women and other men have taken "their" jobs. Similarly, in Vietnam it has been male veterans' clubs that have formed the base of the emergent nonparty opposition in recent years. Government officials have responded by treating male veterans' economic expectations gingerly. Consequently, when the postwar unemployment rate for women markedly exceeds that for men, women's studies analysts would be wise to look for at least part of the cause in managers' and government officials' gendered fears and gendered notions of political anxiety and patriotic gratitude to help explain the job gap.

When any military shrinks, it usually changes its ethnic, gender, and class composition. That is, the kinds of soldiers that the defense officials let go are rarely random. The soldiers who are the first to be demilitarized are likely to be disproportionately from those ethnic and racial groups that the military senior command finds less compatible, even less "reliable." These are often the men from the same ethnic and racial groups that the military was reluctant to mobilize in the first place.[13] In Vietnam, the smaller army of the 1990s tended to be a more thoroughly ethnic Vietnamese army. Especially since the demobilization following Vietnam's withdrawal from Cambodia in the late 1980s, fewer hill tribe women, fewer ethnic Khmer, Cham, and Chinese women would live their lives as the wives, mothers, and girlfriends of the government's soldiers.

In class terms, it is likely to be those soldiers who come from the more affluent social classes who are able to get demobilized earliest: first, because their continued enlistment may arouse the sort of political discontent that governments want to avoid at the end of a war; second, because these are the sorts of young people more likely to be able to find jobs in the postwar economy and thus not so quickly swell the disturbing ranks of unemployed veterans. When foreign investors crowded Hanoi's and Ho Chi Minh City's best hotels, they played their part in this military reconfiguration insofar as they offered private-sector opportunities disproportionately to men already relatively advantaged in the Vietnamese social structure. Thus how the wife of a southern, ethnic Vietnamese educated soldier experiences Vietnam's postwar society might be quite different from how the wife of a northern hill tribe peasant soldier experiences those same years.

There is still a third dimension of a shrinking military's social transformation. That is its regendering. There has been a marked preference by postwar military commanders to demobilize women soldiers before letting go of male soldiers. In the Soviet Union, the United States, and Britain, World War II was fought with thousands of women joining men in the uniformed forces. But after 1945 all three of these governments deliberately demobilized women at a much more rapid pace than they demobilized men. Their presumption was adopted by the male leaders of many liberation armies as well: while both female and male soldiers had been necessary during the war, a postwar, peacetime military could — and should — revert to its "natural" core of male soldiery. These planners imagined the somewhat (not entirely) demasculinized wartime military to have been an anomaly. They consequently designed their postwar military demobilization in order to *remasculinize* the military.[14] In the 1990s new governments in South Africa, Haiti, and El Salvador all were in the process of shrinking their militaries, though analogies with Vietnamese demobilization should be made with caution since the armies of the former had become the objects of widespread loathing, while the Vietnamese army was still held in high popular regard.[15]

If the Vietnamese military continues to consume a significant portion of the national budget and if it continues to carry significant influence in the country's policy-making, then it cannot be to Vietnamese women's advantage to have that important institution devoid of women. Vietnamese women, like those in South Africa and El Salvador, face a critical postwar choice: they can become satisfied with the sort of visibility that museum visitors will see under glass; or, second, they can press the government to recruit more women into a still-influential postwar military; or, third—and most difficult—they can collectively push for a genuinely demilitarized society in which neither military needs nor masculinized presumptions determine historical memories, current job opportunities, or long-term public status.

POSTWAR ECONOMIC RECONSTRUCTION: WHERE ARE THE WOMEN?

Museums, divorces, demobilization—each of these are crucial realms for making sense of women's and men's different experiences of postwar society. But probably the area that most citizens concentrate their attention on is economic reconstruction.

Precisely because postwar economic reconstruction occurs in most countries amid physical destruction and severe financial constraints, it is a process that demands choices. In an environment of shortages, choices are especially likely to have pronounced gendered consequences.

· Who should get the sort of training that requires the most expensive equipment?
· Who should be hired for the first big construction projects?
· Whose aspirations to manage foreign-capitalized firms should be listened to most carefully?

- Whose unpaid work should remain unpaid in order to stretch scarce postwar dollars or dong the furthest?
- Whose sexuality should be the principal target of population control programs in attempts to reduce pressures on food resources and on a fragile labor market?

Each of these questions must be addressed by citizens in any society that is trying to rebuild the country after a prolonged war fought on its soil. The postwar rebuilding process can *widen the gap between the economies of men and the economies of women*, sending out gendered ripple effects far into the future, into a time when the merely physical damages of war have been repaired. After, with the help of the World Bank and foreign companies, the bridges along Vietnam's famous Route 1 were rebuilt, when the Ho Chi Minh City airport's runways had been repaved, when the Mekong and Red River irrigation networks had been restored and new energy stations constructed, the more subtle inequalities between Vietnamese women and men might still remain, possibly more deeply rooted than they had been even before the postwar economic reconstruction began, because each of these reconstruction projects was conducted in a patriarchally gendered way.[16]

If men were considered the "natural" employees on transportation and energy projects, *and* if construction workers had been presumed to be skilled workers deserving of better pay than, for instance, pig farmers or garment factory workers, then every construction project and pig-raising effort and every sneaker and garment factory investment served to rebuild postwar Vietnam in a fashion that widened the gap between men's and women's wages — *even if Vietnam's laws guaranteeing equal pay for equal work had been enforced.*

Precisely because postwar economic reconstruction infuses so much new capital into a society, it is a process that needs to be monitored with a sharp eye for its gendered dynamics. Yet there is a natural inclination to push gender concerns aside. Women as well as men are eager to repair roads and communications networks, to increase agricultural output, to catch up with the rest of the world, which has been spared devastating wartime destruction. In the name of this national goal, women usually are asked by governments (and their fathers and husbands) to put their hopes on "the back burner." They are often made to feel as though they are being unreasonable, even selfish and unpatriotic, if they raise questions about whether as many women as men will be trained for the highest-paying jobs being generated by reconstruction funds. "Later," women are often told. Later, *after* this urgent campaign of economic reconstruction is completed, women's access to the skilled construction jobs, the manufacturing management positions, the administrative policy-making posts will be addressed. But by waiting until after reconstruction — that is, until the post-postwar period — women are likely to lose opportunities for training and income, which will set them back for decades. "Later" is a patriarchal time zone.

CONCLUSION

The postwar era in any country is a time fraught with gendered decisions. Memories are being fashioned in museums out of selected images. Lessons are being set in reports and schoolbooks out of presumptions about masculinity and femininity. Militaries and labor forces are being reconstituted according to officials' gendered anxieties and popular gender-inattentive impatience.

It is precisely in these years when the sounds of guns and helicopters have been replaced by the sounds of farm animals and
construction machinery that women and men could diverge,
could be nudged along paths that would lead them in quite
different directions. Policies about men are always made dependent on policies about women. Policies about women are always
built on policies about men. But this sort of mutual dependency
does not guarantee that postwar decisions will ensure that real
equality emerges when wartime flows into peacetime. The postwar era is a time that calls for acute gender awareness by researchers and policy-makers alike.

CHAPTER 16

Demilitarization — or More of the Same?

Feminist Questions to Ask in the Postwar Moment

To explain why, even after the guns have gone silent, militarization and the privileging of masculinity stubbornly persist, we need to surrender the cherished notion that when open warfare stops, militarization is reversed. One of the insights garnered by feminist analysts from the recent experiences of women and men in societies as different as Bosnia and Rwanda is that the processes of militarization can continue to roll along even after the formal cease-fire agreement has been signed.

Persistent militarization in a postwar society serves to re-entrench the privileging of masculinity — in both private and public life. Thus, if we lack the tools to chart *postwar* militarization, we will almost certainly be ill equipped to monitor the subtle ways in which — democratic rhetoric notwithstanding — masculinity continues to be the currency for domination and exclusion.

In a given social group at any particular time — for instance, the Netherlands in the mid-1600s, Yugoslavia in the late 1990s, Oxfam and the UN in the early 2000s — there are likely to be at work certain processes that bestow influence on those men who manage to meet the currently accepted (versus existing, but commonly disparaged) standards of manliness. The contest between rival models of masculinity has profound consequences for women; each rival form of masculinity requires for its validation the promotion of a particular form of femininity. If a form of masculinity that has as its conforming complement a passive, demure, domesticated model of femininity gains public credibility, then genuine democratization is almost certain to be derailed. Militarized masculinity is a model of masculinity that is especially likely to be imagined as requiring a feminine complement that excludes women from full and assertive participation in postwar public life.

For the past two centuries this rivalry between gendered meanings has been played out in both national and international political arenas. How exactly those rivalries between forms of masculinity that politically marginalize women and those (rarer) forms of masculinity that are confirmed, rather than threatened, by women's vibrant, autonomous public participation actually evolve is determined in no small part by the trends in militarization. The rise or fall in levels of militarization is not caused by lunar orbits. Whether the process of militarization is stalled, reversed, or propelled forward in any society is determined by the political processes that bolster certain notions of masculinity and certain presumptions about femininity over their gendered alternatives.

During recent years I have become convinced that it is not

enough for us to talk about militarism. We must talk about—
monitor, explain, challenge — those multilayered processes by
which militarism gains legitimacy and popular and elite acceptance; that is, we must learn how to track militarization. So let's
look at each — militarism and militarization — and then at their
interaction.

Like any ideology, militarism is a package of ideas. It is a compilation of assumptions, values, and beliefs. When any person —
or institution or community — embraces militarism it is thus embracing particular value assertions about what is good, right,
proper and about what is bad, wrong, and improper. By embracing the ideology of militarism, a person, institution, or community is also accepting a distinctive package of beliefs — about how
the world works, about what makes humans tick.

Among those distinctively militaristic core beliefs are (a) that
armed force is the ultimate resolver of tensions; (b) that human
nature is prone to conflict; (c) that having enemies is a natural
condition; (d) that hierarchical relations produce effective action;
(e) that a state without a military is naive, scarcely modern, and
barely legitimate; (f) that in times of crisis those who are feminine need armed protection; and (g) that in times of crisis any
man who refuses to engage in armed violent action is jeopardiz-
ing his own status as a manly man.

Occasionally these beliefs are put under public scrutiny and
examined; often, though, they are left unproblematized, as if they
were "natural." Whatever one treats as "natural" is close to the
core of one's own ideology.

Now let's look at militarization. Militarism is an ideology.
Militarization, by contrast, is a sociopolitical process. Militarization is the multitracked process by which the roots of militarism

are driven deep down into the soil of a society — or of a non-governmental organization, a governmental department, an ethnic group, or an international agency. There is nothing automatic or inevitable about the militarizing process moving ever forward. Militarization can be stalled by exposure, critique, and resistance at an early stage; occasionally it may even be reversed. It also, however, can be propelled forward after years of apparent stagnation. Most militarizing processes occur during what is misleadingly labeled "peacetime." Thus the 1980s can now, with hindsight, be recognized to be an era in Yugoslav society during which militarizing processes were deliberately being nurtured.

To chart and explain militarization in any place at any time, we need to equip ourselves with the analytical skills to monitor the transformation of assumptions, reassessment of priorities, evolution of values. This is, admittedly, a tall order. I have become convinced that it is an order that can be filled only by wielding an explicitly feminist curiosity. The observer does not have to be — at least at the outset — a self-identified feminist. One just has to start pursuing answers to very specifically feminist sorts of questions. A "feminist curiosity" is a curiosity that provokes serious questioning about the workings of masculinized and feminized meanings. It is the sort of curiosity that prompts one to pay attention to things that conventionally are treated as if they were either "natural" or, even if acknowledged to be artificial, are imagined to be "trivial," that is, imagined to be without explanatory significance.

What follows here is just the beginning of creating a set of necessary questions to which answers must be sought if militarization — and its complementary marginalization of women in public life — is to be accurately monitored and, perhaps, rolled back.

As the war in Iraq dragged on longer than the Bush administration had predicted, some Americans' initial enthusiasm for the U.S. military invasion waned. Here workers are removing a video war game from a local bar in response to its patrons' loss of interest. Did this amount to the demilitarization of some American civilian men's leisuretime activities? (Photo by Evan Richman, © *The Boston Globe*, reprinted by permission)

Feminist Monitoring Question Number One: Do people who can claim to have been "combatants" in either the insurgents' or state's armed forces carry extra weight in the postconflict era when they speak to officials or to the public, *and* does that differential weighting privilege certain sorts of manliness and marginalize most women, regardless of their presumed femininity?

The special objects of feminist curiosity here are the listeners. Pursuing this first feminist question sends one to quite mundane sites. In a postwar Bosnian town meeting, are most residents reluctant to interrupt a male speaker who claims to be a current or past army or militia combatant? Are veterans' claims most likely to receive an elite hearing — by either a civilian Bosnian or UN official in Sarajevo? In informal social gatherings, whose "war stories" are listened to most attentively? In a policy meeting about the return of refugees to their homes in Bosnia, whose view is considered the most authoritative, that of the humanitarian NGO — or the battalion commander of SFOR, the international peacekeeper whose guns and armored cars will wield the necessary threat of force?

There are serious implications for leaving any of these militarized dynamics unnamed and unchallenged, not just in Bosnia, but in Kosovo, Liberia, Sri Lanka, East Timor, or Afghanistan. It matters, for the long-term inclusiveness of the democratizing process, who is listened to by harried, short-handed officials and staff, who is presumed to have the "credentials" to speak, who is deemed to possess the pertinent experience, the relevant skills, the most acute stake, to make their words worthy of attention when so many are vying for attention. *Insofar* as armed combatants in the recent conflict have been mostly male, and *insofar* as it is masculinized combatants who are presumed by their influential civilian listeners to have things to say that (even if unpleasant) must be addressed publicly, the immediate postconflict political process will be on the road to remilitarization without a warning shot being fired. Listening can be militarized. Listening can be masculinized.

Feminist Monitoring Question Number Two: To what extent do those people who wield militarized power (whether or not they wear camouflage or gold braid) become, in everyone else's eyes, the people to whom one must gain access if one is going to have an impact on public affairs? People in positions of militarized authority can threaten to use coercive force. They can label some places and groups "allies" and others "public security threats." They can deploy armed troops here but not there. They can assign armed escorts to some aid convoys but not to others. They can claim "urgency" in tones that others rarely can invoke. They are less likely to be challenged when they resort to secrecy than are their nonmilitarized counterparts. One frequently hears militarized decision-makers fret over the consequences of these common perceptions, even if they, by their own actions, have helped create them. These fretful militarized officials express frustration: so many people come to them for resources and solutions; they "expect us to be social workers."

Insofar as those officials wielding militarized resources and militarized authority perceive their missions to have primacy over all other missions, those officials are fostering a militarized political culture in the postconflict society. *Insofar* as many others (inside and outside decision-making institutions) come to share that belief, the perpetuation of militarization will be fueled further. Moreover, *insofar* as it is widely imagined to be unproblematic for those militarized posts to be assigned to manly men, it will be tempting for everyone in the society to couch their explanations and their needs in the sorts of terms understood by masculinized officials with militarized agendas. This, in turn, is likely to marginalize those officials less willing or less able to speak in these masculinized, militarized terms, and those civic groups who are actively seeking to civilianize postwar society. Some men thereby will be shut out of serious public conversation. Most women will be.

Feminist Monitoring Question Number Three: To what extent

does a given officialdom or a general public assume that security — especially if embedded in the English phrase "national security" — refers to militarized security? For years now, women active in creating peace groups — the Women in Black in Jerusalem and Belgrade, the protesters camping at the gates of missile bases at Greenham Common, England, and Seneca Falls, New York, as well as members of the worldwide organization, the Women's International League for Peace and Freedom, or of Women Monitoring the Peace in the Southern Sudan — have been developing feminist analyses that reveal, first, that security is gendered and, second, that to be realistic about what security entails one has to break down the ideological walls separating "public" life from "private" life.

For many women, the home and neighborhood (and temporary "home," a refugee camp) can be as insecure as a battlefield. In fact, a home or a neighborhood street can *be* a battlefield. When postwar local and international authorities treat "private" violence against women as a nonpriority, as an issue to be put off until "later," as a matter not falling within their own mandate, those same authorities perpetuate a dynamic of militarization in a time of alleged peace.

Through the collection of evidence and its careful analysis, feminist peace activists have demonstrated that men and women, despite their sometimes shared conditions, do not experience identical threats. Their research has revealed that wartime violence translates into quite distinct forms of displacement, intimidation, and privation for women and men, that whatever rewards wartime may generate — and, for some, wartime does generate rewards in security, status, power, and material wealth — they are not equally distributed among the society's women and men.

These women peace activists have found that the sorts of insecurity many women experience in the midst of openly armed conflict are surprisingly akin to the forms of insecurity that women experience when the guns are silent: the lack of resources that can be used to ensure their own physical integrity.

Yet all of this insightful observing and theorizing about security has only just begun to make a modest dent in the orthodox presumption that "security studies" are the studies of militarized decision-making and that a "national security" deliberation is a discussion devoted to the maintenance of a state's militarized well-being.

Domestic violence prevention and prosecution, consequently, are not deemed worthy of urgent attention by "security" officials coping with the demands of postconflict reconstruction. Those engaged in training a new police force, building a new judiciary, or drafting a new legal code, thereby leave the serious strategizing about domestic violence to the handful of feminists inside international agencies and their underresourced allies active in overworked local women's groups. By their neglect, they perpetuate in peacetime one core propellant of militarization: the presumption that masculinized violence is natural.

Trafficking in women, likewise, is rarely treated by conventional "security" officials — international and local — as an urgent concern inside their own bureaucratic bailiwicks. Those officials, instead, more often see only a shrunken list of security issues as appropriate to their finely honed skills and as demanding their scarce attention. A commercialized violation of women's physical integrity — such as organized international trafficking — typically only achieves the conventionally lofty status of a "security" issue when commercialized sex appears to have become a threat to male soldiers' health and discipline. It may be deliberately swept under the policy-makers' rug if police or military personnel are suspected of being directly engaged in the trafficking operations.

Gaining an attentive hearing from officials imbued with this conventional notion of security is very difficult. It leaves "security" deliberations not only militarized, but also highly masculinized, with most women working in NGOs and in international agencies cooling their heels outside the meeting room. This masculinized exclusion is made all the more intense by the shroud of secrecy typically draped over any discussions presumed to be about "security." Given these exclusionary dynamics, it becomes tempting for advocates of urgent action against domestic violence and trafficking in women to adopt a militarized discourse strategy of their own. That is, they may try to pry open the door to the security deliberations room by defining violence against local women as a matter of military discipline or as a question of militiamen's intimidation — when these advocates themselves really believe the issue to be a matter of economic justice, public health, democratization, and human rights. If, by using this tempting tactical ploy, they succeed in getting their toe in the door to security deliberations, they may well discover that, once inside, they have lost control of the original issue. As a result, women's well-being in the reconstructed postconflict society will still be left on the proverbial back burner.

Feminist Monitoring Question Number Four: To what extent does the new (internationally mentored) government's budget allocate disproportionate public funds to that nascent government's security forces? It is true that police forces and military forces do not usually foster identical constructions of masculinity. They also are apt, in postconflict times as in preconflict times, to be recruited disproportionately from rather different social classes and ethnic or racialized communities. Yet, these important dissimilarities notwithstanding, police forces and militaries each conventionally are overwhelmingly male in their composition, and more often than not, they are deeply masculinized in their institutional cultures. In some postconflict countries — for instance, post-1994 South Africa — there has been an organized lobby created specifically to keep watch on the new military, to ensure that it recruits a sizable proportion of women into its reorganized ranks. The same is happening in some countries whose armies contribute to international peacekeeping forces — the Netherlands, for instance. "Success," however, may come in the form of a small percentage of women in the new military. The upper reaches of the command structure, while now less mono-ethnic, may nonetheless be, just as before, reliant on a stubbornly persistent masculinized culture.

If the postwar military and the police forces are rebuilt by local and international officials who shy away from questioning these comfortable masculinized "esprit" traditions and *if* those two institutions are awarded disproportionate slices of the new state's budgetary pie, then the result will be that a disproportionate share of scarce public monies will be invested in the salaries, equipment, morale, and prestige of those parts of the larger state that are least invested in women's voices being heard inside the state. This deeply gendered — that is, masculinized — outcome will be produced even while the elites of the military and police force are routinely pitted against one another in funding contests.

Rivalries between men, whether personal or bureaucratic, do not roll back either masculinization or militarization. Most often, those rivalries merely turn women into silent bystanders. Or, and this is less noticed, they turn women and ideas about proper femininity into cannon fodder for the waging of those masculinized rivalries for political turf or material resources. Being turned into someone else's cannon fodder is not a promising formula for achieving first-class citizenship.

Feminist Monitoring Question Number Five: To what extent is the status of a local woman, any woman, in the postwar setting defined by influential decision-makers chiefly in terms of what they were during the recent war? That is, a feminist curiosity prompts one to keep track of whether certain women's wartime experiences (or the experiences to which anyone paid attention) continue to be deemed the principal basis for defining their present sociopolitical role. For instance, which women are seen by public figures as "heroic mothers"? Which women are talked about in public almost exclusively as "victims of sexual assault"? Which women are seen as the enemies of the newly established state, or of the nation emerging from war?

Employing categories helps us think. Some categories are useful in the making of policies and the nurturing of cultures that foster genuine democratization and demilitarization. But narrow, war-referenced categories into which many women are placed by journalists and decision-makers — even categories that seem to valorize some women — can become the basis for crafting patriarchal and militarized public policies. To act out of a feminist curiosity means to conduct an examination of public policy discourse (memos, television news scripts, campaign speeches, legislative records) to see which categories are imposed to make sense of women's lives in the postconflict societies. A feminist curiosity leads one to be suspicious of a dependence on only those categories that acknowledge women either as silently symbolic or silently victimized.

Feminist Monitoring Question Number Six: Which organizations active in the postconflict society's reconstruction are the most patriarchal? What area of authority, what resources for the remaking of the society do these organizations control? Whose senses of inclusion and well-being do these organizations' operations most perpetuate? By "patriarchal" here I mean something quite specific. Any organization is patriarchal insofar as its internal culture privileges masculinity; insofar as its decision-making is *un*informed by a concern for the actual lives of women as full citizens; and insofar as its policies and actual practices serve to re-entrench privileged masculinity in the wider society. One might take this questioning further, turn a feminist curiosity onto specific influential organizations, peer inside, and ask: Which of its several departments is the most patriarchal, and how does that shape the culture and resource allocation of the organization as a whole?

For instance, take all the international and local organizations operating in Bosnia-Herzegovina from 1995 to 2004. One could launch a comparative study of their relative patriarchal inclinations and impacts. Where, then, on the scale of institutional patriarchy would one place the following?

Office of the High Representative of the Peace
 Implementation Council
World Bank
Dutch battalion of SFOR (the UN peacekeeping office)
Doctors Without Borders (international NGO)

UN High Commission for Refugees

Kvinna till Kvinna (Swedish women's NGO)

Office of the UN High Commissioner for Human Rights

Women of Mostar (Bosnian NGO)

OSCE (the Organization of Security and Co-operation
   in Europe)

U.S. Agency for International Development

International Police Task Force

Catholic Relief Services

Bosnian Ministry of Labor

Bosnian Ministry of Health

each of the several Bosnian political parties

In conducting this investigation one must be sure to include this last set of organizations on our list: fledgling political parties. One of the lessons we have learned from feminists in Chile, Nicaragua, and other postconflict and militarized societies is that the creation of new competitive political parties in the name of the establishment of democracy can perpetuate a subtle form of militaristic thinking and update old forms of masculinized privilege. Women active in electoral politics in countries as different as Sweden, Britain, France, India, and Japan have been revealing through their analyses of their parties just how stubborn patriarchal ways of behaving and thinking can be inside allegedly democratic electoral political parties — of the ideological left as well as of the center and the right. Thus, promoting multiparty electoral politics in any postconflict society is no guarantee that some of the beliefs and values essential to the perpetuation of militarization — especially the belief in the allegedly natural masculine proficiency in public arena competitions — will not be legitimized yet again.

CONCLUSION

We are only beginning to chart the multiple paths that militarization can take. It is a subtle process. What fuels militarization can be disparate and hard to pinpoint. It can move forward before the guns start firing and continue to progress after they have (mostly) fallen silent. Without a determined curiosity, informed by feminist analysis, militarization's causes and consequences will remain below the surface of public discussion and formal decision-making until they are almost impossible to reverse. None of these causes and consequences of militarization is more significant than the entrenchment of ideas about "manly men" and "real women."

If the experiences of women in Bosnia or any other postwar society — local women from the dominant ethnic group of all classes and communities, as well as women from marginalized ethnic groups working with governmental, international, and independent organizations — are taken seriously, we will have a far better chance of detecting how militarization with its complementary privileging of masculinity is perpetuated and perhaps how it might be put into reverse. But taking all of these diverse women's experiences seriously entails asking some pretty awkward questions. Feminist questions are always awkward precisely because they make problematic what is conventionally taken as "logical" or "natural."

Then, there is the question of what to do with the answers. Sandbagging, or even reversing, the current subterranean flows of militarization in Bosnia, Iraq, Congo, Cyprus, or Kashmir will require from us a far more profound commitment to genuinely inclusive democratization than is often called for by bankers, health experts, security officials, lawyers, and electoral strategists. Many of the players in today's postconflict societies may have to surrender an advantage they have been loath even to admit they possess: the privileging of their own status as masculine.

CHAPTER 17

A Feminist Map of the Blocks on the Road to Institutional Accountability

What are the linkages between feminist thinking, violence, terror, and accountability? Briefly, I'd like to try mapping accountability — or, more precisely, the obstacles that make it so hard to hold accountable those institutions (and their decision-makers) whose actions and inactions are responsible for so much of today's violence against women and thus for the insecurity in the lives of women at home and abroad.

Each of these obstacles to instituting effective accountability is best understood if we cultivate a feminist analytical curiosity. So much of what we already know about these obstacles has come directly out of feminist studies of institutional cultures, that is, investigations of the patriarchal assumptions and behaviors that shape institutional cultures — the cultures of legislatures, the cultures of corporations, the cultures of militaries, the cultures of police forces, the cultures of UN agencies, the cultures of law firms, the cultures of NGOs, the cultures of scientific labs, the cultures of labor unions, the cultures of state bureaucracies, the cultures of universities, the cultures of social movements.

Thus, to make sense of what we must dismantle in order to achieve accountability for every institution that currently perpetrates, or is complicit in, violence against and intimidation of women will require paying careful attention to feminist analysis. Here is the beginning of what I realize is a still-in-progress list of the obstacles on the road to institutional accountability:

> *The Culture (one might even say, cult) of Secrecy:* Maintaining such a culture requires tight bonds among the insiders, bonds so often welded together with forms of masculinity.

> *The Culture of "Imminent Danger":* This culture is sustained by the classic patriarchal caveat that women are in the sort of danger from which only rational men can protect them.

> *The Culture of Solidarity:* See the first item above. Consider every feminist study of every masculinist nationalist movement. Think about the American navy's 1990s Tailhook scandal. Stir in a ladleful of brotherhood.

> *The Presumption of Normalcy:* "Boys will be boys." "Cheap labor." If normal is still too porous, the practitioners of normalcy will raise the bar to the level of "natural." Dig out a dog-eared copy of Virginia Woolf's *The Guineas* if feminist memory fails here.

> *The Presumption of Triviality:* Anthrax scares are not "serious" so long as the anthrax scares are directed only at abortion providers. Trivializing is a political action. It is worthy of continued feminist monitoring. See the Human Rights Watch and Amnesty feminist reports since the 1990s on

the long-standing institutional ignoring of sexual violence against women in refugee camps for a refresher on how otherwise well-meaning organizations convince themselves that certain conditions naturally fall below the collective radar.

The Culture of Expertise: Whose credentials allow them to be called as public witnesses? How many Women in Black (in Spain, Israel, the United States, Italy, Yugoslavia) are in CNN's and Reuters' Rolodexes? How many feminists who conduct research into all forms of violence are deemed by policy-makers to be experts on "security"? The narrow and naive conventional definitions of relevant knowledge produce a shallow questioning of institutional practices that rarely gets to the core of why that institution's elite as well as rank-and-file staffers think about the world in the patriarchal ways they do.

An Institutionalized Short Attention Span: Telltale signs: watching the conflict only until the leading male actors sign the cease-fire; pulling the newspaper's or network's journalists after the most "newsworthy" military engagements wind down; not knowing how to listen to the silences. Why was it at least two years after the 1994 ethnic violence in Rwanda before the extent of the rape of women was made public? Which political parties' accountability, and which local Rwandan radio station's accountability, would never have become a political issue had not nurses, human rights investigators, and local women's group members used their own feminist curiosity to make these assaults on women visible?

Both the direct institutional actors *and* the more shadowy complicit institutional actors need to be held accountable for the insecurity into which they throw so many women's lives.

It is feminist researchers, wearing many different sorts of hats, who will make us smart — realistic — about how the workings of masculinist ideas and patriarchal cultures inside organizations create and stubbornly sustain the blocks on the road to accountability — public accountability, accountability to women as well as men, accountability as citizens of states and as citizens of this interdependent world.

CHAPTER 18

When Feminists Look at Masculinity and the Men Who Wage War

A Conversation between Cynthia Enloe and Carol Cohn

We (Cynthia Enloe and Carol Cohn) first met in Finland in the frigid January of 1987. We were among women from more than twenty countries who had gathered for a forum on women and the military system — and we turned out to be sharing the government-run Siuntio Health Spa with a group of World War II veterans and their families.[1] Cynthia's pathbreaking 1983 book on the militarization of women's lives titled Does Khaki Become You? *illuminated the lives of members of both groups and, in many ways, opened the conceptual space for our international forum to take place.[2] Three years later, the U.S. edition of Cynthia's* Bananas, Beaches and Bases: Making Feminist Sense of International Politics *came out.[3] It turned many of the assumptions in the academic study of international politics on their head, revolutionizing our ideas of what should even "count" as "international politics," illuminating the crucial role played by notions of "masculinity"*

*and "femininity" in international relationships, and sparking a vibrant
project of feminist critique, research, and theorizing in the study of international relations.*[4]

*As colleagues in the small world of feminist international relations
theorists, we have had many occasions since 1987 to discuss our over-
lapping interests in militaries, masculinities, international organizations, and gendered conceptions of security. In the spring of 2002, we sat
down at Carol's kitchen table to explore the directions feminist analysis
of international politics might take in the changed, and unchanged,
"post–September 11" world.*

Carol Cohn (CC): Cynthia, what do you think we still don't
know enough about in the realm of international politics?

Cynthia Enloe (CE): Like you, I, of course, see the "international" as embedded in the national and in the local. And, like
you, I also see — or, better, have been taught by other feminists to
see — the "political" in many spaces that others imagine are
purely economic, or cultural, or private. With those provisos, I
think we really don't know enough about how masculinity operates; but to carry on that exploration, we have to be women's-
studies-informed. This is not masculinity studies.

CC: Because understanding the dynamics of masculinity requires
being curious about the complex workings of femininity?

CE: Yes, I really believe that. I think more and more about marriages, about particular masculinities — especially of the sort that
states think they need — about how they're being confirmed by
women in their roles as wives. Those women, of course, are not
always willing to fulfill the state's needs! Your own classic article

about the American male intellectuals who designed Cold War nuclear strategies is so revealing about the ways in which certain forms of masculinity get confirmed by certain highly deflective modes of discourse.[5] You were surrounded by men during that study, operating as a sort of mole in a hypermasculinized subculture. But looking back, do you think it mattered that you were a *feminist* scholar doing this research on Cold Warrior discourse?

CC: When I was there, I tried very hard to shed my analytic lenses — even though we all know this is never completely possible — and to just pay careful attention to what was happening around me. What was clearly important, however, from day one, was that I was seen by these defense strategists as a *female* scholar. For example, I think many men were much more willing to talk with me, to answer my "dumb," naive questions with great openness, both because of a kind of genuinely chivalrous generosity and because it was in a sense "normal" for a female to be asking such basic questions. Also, it was relatively easy for me personally to deal with being in the "nonexpert" position. A male colleague who also did interviews with powerful nuclear decision-makers told me somewhat ruefully that he and the men he was interviewing would sometimes get into a kind of competitive "who's-the-bigger-expert-here?" deadlock. It was probably quite productive that my relationships with these men did not provoke that kind of dynamic in either one of us!

CE: Yes, delving into masculinized cultures does turn the usually maddening presumptions about the "naive little lady" into an advantage — it was easier, though, for me to carry this off back in the days when I used to wear sleeveless sundresses!

Today I also want to know how the genderings of institutional cultures work inside international aid organizations. I want a feminist analysis of Doctors Without Borders, Oxfam, the International Red Cross. This is part of my current interest in what it takes to genuinely *de*militarize a society — and the intimately connected question: how do postwar societies manage, after the peace accord is signed, to reestablish masculinized privilege in their political cultures? These humanitarian peace-building groups have become crucial in every demilitarizing process. For instance, feminists inside Oxfam UK are asking *both* what Oxfam's postconflict operations' impacts are on local women *and* what are the politics of femininity and masculinity inside Oxfam itself. Suzanne Williams, a British feminist and a longtime staffer inside Oxfam UK, asked me to come up to Oxford in the spring of 2002 for a noontime conversation with about fifty Oxfam staff people. I remember thinking, "Oh, this is my chance to pursue my curiosity!" So I asked, "Okay, group, I don't know enough about Oxfam; do tell me what's the most masculinized of all Oxfam's departments." They thought a minute, whispered among themselves, and then came up with their answer: the Emergency Aid Department. Why? Because their staff handles water pipes. If you're the ones delivering water to refugee camps, you get the Land Rover first; you're doing the heavy lifting; your daily work is surrounded by the aura of urgency; you're doing a job that calls for technical expertise. Put it all together and laying water pipes in the Congo or Kosovo becomes a distinctly "manly" enterprise. Now it's important to remember, the Oxfam water pipe guys are noncombatant, antimilitarist men, providing essential humanitarian aid to people who have been driven out of their homes and into refugee camps in wartime. A bit later, I asked these smart, worldly, dedicated folks, "Okay, so what's the least masculinized department in Oxfam?" One woman sort of chuckled and ventured, "Development Education." Everybody in the room nodded, "Yeah, yeah." "So, that means it's the most feminized?" "Well, I don't think about it that way, but yes."

CC: You know, in my research at the UN, I've heard the Third Committee of the General Assembly — that's the committee that works on social, humanitarian, and cultural issues — referred to in-house as the "ladies' committee."[6] On the other hand, the Security Council remains an overwhelmingly male and masculinized preserve, although there have been some very important contributions from women ambassadors in the last few years.

CE: The "ladies' committee" . . . good grief! What you're now uncovering inside the UN makes me all the more convinced that we need to launch explicitly feminist investigations of institutional political cultures. Let's have a feminist analysis of the two International War Crimes Tribunals at the Hague and in Arusha [Tanzania] — I wonder if the two are identical? In the Hague we have Carla del Ponte (Swiss) coming right after Louise Arbor (Canadian), two women serving as the tribunal's chief prosecutor. That is pretty amazing! If we really took them seriously, not just as "remarkable women," what would we reveal about this fledgling new world order — and about what it will take to make the brand-new UN International Criminal Court work for women? Could it be that we're on the verge of creating, through the International War Crimes Tribunals, institutions that are less masculinized than the UN Secretariat, the World Trade Organization, the World Bank, or the International Monetary Fund? How could we *tell?*

CC: That's a really provocative and important question. And I think that the feminist questions you've proposed for monitoring postwar demilitarization are an extremely useful example of how to approach it.[7] So, once we get feminist analyses of international institutional political cultures, what do we have?

CE: A lot more realistic notion of how the world operates. That translates into a far more accurate causal explanation for patriarchy's remarkable global malleability.

CC: In my initial conversations with women in NGOs [nongovernmental organizations] around the UN, I've found that if I ask questions like, "What gets in the way of DPKO [the UN Department of Peacekeeping Operations] dealing with gender better?" the answers first tend to be about individuals — "The guy who headed that operation didn't want to have to have a gender advisor," or "These particular people on the budget committee won't support it," or "That guy didn't make a strong and compelling enough argument to the budget committee," and so on. "Institutional culture" is not usually what they bring up first, although they will, in fact, speak quite pointedly about it when you ask.

CE: Maybe it's because these women are lobbyists, nudging, pressing UN departments to pay attention to women's needs and to give women a seat at the proverbial table. I know you've been paying close attention to the UN-focused activists from the Women's International League for Peace and Freedom and other NGOs. Well, if you're a WILPF lobbyist, perhaps you think, "Oh, thankfully X is no longer the deputy head of mission. Now there is somebody who will at least let us in the door." It is also a more hopeful way of thinking. You can imagine, if this man or that woman gets transferred, we can get access to lobby for women's concerns. And that does matter. But I always wonder about the institutional passivity. Who, when he was evaluated for promotion, never even thought to ask WILPF whether they thought he was an effective UN official? Which institution-wide assumptions or priorities or rewards let him ignore DPKO's gender mandate so cavalierly?

CC: And who made the decision that there needn't be accountability mechanisms regarding implementation of gender mandates? Cynthia, a minute ago you spoke of "patriarchy's global malleability." You are quite purposeful about using the term "patriarchy." Tell me why.

CE: Well, I can remember the first time I ever heard "patriarchy" used — it terrified me. [*laugh*] It sounded so ideological, heavy, and — I don't know — all the things that at that age I wasn't. It was Jean Grossholz who used it. Jean was mobilizing people behind the scenes at the first Wellesley conference on women and development, which was turned into one of the very early special issues of *Signs*. I think it was 1980. I remember Jean going around and saying to people during coffee breaks, "We *have* to talk about patriarchy." And I thought, "Oh no, not patriarchy — I don't know what patriarchy is, and furthermore, it's not the kind of language I use!" Today I can't imagine trying to think, seriously, about the constructions of power and the systems by which power is both perpetuated and implemented *without* talking about patriarchy.

When I use "patriarchy" I try to be very clear and to give lots of examples. I try to remember what I was like when I first heard

Jean use the word, and I remember how scary it sounded, right? It certainly sounds scary to many academics and policy-makers today who don't want to be seen as out-there feminists. I can understand why they would much rather use "gender hierarchies" (that's if they're really tough), or maybe just "gender divisions of labor," or simply "discrimination," or "inequality."

In my teaching and writing, I try to be as precise and as concrete as I can be, which requires an endless curiosity! "Patriarchy" is not a sledgehammer being swung around a raving feminist head. It is a useful investigatory tool; it sheds light on complex, dynamic relationships at the same time as it reveals patterns of causality.

CC: But let me pursue that a little. If you say "Is X patriarchal?" for people familiar with the term normally the response would be, "Well, of course — find something that isn't!"

CE: Yeah, right.

CC: But what they might mean is simply that men are on top, men are in power. So saying, "It's a patriarchy," wouldn't really shed light on the institution. The term is, for lots of people, a thought-stopper. So why does it seem like such a *thought-opening* question to you?

CE: Because employing the concept of patriarchy in your investigations means you have to ask about the daily operations of both masculinity and femininity in relationship to each other and to the workings of power. It is not men-on-top that makes something patriarchal. It's men who are recognized by others as meeting certain standards of manliness and who claim for themselves a certain form of masculine identity, for the sake of being more valued, taken "seriously," and being trusted as "the protectors of and controllers of those people who are less masculine," that makes any organization, any community, any society patriarchal. Any group or institution becoming patriarchal is never automatic; it's rarely self-perpetuating. It takes daily tending. It takes decisions — even if those are masked as merely following "tradition." The perpetuation of a partriarchal institutional culture relies on many women finding patriarchal relationships comfortable, sometimes rewarding. You and I in our own work have found women who would much rather not rock the patriarchal boat — often for good reasons. Patriarchal structures and cultures have proved to be so adaptable! That's what's prompted me to watch them over time — the British House of Commons, sneaker companies, the Israeli military, Chilean political parties, Bosnia's and Afghanistan's new governments. Patriarchy isn't "old hat," yesterday. Patriarchy can be modern, "hip," a model for tomorrow.

CC: In the two institutions in which I've most recently done work, the word "patriarchy" is never used, but "gender" is all over the place. In the U.S. military, it is "gender integration." At the UN, it is "gender balance" and "gender mainstreaming." Although many people see "gender" as a more neutral, less inflammatory word than "patriarchy," in these institutional cultures, "gender" is apparently often heard in a way that is just as alienating and thought-stopping, evoking/representing "political correctness." The other thing that strikes me is that, in these institutions, where attention to gender has been mandated, "gender" remains an extremely opaque word. At the UN, for example, everyone is supposed to integrate a "gender perspective" into their programs, but many people simply don't have a real clue what that means. And the training that might make it clearer has been in short supply. But all of that is really about the practical effects of using specific words rather than the actual conceptual or analytic difference between "patriarchy" and a term such as "gender system."

CE: I keep using "patriarchy" because it reminds us that we're investigating power.

CC: You and I have talked about how highly resistant many people in the fields of international politics and international relations are to feminist analyses and to undertaking feminist-informed research. To some degree that's a reflection of the structure of rewards in academic and political institutions.

CE: Right.

CC: But this resistance is also conceptual. Their explanatory political models were constructed *without* women, and *without* men-as-men, so "inserting gender" then appears to them to be both difficult and unnecessary.

CE: I think one needs to start with the unsettling, candid question, "Do I *really* understand what is going on?" Yes?

CC: Yes. But it is often not easy to see that you have so far never seen — especially when you are working within a paradigm dominant in your field. What enabled you to see that *you* didn't really know what was going on? What led to *your* "aha!" moment?

CE: It came in fragments. The first glimmer came when I was doing the index for the book right before *Khaki* — that was *Ethnic*

Soldiers.[8] I learned so much researching it. It was my last non-feminist book — of course, I didn't know that at the time! Working for four years on *Ethnic Soldiers* taught me always to ask the ethnic question. But I didn't know then to ask the "where are the women?" question.

I can actually picture this. *Ethnic Soldiers* was going to be published by Penguin, which was great because it was going to be a trade paperback, and I had a very socially conscious editor there. At the indexing stage, I was in Norway, on a fellowship at PRIO, the Peace Research Institute of Oslo. This was in October 1979; it began to get dark by midafternoon. I was sitting in a coffee shop near PRIO, with my pink index cards and my green index cards. I was doing the index — the headings, the subheadings — realizing that indexes were really very political because they reflect what you want to make visible. Feminist pals had been nudging me to read Adrienne Rich's *Of Woman Born* . . . and it had had a big impact on me.[9] All of a sudden I had this fantastical imagining — I was sitting there in Oslo as the twilight was dimming, and I imagined Adrienne Rich (whom I had then never met, and never expected ever to meet) would walk into a bookstore. She would see *Ethnic Soldiers* on a bookshelf, would pull it off, and do what (I was then learning) feminist book buyers always do — turn to the index, and go to the W's. She'd find there were no "women" in my W's — only "Walloons," "World War I," and "World War II." And in my fantasy she'd immediately put the book back on the shelf.

CC: [*laugh*]

CE: I was fantasizing this at the post-page-proof stage, so I couldn't go back and rewrite anything in *Ethnic Soldiers.* I just prayed, "Please, dear God, maybe I mentioned women *some*place in this five-hundred-page typescript?" And I found, by luck, I had used "women" — twice. Once when thinking (briefly!) about Nepali women married to Gurkha soldiers, and again when thinking about the Rhodesian white-dominated regime starting — in desperation — to enlist white women into their military, rather than recruiting more black men.

CC: Two things immediately strike me about this story. First, *there's* the question you've asked ever since — "Where are the women?" Second, you started by saying that one needs to ask, "Do I really understand what is going on?" But, of course, in the story you just told, asking that question wouldn't have helped, would it? You didn't think that you didn't know what was going on when you wrote that book, right?

CE: You're right.

CC: It was actually a very different process that got you there — a social one, just as grad students' questions are socially shaped by their relations to professors, their departments, job markets. In this case, you imagined someone whom you admired and pictured what her reaction to your book might be.

CE: My imagining Adrienne Rich in a bookstore didn't immediately change my writing or my research. But soon after that I was being pushed by the wonderful students at Clark University to start teaching a course on the comparative politics of women. I think that the embarrassment I felt as I imagined Adrienne Rich's curiosity and *her* dismay at my lack of awareness made me a little more open to students' suggestions. Soon I began to let my teaching — and I love to teach — begin to affect my research more. So sometimes embarrassment is really fruitful! Then there are also friends. It was feminist friends' encouragement that led me to start reading things I hadn't been reading, far from political science though deeply political.

CC: I love the idea of *"fruitful* embarrassment." What do you think are the social contexts that make that possible?

CE: I've thought about this a lot, and I know you have, too. It's about reimagining this thing called a "career." How to not position oneself holding a Plexiglas shield in front of you. How to gain confidence from expressing surprise, how to gain confidence from admitting, "I should have thought of that, and I didn't!" From very early on in this thing called a career, I've tried very hard not to act out of defensiveness. It's so demobilizing, draining of energy, and privatizing; it doesn't let one listen well enough, or reach out, or be part of a community. Defensiveness plays right into the narrowest, least fruitful form of careerism. Careers are okay, in the sense that one wants to grow, to have the sense that you are moving forward in your own thinking — even having a bit more influence along the way, if it's a good kind of influence — in one's own little pool. But *careerism* — that is about "Oh, I better not let anybody see what I don't know." Or "I better pretend that I know more than I do." We all have those feelings. But I really try not to let that be what I express. Once I try to express the curiosity, and the "Gee, I never thought of that, tell me more, I need to rethink that," once I express it, even if it is not what is going up and down my spinal cord, it's easier to actually do it.

I remember once doing a noontime thing at Harvard, for the Department of Government. A senior male faculty member was there; everyone was very aware that he was there and that he didn't usually come to anything that had "women" or "feminism" in the title. After my talk he asked a question, a little skeptical, a little amused. You could almost feel a collective shiver go down the spines of everyone in the room as they together silently thought: "Oh, my God, what if she doesn't measure up?" Everyone was thinking, "We're having a feminist talk at Harvard. We need Harvard's credibility, its senior male faculty's credibility to ensure our own careers." I felt really responsible. So I just turned to everybody before I answered him and said, "Breathe. It's okay. We're just having a discussion. This is an interesting question, not a test. We're not in a gladiator arena." We might have been, mind you! But I decided that we would pretend we weren't.

CC: Cynthia, one thing that everyone who knows you comments on is that you are amazingly generous to your feminist colleagues and graduate students. Why are you?

CE: Oh, a lot of people are.

CC: But you are to a remarkable degree. Why?

CE: Because I think we're all in this together. Because I know that 95 percent of everything I know, I know because somebody else has done the work. I'm totally dependent on other people feeling confident enough, empowered enough, energized enough, and funded enough that they can do the work that will help make me smarter. Also, I actually want to have a lively set of experiences with people. It makes academic life more fun; it makes it more interesting, worth doing. I'm not the sort who wants to go to a log cabin in the woods and think my own little thoughts by myself. This means it really matters to me to change institutions, to change the cultures in our departments, in ways that give people who are coming along, just like other people did for me, a sense that, together, you can change cultures; you don't have to buy into the existing culture. I think about institutional cultures a lot. I think they're changeable, though it's surprising what one has to figure out in order to make those transformations stick. This is why the host of women's caucuses we've all created in so many professional associations, and all the new feminist journals we've launched with their formats and processes self-consciously crafted and nurtured, are so significant. Each and every one of them, I think, is a feminist experiment in creating healthier professional institutions — in the process, we're trying to transform the very meanings of "professionalism" and "career."

CC: I've noticed that in your books you draw a lot on works by historians and anthropologists.

CE: I continue to be especially influenced by feminist-informed, historically minded ethnography — no matter what is the writer's formal disciplinary home. At my favorite Cambridge café, "The Newtowne," I read every publisher's new catalog! I've been influenced by so many feminists using an ethnographic approach: Seung-Kyung Kim's work on South Korean women factory workers during the 1980s pro-democracy campaign; Diane Singerman's study of women, men, and the state in one Cairo neighborhood; Anne Allison's terrific participant observation of corporate businessmen's interactions with hostesses in a Tokyo drinking club; Purnima Mankekar's subtle insights into lower-middle-class Indian men's and women's viewings of nationalist prime-time TV sagas.[10] Oh, and then I love Cathy Lutz's study of town life around Fort Bragg — that's the huge army base in North Carolina — Jennifer Pierce's eye-opening insider's account of how masculinity continues to get privileged in two large San Francisco law firms, and Hugh Gusterson's ethnography of life in a California nuclear weapons lab.[11] And more! Then I take these and almost literally put them side by side with Joni Seager's astounding feminist world atlas.[12] Doing this makes me think in thickly local and broadly comparative ways simultaneously. Over the years I also have been deeply affected by Hannah Arendt.[13] She was the first to make me rethink just what is "politics." I heard her in person — twice!

CC: You did?

CE: Yes! Talk about formative times! I was an undergraduate at Connecticut College; it was maybe 1958 or 1959. And I had a professor, Louise Holborn, wonderful woman, a German emigré and my comparative politics teacher. And she said we all *had* to come to the all-campus lecture by Arendt, we who had never heard of Hannah Arendt! Here was Arendt, by this time an older woman, kind of jowly, still speaking a very German-accented form of English. I remember this clearly — I *did not* understand what Arendt was talking about, *and* I was absolutely mesmerized. Both! I took notes like crazy. She probably was talking about totalitarianism, at that point in the late '50s. I remember going to the little campus coffee shop afterward; I just sat and I thought and thought . . . it was so exciting! Arendt was so serious. I was surrounded by women faculty members who were serious, but I had never seen seriousness like that . . . I thought it was wonderful! I thought it was just wonderful.

A few years later, out at Berkeley, I took political theory from Sheldon Wolin, a wonderful teacher. He was a great admirer of Hannah Arendt, who in the 1960s — when I was at Berkeley — was writing provocatively rich essays for the *New Yorker* and in the *New York Review of Books*. I tore out each essay and still have every one of them! When I've taught seminars on Hannah Arendt, I've brought those now-yellowing articles into class and said, "You all know what political thought looks like? It has ads down the side. It has cartoons in the middle. It appears on the newsstand. Political theory isn't something that just comes out in a university press book, that you buy in an academic bookstore. Political theorizing is—well, should be—part of the hubbub of the public arena." See, I get excited even thinking about it! So, the second time I heard Arendt was thanks to Sheldon Wolin. I was a graduate student at Berkeley, and Sheldon Wolin had organized an APSA [American Political Science Association] panel on revolution. Remember, this has got to have been around 1963 when we were all talking about theories of revolution. The panelists gave their written papers, then Sheldon Wolin looked out in the audience to start the discussion. There were about fifty people there—it wasn't a featured panel. Wolin spotted Hannah Arendt and called on her. She just stood up in the audience and said, "I've been taking some notes." [*laugh*] It was great! And out came, of course, the most thought-provoking ideas. I mean, they weren't arrogant; they didn't sort of wash over all the panelists; they were engaged. What I loved was that she was a member of the audience, an audience participant. And that is exactly where political thinkers should be, right? Not just up on the panel, but rising out of the audience. I wish Arendt were still alive, writing in the *New Yorker!*

CC: I wonder what she would have written about "September 11"? Did the events of September 11, 2001, change what you want to be thinking about?

CE: I don't think I'm knowledgeable enough yet to think very clearly about the actual men who took part. I would have to think about where masculinity comes into it, and the ways in which masculinity gets mobilized. *Frontline* on PBS has had some very slow-moving, thoughtful, jigsaw-puzzle kinds of biographies of two or three of the men, and I found them very helpful. To be honest, I — this doesn't mean other people shouldn't be interested — but I myself am not *very* enlivened in my own curiosity about men or women, but especially men, who engage in what is now defined as terrorism. I think this distancing may be due to feeling determined not to be seduced into thinking that those men in terrorist groups are more interesting than men who look much more conventional, much more institutionalized, more apparently rational, and *seemingly* nonviolent. There is a temptation — and this is simply the strength of narration — to find Timothy McVeigh (the Oklahoma City bomber) or Mohammed Atta (one of the World Trade Center attackers) much more intellectually enticing than a person who usually goes nameless, for example, yet flies — or designs — a B-52 bomber. Curiosity about the rank-and-file terrorist so often can distract us from asking where power really lies. I don't mean that people who engage in murder, singly or multiply, shouldn't be thought about a lot. In fact, I am learning a lot now from a women's studies doctoral student who's using a feminist approach to understand women joining terrorist groups. Personally, though, I am more interested, for example, in understanding the Koranic boys' schools in Pakistan. I've been trying to read a lot more about why Pakistani mothers and fathers are pleased to have their young sons receive shelter, food, and learning that is valued at these schools. I'm very wary of demonization. I am interested in the processes of gendered alienation; I am interested in socialization; I am interested in the larger processes at work without treating individuals as abstractions, as lacking in consciousness.

The awful violence of that September 11 engaged my emotions; I certainly felt a sense of horror and worried intensely about people I knew in New York. But the terrorists who hijacked those four planes? They aren't the main objects of my curiosity, because I think they are more the symptom than the cause of extreme alienation that allows violence-wielding insurgencies to grow. I also think ultimately these men (and a few women) are nowhere near as capable of affecting our ideas, our lives, the structures and cultures in which we live, as are a lot of other people who wield influence but who look not very narratively interesting to many of us. I'm pretty interested in bland people, I guess! I want to know more about those people whose blandness is part of what's interesting about them — the rank-and-file men in conventional armies, the women who work as secretaries in aerospace corporations. Or Kenneth Lay, the CEO of Enron; nobody 'til the winter of 2001–2 thought he was as narratively "interesting" as Timothy McVeigh. I'm interested in Kenneth Lay and the institutional culture he and his colleagues created that destroyed everybody's pensions. So, yes, I put up a bit of an intellectual firewall between my curiosity and certain popular — and state-crafted — diversionary narratives. When reporters phone to talk about, for instance, women terrorists, I try to lead them to consider other politically fruitful puzzles.

CC: Interest in the Koranic boys' schools, the *madrassas*, fits right in with your interest in institutions — both in how different kinds of masculinity are constructed within institutions and in how masculinity is mobilized to achieve the institutions' ends. But the question of what is the difference between somebody who goes through those *madrassas* and engages in these violent acts versus someone who goes through the same school and doesn't — that is not especially interesting to you?

CE: For me, not intensely. But I'm not saying my interests are what everybody should be interested in. Some of the best pieces of reporting coming out of Afghanistan in the midst of the bombing were by a *New York Times* journalist named Amy Waldman and later by her colleague Carlotta Gall. I'm going to have to write them fan letters! For instance, Amy Waldman and Carlotta Gall wrote such smart analyses of how the warlord system works. I'm very interested in warlords, in warlordism. A lot of men are oppressed by warlords, yet other men really derive a sense of pride and satisfaction, as well as rifles and daily food, from attaching themselves to the coattails of men who thereby become warlords. Warlords have much in common with American party machine bosses. Well, in the wake of the American-led invasion of Afghanistan, Amy Waldman paid serious attention to women in these processes that have nurtured warlordism — and also the Taliban regime — and Al Qaeda. She asked: Whom did these men *marry*? The foreigners, particularly the Arab men who had come to Afghanistan as Al Qaeda fighters, and the Afghan, mainly Pashtun, men who became part of the Taliban — whom did they *marry*? How did these men construct their own notions of themselves as masculine? A certain kind of warrior ethic and identity requires a man to be deliberately celibate, while other warrior cultures put a premium on the warrior-as-husband. Amy Waldman started going around the neighborhoods, talking with women and men, about the process by which young women were pressured into marriages with Taliban and Arab men. She found that some mothers and fathers had been given money to persuade them to give up their daughters to be wives of Afghan and Arab fighters, though oftentimes the parents didn't feel like they had a choice.[14]

So I thought, all right, let's talk about warlordism and marriage as if that connection actually mattered, as if marriage also were a transaction of power that created a social system that allowed the Al Qaeda Arab male fighters, the Afghan Taliban fighters, and the anti-Taliban Afghan warlords (the U.S. allies) — each — to confirm their own masculinities in wartime. And let's ask who were these women and how did they cope with these marriages? And how did their fathers and uncles and brothers think about them? This was one of those articles that turned on a lot of lights. It reminded me that to make sense of any militarized social system, you *always* have to ask about women. They're not a minor sidebar interest.

CC: What other questions did your feminist curiosity turn to as being really important questions to ask — in relation to not just the events of September 11, 2001, but everything that has come in the two years following?

CE: Looking at U.S. society, I became intrigued with the gendered sprouting of American flags. Thinking about those flags pushed me to think about, on the one side, private emotions, particularly grief, grief for people whom you don't know, and, on the other side, constructions, reconstructions, and perpetuations of a militarized nation. The connection between flag waving/wearing, altruistic grieving, and the militarization of a nation can only be fathomed if one asks feminist questions. Back in October 2001 I happened to be talking to a woman at a campus social gathering. She was a staff woman who came up to say "hi." She wore on her lapel one of those jeweled American flags. I didn't look at it and grimace — it would be terrible if I had. Still, looking down at her flag pin, she immediately said, "Oh, you know I'm wearing this not to say anything political, but I had to find some way to express my sadness, and my feelings of solidarity with the people who've lost so much." I was very embarrassed that she felt she had to explain her wearing the flag pin to me. Did I come across as judgmental?

Later I thought that maybe especially people who don't have much power — certainly many women who are in staff support positions in universities don't possess much power to shape the expression of ideas and meanings — maybe they have to search for a way to make a public expression of grief that won't be misinterpreted — that somebody else won't co-opt, expropriate, exploit. Women are in that position so often, and so are a lot of men without power, but women are in that position so often because — and this comes back to how patriarchal cultures operate — because their *ideas* about grief are not taken very seriously. Their *expressions* of grief are treated as important symbolically, but not their ideas about grief, and certainly not their ideas about how grieving should shape public policy. So, in that circumstance, how does a woman reduce her complex ideas to a pin she wants to wear on her lapel?

CC: How have your reflections on the relations between grief and patriotism shaped your approach in your public talks since September 11?

CE: I try to talk about grieving as it connects to the multiple forms of security, especially to what feminists have taught us about "national" and "security." I try to describe other countries where people see as strange what Americans take to be normal.

CC: Such as?

CE: The presumption that the military as an institution is the bulwark of "national security" — it's not just a U.S. idea, but it's such a distinctively American late-twentieth/early-twenty-first-century presumption. It certainly is not, however, a Canadian presumption, not an Italian presumption, not a Spanish or Japanese presumption. And then I try to suggest how asking *feminist* questions helps me make sense of things that otherwise are very puzzling. I want to present feminist questions as a tool. And usually I'll try to get people to talk about the images they've seen of Afghan women — and did they know that there are Afghan feminists, and why does it seem so hard to take on board the idea of Afghan forms of feminist organizing, strategizing, analyzing?

CC: What did you think of the "women's week" in American presidential politics [in November 2001], when Laura Bush was out talking about Afghan women?

CE: You know, in some ways, I found it very embarrassing, absolutely insulting. It was not Laura Bush's or even George Bush's message. It was White House strategist Karen Hughes's message, her effort to close the American electoral gender gap between Democrats and Republicans. (Bush had attracted significantly fewer women's votes in November 2000 than had Al Gore.)

CC: Yet in some ways, this public relations maneuver seemed to work for them. I was struck by all the women who supported U.S. military action *because* of the oppressed condition of Afghan women — something that was news to many of them.

CE: You know, when researching *Bananas*, I became fascinated with the World's Fairs of the 1870s, '80s, and '90s. One of the things that was used to promote the value of Americans' colonization of the Philippines was expressed in the tableaus that were put up on the midway in the World's Fairs. The "benighted woman," usually carrying a heavy burden, was put there by the fair designers to make the American fairgoers think, "Oh, that's terrible," to sympathize and thus feel reconfirmed in their own advanced civilization. The oppression of women, for at least the last one hundred fifty years, has been used as a measure of how enlightened any society is, without much deeper commitment to deprivileging masculinity. That's why you have to have a *feminist* understanding of orientalism.

CC: No one could ever accuse me of being an optimist, but let me push this. Now that the position of women has been publicly inserted in American national security discourse, now that it has been rhetorically marked as a supposed concern of male national political elites (no matter what their motivation), do you think there is even the slightest chance that that new discursive legitimacy of talking about "women" and "national security" in the same breath can be used as a wedge for political good?

CE: Here's my sense — but we're all going to have to keep watching this. If Afghan women, like Kosovar women, Bosnian women, and East Timorese women, do manage to make serious gains in demasculinizing the reconstructed postwar Afghan society, it will not be because of tokenist, exploitative discourse maneuvers by George W. Bush or Britain's Tony Blair or their political strategists. It will be because, first, Afghan women themselves have organized. Second, because there has been so much serious, feminist-savvy, detailed work going on inside international groups such as Oxfam, Human Rights Watch, Amnesty, and WILPF, as well as inside UN agencies — UNDPKO, UNICEF, and the UNHCR [Office of the United Nations High Commissioner for Refugees]. Most of us in our research and teaching barely know all the things that you, Cynthia Cockburn, Dubraka Zarkov, Dyan Mazurana, Angela Raven-Roberts, Sandy Whitworth, Julie Mertus, Suzanne Williams, Wenona Giles, Jennifer Hyman, and others are trying to teach us about how feminists are making inroads into the masculinist operations of international and local institutions operating in Afghanistan and other "postconflict zones."[15]

CC: My wondering if there could be any positive impact comes from my conversations with NGO activists about Resolution 1325, the UN Security Council's landmark resolution on women, peace, and security, passed in 2000. While the Security Council may have anticipated simply another thematic debate, women's NGOs ran with it; they publicized it, printed and distributed copies of it, and got the word out to women's activist groups in many different countries. So now, 1325 has an active constituency who monitor and push for its implementation. Women's groups are really using it as a tool. For example, in the resolution, the council committed to consult with women's organizations when on field missions. So on the council mission to Kosovo, the women got to meet with the council members and present them with a letter critiquing the UN mission's Gender Unit and pass on information they wanted the council to have — although the meeting *did* end up occurring at 11:00 p.m. in a diplomat's hotel room! Another example — before Lakhdar Brahimi, the UN's special representative to Afghanistan, left New York to start talks about an interim Afghan government, women's NGOs provided him with a list of Afghan women's NGOs they felt he should consult with — and he did. And 1325 isn't just having an impact on UN activities; women are also using it to put pressure on their own governments. I spoke with a woman from the Russian Committee of Soldiers' Mothers, for example, who told me that when they first got the resolution in the mail, they looked, thought, "Oh, just another Security Council resolution," and didn't bother to read it. But later, someone looked — and they've found it to be a gold mine. "Now," she says, "when we go to talk to political or military leaders, we take it with us. And because the Russian leadership is now very concerned about their international legitimacy, they feel that they have to listen to us, because that's what the resolution says."

CE: So it's not a high-tech aerial bombing campaign that's improving women's lives.

CC: Right. But is there the least possibility now of a parallel move? Despite the motivations of the Bush government, could this opening of rhetorical space for talking about women's lives and "national security" in the same breath be seized upon by women activists for ends that go far beyond the intentions of Bush's policy advisors and speechwriters?

CE: It's really risky for anyone who's trying to understand cause and effect to imagine that the military campaign strategists who were desperate for international legitimacy and thus grasped onto whatever they could — and girls being denied schooling happened to work very nicely, thank you — had that as their strategic objective. Maybe sometimes it's a risk that it's worth feminists taking. After all, we aren't served up many chances to get our foot in the patriarchal door. Still, so many feminist studies of imperialism, colonization, World's Fairs, warfare, the global spreadings of Christian missionary work, and expanding capitalist markets are here in front of us now to flash a blinking yellow cautionary light. That is, when on occasion women's liberation is wielded instrumentally by any masculinized elite as a rationale-of-convenience for their own actions, we should go on high alert; they'll put back on the shelf this rationale-of-convenience just as soon as it no longer serves their deeper, longer-range purpose.

CC: So, in those weeks after September 11 and before the bombing in Afghanistan started in October 2001, what did you say when you were asked for a feminist response to the question "What should 'we' do now?"

CE: I didn't have it all worked out — I found myself saying, well, first of all, let's really think about what is the *appropriate* response, and what, in the long term, is the most useful response. And especially if we're Americans, let's think comparatively. Can we learn some lessons from the women of Srebrenica, the Bosnian town where five thousand men were massacred by Serbian militias in 1995? Or, what if the September attack had happened in Brussels, seat of the European Union? Would we all assume it was reasonable for the Belgian air force to take to the skies, heading for Southwest Asia? Feminists have taught us to be very, very careful before we adopt a response to grief, loss, and anger that is a *statist* response, especially a militarized statist response.

What did you say during those weeks?

CC: My starting place was that we needed to analyze *why* military violence seemed like a good response — or why it seemed so impossible for Americans not to strike back. We can't take it as self-evident.

I've been very influenced by working with Sara Ruddick on a "feminist ethical perspective on weapons of mass destruction."[16] She has written that the efficacy of violence is overrated, while its costs are consistently underestimated — although I actually believe that more than she does at this point! Anyway, I think that response to September 11 is really a prime example. The seemingly "self-evident" (to a lot of people) need to strike back is partly based on the assumption that it will "work," that it will be the most effective form of response. People assume that military violence will, in general, work a lot better than a negotiated political solution or a response based on the enforcement of national or international law or on economic actions.

I think that assumption needs to be examined, challenged. Even if you see the question of whether to use military force as a strategic, pragmatic question, apart from moral consideration, I am not at all sure that it *is* an effective response to terrorists or the causes of terrorism — even from a purely U.S. perspective. What I am sure of is that the human costs will be enormous, including the spread of further violence, and that in the long run the political consequences both for the United States and for many Arab women will be quite damaging.

I think one reason it's so hard politically to even examine the assumption that "striking back" is the best option is that ideas about masculinity are so intricately and invisibly interwoven with ideas about national security. So-called realist strategic dictums for state behavior sound a lot like dictums for hegemonic masculinity.

CE: You mean, "We have to do something."

CC: And: "The risks of inaction [read 'passivity'] are far greater than the risks of action," and "We have to show we are strong," and "We have to show them they can't push us around," and "We aren't going to take this lying down," and "We can't let them think we are wimps."

CE: "It's our honor." Americans in the early twenty-first century have created what seems to me to be a deadly combination for themselves (ourselves!) — possessing such disproportionate power combined with a culture of diffuse fear, a cultural sense of being vulnerable. It gives me the shivers.

CC: But I think the problem is more than the sense of being vulnerable. It is the refusal to acknowledge the *inevitability* of our vulnerability. After all, vulnerability is a fact of human and political life. The attempt to deny its inevitability is what has led to the development of weapons of mass destruction "as deterrents," to massive investments in "national missile defense" and other baroque weapons technology, while we refuse to make serious investments in dealing with the worldwide HIV epidemic, or starvation, or poverty around the world. It has led to U.S. partnerships with oppressive regimes and multiple military attacks on other nations — Iraq, Iran, North Korea — even as we speak! And all of these, of course, are part of what creates the desperation and anger that are the seeds of terrorism.

My fantasy is that if we acknowledged the impossibility of making ourselves invulnerable, of constructing Reagan's Plexiglas shield, we would have to have policies that fostered and strengthened goodwill and interdependence, that invested in making the planet a livable place for people in all countries, that aimed at disarmament instead of weapons "advancement" and proliferation. And my fear is that we won't acknowledge it, because these assumptions about strength and weakness, and vulnerability, are simultaneously engaged at the very personal, identity level but also built right into beliefs about national security and into national security doctrine — as though they reflected "objective reality" and in no way stemmed from deeply felt and held identities.

So stopping to try to disentangle emotions and assumptions about violence and its efficacy was the starting place for me. Ultimately, I want to ask what it will take to change the discourse, to alter the meanings of strength and justice in the international political arena.

CE: You know, having conversations like the one we've been having makes me more convinced than ever of the necessity of crafting, and teaching others to craft, a feminist curiosity. I guess that my conviction comes from our living at a very particular moment in world politics and feminist politics; we're living in a world where American militarized policy carries more clout — disproportionate clout — than ever in world history, while we're also living at a time when feminists in the United States are more conscious than ever that we'll only be able to understand the world if we take seriously the insights of women from Finland to Fiji!

CHAPTER 19

Updating the Gendered Empire

*Where Are the Women
in Occupied Afghanistan and Iraq?*

Empire. Until not long ago the study of empires was the purview of academic historians. Some historians, though, especially male historians, recently managed to draw considerable attention from thoughtful magazines and television's serious talk shows for their hefty new or reissued books on empire.[1] Sales figures began to rise and media invitations rolled in. Readers and viewers were beginning to look for parallels to contemporary international affairs. We often try to sort out puzzles by thinking through analogies. Analogies are powerful. If we get our analogies wrong, our explanations are likely to be askew. In the wake of the U.S. military invasions of Afghanistan in 2001 and Iraq in 2003, those experts invited to speak in the public arena began to summon British and even Roman history in order to ask: Are we today seeing the emergence of a new empire?

As the U.S.-led wars in Afghanistan and Iraq dragged on,

there were good reasons not only for media commentators and political decision-makers, but also for ordinary citizens to become curious about past experiences of empire. History teachers began to feel vindicated. Victorian wasn't just stuffy furniture. Caesar wasn't just a salad dressing.

Does the global reach of the present United States military, political, cultural, and economic influence have the cohesiveness, the expansiveness, and the sustainability to amount to an "empire"? Or, to put it more concretely: If we compare the U.S. role in the world today — its invasions and political occupations of Afghanistan and Iraq; its diplomatic roles in the former Yugoslavia and Liberia; its global network of military bases stretching from North Carolina and San Diego to Guam, South Korea, Okinawa, Uzbekistan, Kuwait, Iraq, Turkey, Bosnia, Germany, and Britain; its refusal to ratify a host of new international treaties; its manufacturing, trading, and banking practices from Poland to Indonesia — with those military, cultural, economic, and diplomatic practices of earlier Roman, Persian, Hapsburg, Ottoman, British, Belgian, Russian, Chinese, Japanese, U.S., French, Spanish, and Dutch empires, do we risk comparing an orange with apples? *Or* are we perhaps on firmer ground, comparing a new apple with a host of earlier apples?

Despite their remarkable absence from interview shows and op-ed pages, scores of feminist historians have given us fresh, detailed accounts of how both women and notions of femininity were pressed into service by earlier empire-builders.

Where were the women? Thanks to three decades of sleuthing by feminist historians, we now know where to point our analytical binoculars. We know not to look just at the gilded diplomatic halls, the bloody battlefields, and the floors of stock exchanges. We have been taught by these pioneering feminist historians to point our glasses farther afield. If groundbreaking feminist historians — Philippa Levine, Piya Chatterjee, Kumari Jayawaradena, and others — were invited to submit feature articles and to give mainstream media interviews, they would urge us instead to look inside brothels, to peer into respectable parlors, to press our noses against the sooty windows of factories, to keep an eye on sexual relations on tea plantations.[2] All of these sites, it turns out, though far from the official centers of imperial power, have been sites of empire-making. That is, empires are built in parlors. Empires are built in brothels. Empires are built in allegedly "private" places. Given that, we need to examine the current possibility of a U.S. imperial enterprise from the vantage points of parlors and brothels. To make sense of putative American empire-building, we have to become much more curious — curious about the marriage aspirations of factory women, about the gender dynamics inside soldiers' families, about sexual policies of the U.S. military forces in Afghanistan, Uzbekistan, Iraq, and Kuwait. And that is just the beginning. Reports now labeled "human interest stories" have to be considered as serious commentaries on foreign policy.

These thoughtful, worldly feminist investigators also have shown us how diverse and complex women's actions and feelings have been within empires. Women as tea pickers, women as nannies, women as teachers, women as wives, women as explorers, women as missionaries, women as activist reformers, women as mothers, women as educators, women as mistresses, women as prostitutes, women as textile factory workers, women as writers, women as overseas settlers, women as anticolonial nationalists —

each in their own way played crucial, yet overlooked, roles in greasing (or clogging) the wheels of an imperial enterprise. The roles each group played were "crucial" because so many empire-builders designed international power-extension strategies that relied on particular ideas about where different sorts of women "naturally" were meant to be. The imperial strategists may have been men, but they were men who thought (and worried) a lot about women. The imperial strategists — and their male opponents too — may constantly have weighed varieties of masculinity, but they could do so only by trying to rank and manipulate the varieties of femininity.[3] By not asking about women in this current, possibly imperial enterprise — except, that is, for the Western media's seeming addiction to the visual image of the veiled Muslim woman — the commentators now capturing the public limelight are making both themselves as men inside empires and other men and masculinities in empires virtually invisible. Feminists all over the world have learned how risky *those* sins of omission can be.

WILL THE WOMEN STAND UP?

In the 1980s, at a meeting in Happy Valley, Labrador, a group of Native Canadian women of the Innu community brought together several dozen women, mostly from other parts of Canada, to discuss the effects that a NATO air force base was having on their lives. The term "empire" was not used. Yet fueling this collective conversation was a shared feminist curiosity about how unequal international power relations between allied masculinized governments depend not only on certain relationships between men and women but also on global presumptions about where women will be — and where they should stay. The Innu women were helping us to "unpack" NATO.

One morning the Innu organizers cleared the meeting hall of chairs and asked each of us to imagine ourselves to be a particular woman who was playing a role, maybe even unconsciously, in sustaining, questioning, or resisting this NATO air force base. As each of us thought of a woman, we took on her persona, spoke to the group in the first person as that woman, and joined others sitting on the floor. The floor soon became a complex world of militarized relationships among diverse women. Within an hour that late-winter morning — it was April, but the ice was just receding on the nearby lake — we had populated the wooden floor with women from Canada, the United States, Britain, and Germany, with women married to air force officers, local Innu girls dating young fliers, other Innu women camping on the NATO runways to protest low-flying training flights, Canadian feminists in Toronto unaware of the Canadian government's alliance policies in "remote" Labrador, women from the Philippines eager to share their own experiences of foreign military bases, and more.

More recently, in Tokyo and Okinawa, groups of us tried a similar feminist exercise, inspired by the Innu activists' innovation. Our aim also was to make women visible in international power politics. We sought to piece together a map of where women are in sustaining, questioning, and resisting the unequal U.S.-Japan military alliance. Any assessment of American empire-building today must look closely at the dynamics sustaining this unequal alliance. This time we couldn't move the furniture, so we stood up. Women and men in the audience, one by one, imagined themselves a particular woman living her life inside this alliance. As we took on the persona of a particular woman, we got onto our feet and spoke out:

> I am a young African American woman proud to be serving in the U.S. Marines stationed in Okinawa; thank God, I didn't take that job at Wal-Mart.

> I am an Okinawan woman, and I think I'm becoming what you might call an Okinawan nationalist because I'm growing more resentful of officials in the Tokyo government who routinely override our Okinawan concerns when they agree to allow so many U.S. bases to operate here on our land.

> I am a young Japanese mainland college graduate. As a woman, I've decided that enlisting in the Japanese Self-Defense Force will offer me more career opportunities than a dead-end job working as a corporate "office lady."

As some people stood up, others in the audience began to think of more women whose feelings, ideas, and actions were shaping — though scarcely controlling — the current U.S.-Japanese military alliance, a government-to-government agreement that was projecting American military dominance throughout Asia and the Pacific and as far away as Afghanistan. Our "map" was becoming bigger and more complicated with every person who stood up:

> I am a Yokohama high school student; my friends and I are dating American sailors to improve our English.

> I am a dairy farmer in Kyushu. I care personally about Article Nine, the peace article of the Japanese Constitution, so, in between my daily milkings and stall muckings, I write a small newsletter to tell other Japanese people what it means to live next to a fighter air base. One Friday a month I go and sit outside the gates of the Self-Defense Force fighter plane base;

sometimes a dozen people come to join me; other times I'm sitting there all alone.

Over on the other side of the hall another Japanese young woman then stood up:

> I am an American white woman married to a U.S. Navy officer. I'm surprised that the navy's family housing here in Japan is so much nicer than what I have to endure at the base back in the U.S. Maybe I'll urge my husband to reenlist after all.

Then another:

> I'm one of those guides you see up in the front of tourist buses all over Okinawa; but recently I've retrained myself to become what's called a "peace guide." Now as my tourist bus travels around the countryside, I point out to visitors all the good farmland and beautiful coastal beaches that have been taken over by American military bases.

Way in the back a young man stood up:

> I'm just a housewife. My husband runs a small construction company, which makes me feel so nervous because the Japanese economy has been in recession now for over a decade. I don't like our government offering to send Japanese soldiers to help the Americans occupy Iraq, but I feel relieved that my husband's company just won a government contract to build a new road leading to a U.S. base. How should I reconcile my mixed feelings?

A graduate student at a Tokyo university was sitting toward the front of the room. She waited until the end and then stood up. She turned around to look at others in the large lecture hall:

I'm just starting my doctoral dissertation in political science. There aren't many Japanese women teaching international relations, so to get a university job, I'll need to have the full support of my dissertation supervisor. He's quite well known in the field. Listening to everyone talk here tonight, I now want to change my dissertation research focus so I can look at the lives of Japanese girls and women living near a military base. I want to find out how they relate to the base and what that means for how they imagine themselves in Japanese political life. But my faculty supervisor won't think that asking these questions amounts to doing "real" international politics. How can I persuade him?

These collective acts of Innu, Okinawan, and Tokyo feminist imaginations revealed to all of us several important political realities. Each revelation is relevant to our current thinking about where women are in pursuing — or subverting — any imperial enterprise. *First*, women are intimately engaged in the little-noticed daily workings of those unequal international military alliances that are the backbone of nascent or mature empire-building. *Second*, women's roles in these large structures of international power are far from uniform. In fact, some of these women might view some of the other women who are engaged in the same global structure as too remote or too unsympathetic to become potential partners because of their class, ethnicity, nationality, ideological location, or even just their job. This, despite the fact that some of these women live their daily lives within just a mile of each other.

Third, every one of these women, nonetheless, is where she is on the globalized political map because of dominant notions about femininity and ideas about how she, as a woman or a girl, should relate to men and to masculinized foreign policies. *Fourth*, many women are privately ambivalent about the complicit roles they play in these unequal international power structures; some of them are actively self-conscious about their ambivalence. *Fifth*, while most of these women never make the headlines, they are counted upon by foreign policy-makers to keep playing their supportive, or at least passive, roles. Today's unequal international alliances depend on that.

AFGHAN WOMEN STAND UP

While spending several months in Tokyo's Ochanomizu University in early 2003, as the Bush administration mobilized to invade Iraq, I had the good fortune to meet and listen to one of the handful of Afghan women who had been appointed to senior posts in the interim government created in the wake of the U.S.-led military invasion of Afghanistan. She herself was not a cabinet minister. Only two of the twenty-seven members chosen for cabinet posts in the interim administration of President Hamid Karzai were women. But she was a deputy minister, with considerable responsibility for shaping the policies and institutions of the post-Taliban state. She was now in her fifties and had been a professional woman before the Taliban's ascendancy. Before that she had fought with the insurgent Afghan *mujahideen* forces against the occupying Soviet army.

As this story will suggest, it seems wise even today not to mention her name or even her precise post. She was in Tokyo at the invitation of the Japanese government, specifically of Japanese women working inside the government's overseas aid program, a program coordinated with the United Nations relief efforts in postinvasion, post-Taliban Afghanistan.

While passionate about the need to invest in girls' and women's training and empowerment, this Afghan woman official did not see herself as a natural ally of the Afghan women's organization best known outside of the country, the Revolutionary Association of the Women of Afghanistan, or RAWA.[4] Afghans (like the Vietnamese, Filipinos, and Tanzanians) have experienced not just one, but several waves of imperialist occupation: Persian, British, Russian, and now American. Creating a sense of national identity in countries such as Afghanistan has meant for many women advocates crafting comparative judgments about both past and present foreign rulers and about rival male-led local parties, each claiming to represent the nation, each claiming to know what is best for the nation's women.

One activist local woman's savvy use of openings created by the latest occupying power looks to another activist local woman like collaboration with the enemy, betrayal of the nation. Neither woman controls the masculinized political contest. Having to make such choices, often in the midst of war, displacement, and confusion, does not breed trust among women.

Thus this woman as a deputy minister, so eager for support in her efforts on behalf of girls' and women's empowerment in the midst of the U.S.-led occupation, voiced distrust of the women active in RAWA. She distrusted their local and international politics, even though RAWA's women activists had taken risks to do this work, as she also had, both inside Afghanistan during the Taliban's rule and in the increasingly politicized male-run refugee camps over the border in Pakistan.[5] She imagined, nev-

ertheless, that the women active in RAWA had been too sympathetic to Kabul's 1980s Soviet-backed secular regime. So now,
during the current U.S.-backed regime, this woman was not only
seething with frustration at the patriarchal resistance she en-
countered daily from the men at the top of the Karzai regime,
she was simultaneously keeping an arm's length distance from the
activist women of RAWA.

Imperialism does this. It can send out fissures among the advocates of women's rights.

During one of these Tokyo discussions, the Japanese woman
who hosted this Afghan deputy minister whispered, "In all the
times I have met with her in Kabul, I have never seen her smile."
Now, after two weeks in secure Tokyo, enjoying daily conversations with Japanese specialists on women's and girls' health,
economy, politics, and education, she seemed to be letting down
her guard. She dared to smile. She even made a joke. She had
good reason, though, to maintain her deadpan "game face" when
she was doing her risky work in Kabul. Not long before, her son
had been beaten severely on a street in Kabul by a group of
unidentified men. Before he lost consciousness, he heard his assailants warn him, "Tell your mother to get out of the place
where she doesn't belong." The message was clear: a year and a
half after the U.S. military and their Northern Alliance partners
toppled the Taliban regime, any woman who dared to take on a
modicum of political authority was still endangering not only
herself, but members of her family. This woman was not easily
cowed. Following her son's beating, she became angrier and
more committed. But smiling was a luxury that an activist woman
still could ill afford in Kabul.

Listening between-the-lines to the conversations between this

Afghan deputy minister and the Japanese aid officials hosting her prompted one to ask more questions about the genderings of militarized occupation.

Security — how to measure it, who gets to define it? These issues became contested during the U.S.-led occupation of Afghanistan. It was in the name of what it called the pursuit of "national security" that the Bush administration mounted its invasion of Afghanistan in 2001. In the months following the invasion, now in the name of concentrating its own military forces on combat missions to eliminate the remnants of both Taliban and Al Qaeda armed forces, the U.S. government rejected repeated requests by the UN secretary general, international relief agencies, the Karzai administration, and local Afghan women's groups to extend the reach of the international peacekeeping force — a NATO force, though nominally operating under a UN mandate — beyond the city limits of Kabul. The woman deputy minister told her Japanese hosts that one reason it was proving so difficult to achieve genuine parity between newly recruited male and female teachers was that many men in government claimed that the school districts outside the capital remained too dangerous for women teachers and principals to be appointed.

Danger — when governments claim danger, does the deepening of masculinized authority follow?

Combat — why has a "combat mission" repeatedly trumped peacekeeping and policing in the hierarchical game of competing masculinities? For the first two years of the U.S. military operation in Afghanistan it appeared as though the American military's civilian superiors in Washington wanted to ensure that American soldiers in Afghanistan stayed firmly in control of the hallowed "combat" mission. The supposedly "softer" masculinized missions of policing and peacekeeping seemingly were best left as the responsibility of German, Canadian, and Dutch men.

This story of the rarely smiling Afghan woman official might be taken by some Americans as a vindication of the Bush administration's militarized, expansionist foreign policy: that is, the violence perpetrated against women by the Taliban regime in the late 1990s was so extreme that only a foreign-led militarized response and foreign occupation were appropriate. In fact, many Americans had only the vaguest notion of where Afghanistan was, or what the longtime U.S. government involvement in its twenty-year civil war had been, or how its Taliban-controlled government was related to the clandestine operations of the insurgent movement led by Osama bin Laden. Consequently, for these American voters, forging a link between the geopolitics of counterterrorism and the liberation of benighted women proved especially helpful in constructing their own informal narratives of the causes for the 2001 U.S. invasion of Afghanistan. The fact that there were *any* women in the postinvasion Karzai interim government and that those women remained under threat only served to entrench many Americans' justifying narrative.

But there is an alternative interpretation. To explore this alternative, we need to ask another Afghan woman to "stand up." This is a young woman living in the Afghanistan province of Herat. Her mother is literate, having attended school in the 1970s, a time when the Afghan regime then in power cited the education of girls as a primary strategy for national modernization. Thus she is eager for her daughter to attend school. But mother and daughter remain subject to public intimidation in Herat if they voice such aspirations. This young woman's life two years after the U.S. invasion is not governed by the American,

UN, and Afghan officials working in Kabul. Her life — her sense of security, physical mobility, personal identity, public identity, educational and economic opportunities — is governed by the self-proclaimed provincial governor of Herat, Ismail Khan.

English-language commentators have called Ismail Khan a "warlord." The label makes Khan sound archaic. It is a label that dampens our political curiosity. In reality, the power Khan and other Afghan regional "warlords" wield in postinvasion Afghanistan derives from two very modern resources: first, Ismail Khan commands a sizable army of his own, equipped with modern weaponry; second, he is deemed an "ally" by the U.S. military.[6]

Herat's Ismail Khan had contributed his troops to a loose amalgam of militarized Afghan opponents, first of the Soviet army in the 1980s and then of the Taliban regime. His forces and those of the other "warlords" are now called the Northern Alliance. The name makes them sound akin to NATO. These Afghan regional commanders were useful to the U.S. government during its own rivalry with the Soviet Union during the Cold War, and they became useful again when the United States decided to wage war against the Taliban and Al Qaeda. In October 2001 the Northern Alliance's commanders and all-male militias — despite their interethnic tensions, they share a history of opposition to the modernizing, secularizing reforms of the 1970s Kabul government — were selected by Washington's war-planners to be their most trusted, effective military allies on the ground when they devised their invasion of Afghanistan in the aftermath of the attacks on New York's World Trade Towers and the Pentagon.

Which men the expansionist foreign elite chooses to become their trusted local allies will almost certainly have repercussions for local women. Moreover, which men an invading force selects as its local allies will either enhance or, more commonly, undermine the viability of those foreign expansionists' use of "women's emancipation" as a moral justification for their expansionist enterprise. When U.S. policy-makers in Washington selected Ismail Khan and his fellow Northern Alliance antimodernist regional commanders as their most promising allies, they did not employ "the empowerment of Afghan women" as their chief criterion. Instead, the Washington strategists used "ground-level military capability" and "previous experience of cooperation with us" as their principal criteria for choosing their Afghan allies.

The criteria that any expansionist government uses when it chooses its local allies are much better predictors of the expansionists' postinvasion commitment to women's advancement than is any *post hoc* discourse of moral justification.

Furthermore, which men the invading force chooses as its primary local allies will also privilege certain forms of local masculinity. This was true in earlier imperial enterprises, and it is true in any putative imperial enterprises today. Internationally ambitious governments typically have sought local allies as they expanded the reach of their power and authority. Stories of the Spanish expansion into Mexico; the Dutch expansion into what is now Indonesia; the British expansions into Malaya, India, and Egypt; the U.S. expansion into the Philippines; the French expansion into Vietnam — each testifies to this common expansionist strategy of forging unequal local alliances-of-convenience. Empires, that is, are crafted out of unequal alliances between the ambitious imperialists and those local actors who calculate, often mistakenly, that they will be able to extract strategic gains for themselves even out of a clearly imbalanced alliance. Bedfellows are not all equal. All masculinities are not equal.

Virtually every one of these imperializing alliances was between men. This fact is not trivial.

In postinvasion Afghanistan, the likelihood of the young Herat woman experiencing meaningful liberation, of the sort wishfully imagined by so many Americans who lent their moral support for the U.S. invasion of Afghanistan, has been *made* dependent on a deeply masculinized local provincial regime whose power is ensured by its deeply masculinized foreign institution, the U.S. military.

Several independent human rights researchers investigated what happened to Afghan girls and women between 2001 and 2003. What these researchers discovered, not only in Ismail Khan's Herat, but in many other provinces outside of Kabul where Northern Alliance commanders have used their militias and their intimate ties with American soldiers on the ground to consolidate their grasp on the levers of local power (and money), is that the military strategy that the Bush administration adopted to conduct its invasion has hobbled, not facilitated, the genuine liberation of most of Afghanistan's women and girls. These observers noted the apparently easy rapport that had developed between the male American Special Forces soldiers — the Special Forces being perhaps the most masculinized of all U.S. military units — and the local governor's militiamen, perhaps due to their shared identity as "combat-tested men." The investigators also noted that, despite their opposition to the Taliban regime, Ismail Khan and the Northern Alliance commanders were committed to a very patriarchal form of post-Taliban social order. Ismail

Khan thus shared with the Taliban's and Al Qaeda's male leaders a belief that controlling women's marital and sexual relations was important for sustaining a hold on power.[7]

The Northern Alliance and its relationships with the U.S. military warrant feminist-informed investigations for several reasons. We need to know in precisely which ways shared masculinity has facilitated the sustaining of this alliance between Herat's "warlord" Ismail Khan and the U.S. field commanders. We also need to know in exactly which ways, other differences notwithstanding, shared masculinities created easy rapport between the American and Afghan Northern Alliance commanders' rank-and-file men, assisting both in consolidating their authority in their respective daily operations. In addition, we need to explore the ways in which this two-layered masculinization served to entrench the Northern Alliance regional commanders' own notions of subordinate femininity.

Further, in our investigation of contemporary American expansionism, we need to pay serious attention to the rivalry between the Northern Alliance commanders' model of masculinity and the models of masculinity being projected by the Kabul-based senior civilian officials in Hamid Karzai's cabinet. Some Afghans declared this to be a contest between the "warlords" and the "neckties." Men such as Ismail Khan could claim that the "neckties" sitting in Kabul had become the "lackeys" of the U.S. and other foreign donors (the UN, the European Union, and Japan). Khan and the other warlords — despite their intense ethnicized distrust of each other — on the other hand, could claim to be combat-tested veterans, commanders of men, men who had wielded manly violence and risked their lives to defend the nation. The warlords thus could drape over their patriarchal shoulders the mantle of masculinized nationalism. Their ability to control the women in their provinces and to act as the guardians of "true" Afghan femininity had become a crucial component of their ability to mobilize their own male armies and to collect their own tax revenues.

On the other hand, the "neckties" — represented especially in President Karzai's minister of finance — could claim to be Men of Reason. "Reason" and "combat" — both have been used repeatedly by men of myriad cultures to compete with other men for the political brass ring: being recognized as the most manly of public men. The Afghan men in neckties could thus see themselves as builders of a new centralized constitutional state, a political order based on laws and budgets, not on artillery and armed road blocks. The necktie wearers could portray themselves as being able to represent the nation's interests where it counted, not on some desolate battlefield, but in the corridors of the most important masculinized international arenas, the United Nations Security Council, the U.S. State Department, the World Bank, the European Commission.[8]

One might think that any form of dominant masculinity might be better for most women than the warlord variety is. In practice, however, Afghan women hoping for the access to education, public voice, and economic opportunities that U.S. officials promised for women commonly have found that there is little space left for autonomous women in such a warlords vs. neckties masculinized contest. In such a contest, women are deemed crucial by the rivals, but merely as symbols, subordinates, admirers, or spectators. Men rivaling each other in the arena of politicized masculinity always have needed to ensure that "their" women will play those politically salient feminized roles. That is not liberation. That is not authentic citizenship.

Wait. Now another Afghan woman is standing up. She is Suraya Parlika. Trained as a lawyer, she has led the Afghan women's lawyers association based in Kabul, one of several non-governmental organizations founded by women in the wake of the fall of the Taliban regime. In late 2003 Suraya Parlika decided to monitor the commission assigned to draft Afghanistan's new constitution.[9] She and her colleagues were thus prepared not only to read the fine print of the newly drafted Afghan constitution, but also to write constitutional proposals of their own. Coming to the meeting, Suraya Parlika and her colleagues each chose to defy intimidating personal threats against Afghans daring to introduce the discourse of human rights into local politics.[10]

Suraya Parlika and her co-organizers took the unusual step of inviting — and persuading the Karzai government to temporarily release just for this purpose — three women prisoners: Eqlima, who had been jailed on charges of running away from an abusive uncle's home; Mina, who had been arrested for running away from a "husband" to whom she had been sold; Rosia, who had been imprisoned for fleeing her father-in-law's house after being forced to marry her brother-in-law after her own husband's death. Parlika and the other activist women invited these three imprisoned women to their conference because they believed that a country's constitution could not be fairly and realistically drafted *unless* its provisions flowed from an understanding of the experiences of debilitating gender power imbalance that actually shaped the daily lives of women and girls.

With her co-organizers, Suraya Parlika was going far beyond Abigail Adams's much-quoted eighteenth-century modest admonition to John, her constitution-drafting husband: "Remember the ladies." These Afghan women activists were drawing lessons from their own twentieth-century Afghan experiences of living with constitutions written, constitutions amended, constitutions partially implemented, constitutions left unimplemented. Like women activists recently in South Africa, Cambodia, Palestine, Rwanda, and East Timor, and like feminists active in UN peace-keeping operations around the world, these Afghan women meeting in postinvasion Kandahar had become convinced that the writing of a new constitution must become women's business. Any constitution, after all, is a blueprint for a state's power and authority, a design for distributing powers and responsibilities within the state's institutions, and a map of citizens' limitations, rights, and responsibilities.

Since every stroke of the constitutional pen can either em-power women as full citizens or turn them into marginalized de-pendents of male citizens and a patriarchal state, drafting and rat-ifying a constitution must be processes that include politically conscious women, preferably in equal numbers with men around the drafting table and in the ratifying assembly. If that fair repre-sentation proved impossible to achieve, then, these women had concluded, women had to be on the alert, mobilized right outside the drafting room door. In fact, the 2003 Afghanistan constitu-tion-drafting commission did include seven women among its thirty-five appointed members — a significant presence, though men remained a decisive majority. Thus Suraya Parlika and her colleagues used their four days to listen to the stories of Eqlima, Rosia, and Mina and then to draw up their own constitutional proposals.

Here are the provisions Parlika and her colleagues concluded had to be explicitly included in the new Afghanistan constitution if it were to ensure Afghan women's participation in public life as fully autonomous and effective citizens: (1) mandatory education for girls through secondary school, (2) guaranteed freedom of speech for women, (3) insurance that every woman would be free to cast her own ballot and to run for elected office, (4) insurance that women would have equal representation with men in the government's new legislature, (5) the appointment of an equal number of women and men to judgeships, (6) entitlement of women to pay rates equal to those of men, and (7) a guarantee that women would have the right to exert control over their own finances and to inherit property.[11]

All of these provisions, individually and taken together, would not only upset political convention, but fundamentally rearrange the relationships between women and men in the sphere commonly imagined to be "private." Yet the women conferees weren't finished. After listening carefully to the stories of Rosia, Eqlima, and Mina, Parlika and the other activists pressed for additional provisions in the new Afghanistan constitution: (8) permission for women to bring criminal charges against men for domestic violence and sexual harassment, whether those violations occurred in a public place or inside a home, (9) a ban on the common practice of family members handing over girls and women to another family as compensation for crimes committed by the former against the latter, (10) raising the legal age of marriage from sixteen years to eighteen years, (11) the right of women to marry and divorce "in accordance with Islam," and (12) a reduction of the time that women would have to wait to remarry if their husbands abandoned them or disappeared.[12]

These twelve provisions did not add up to the vision of a post-Taliban "good society" for which most Northern Alliance male commanders had been waging their wars. Those Northern

Alliance commanders, several of whom had served as governors and cabinet ministers in the interim government, were among the influential men who tried to wield influence over the large national council, the *loya jirga*, that convened in Kabul in December 2003. This was the national assembly designated to consider — and amend — the draft constitution. The success of Parlika Suraya and her allies in pressing for a new constitutional state that was structurally and ideologically designed to fulfill the promise of women's liberation depended in large part on whether the U.S. government still imagined the Northern Alliance commanders to be its chief partners in expanding the American security net's global reach. It remained unclear who American officials would choose as their best allies to achieve American and global "security": the warlords, the neckties, or the women activists.

In January 2004 the *loya jirga*'s delegates, after heated debate, passed a draft constitution. At the heart is ambiguity. On the one hand is the guarantee of women's and men's equality. On the other hand is the pledge that Afghanistan's future law-making will be "informed by" the principles of Islam, which when interpreted by conservatives, treat such gendered equality as anathema. Who will support Afghan women activists when they press the new government to enforce the constitution's first guarantee?[13]

WHERE ARE THE WOMEN IN THE U.S.-DOMINATED OCCUPATION OF IRAQ?

Three women who might help us better understand the U.S.-British military invasion of Iraq and its drawn-out militarized occupation are Raja Habib Khuzai, one of three Iraqi women members of the U.S.-annointed Governing Council; Nimo Din'Kha

Skander, a woman who operates a small hair salon in Baghdad; and Kawkab Jalil, one of the women activists who have begun organizing independently to advocate for women's participation in the U.S. occupation era's emerging political system.

These three women do not represent all of the women in Iraq, nor would they make such a claim. But if we start to take seriously at least these three distinct, complex, thinking women, we are likely to make visible where women are and where femininities are in the consolidation or, alternatively, the subversion of the U.S. expansionist enterprise. That, in turn, should shine a bright light on where the men are and where rival masculinities are in Iraqis' U.S.-dominated postinvasion lives.

Raja Habib Khuzai takes the floor. She is a medical doctor and maternity hospital director, a skilled professional. Until September 2003 Khuzai was one of three women on the twenty-five-member Iraqi Governing Council. After September she was one of only two. On September 20, 2003, her colleague, Akila al-Hashimi, was gunned down by unknown assailants in broad daylight as she was leaving her Baghdad home.[14] Akila al-Hashimi, then fifty, had been a career Iraqi diplomat. She was described by journalists as a "member of a prominent family of Shiite clerics" and a "force for peace and tolerance."[15]

Both Akila al-Hashimi and Raja Habib Khuzai had been selected to serve on the U.S.-approved Governing Council in early July 2003 as a result of what was reportedly intense behind-the-scenes bargaining, bargaining not unlike the sort that had produced the interim cabinet of Afghanistan president Hamid Karzai a year earlier. The need to use the maddening passive tense — "had been selected" — in the previous sentence is telling. To date, we do not know precisely what dynamics shaped this

Baghdad bargaining and its eventual outcome. But in virtually every political system we know about, the less transparent any process of political bargaining is, the more likely it is to be governed by presumptions of masculinized politics.

The cause for this masculinization is this: closed-door bargaining is less vulnerable to popular pressure and popular scrutiny. Those who wield the most influence in such backroom political transactions are those who come into the process with resources that can be converted into political currency. First are those who have organized public support — based on religion, ethnicity, or political party affiliation. In Afghanistan rivalries between self-declared male leaders of the Pashtun majority and the Uzbek and Tajik minorities became central in the bargaining. Similarly, in Iraq the ethnicized and sectarian male-led organizations of Shiite and Sunni Muslims, Kurdish ethnic communities, and Kurdish rival political parties were seen as the salient divisions that required juggling on the Governing Council. That is, organized ethnic, religious, and ideological divisions were thought by the crafters of the new Afghan and Iraqi governments to be the salient bases for representation. Gender was deemed by these same men to be simply symbolic, a step above trivial. Second among the individuals enjoying an advantage in closed-door bargaining sessions are those who have ready access to weapons and to armed men. Third are those with economic resources — companies of their own, trading connections, open lines to donors, bank accounts abroad. And fourth among the advantaged bargainers are those people who have earned credibility in the eyes of those foreign men orchestrating the bargaining. In the case of the formation of the postinvasion Iraqi Governing Council, that meant credibility in the eyes of the American oc-

Pictured here are those Iraqi opponents of Saddam Hussein's regime whom U.S. officials chose to invite to London in December 2002 to design a "post-Saddam" regime. Both American officials and political commentators noted the religious, ethnic, and party diversity of the invitees, but they failed to find the group's masculinzed uniformity significant. (AP Photo/ Alastair Grant, courtesy AP/Wide World Photos)

cupation officials and their superiors in Washington. Some players in any backroom bargaining possess all four convertible resources. In most political systems all of these bargaining chips are kept out of the hands of all but a very few women.

The bargaining process that produced the 2003 Iraqi Governing Council had been going on among a virtually all-male cast of characters in various forums since December 2002, months before the Bush administration and its British allies launched their military invasion. At the December 2002 London meeting convened by the Bush administration, sixty Iraqis were invited. They were deemed by Washington strategists to be key players in the opposition to the Saddam Hussein regime. Of the sixty, three were women. In May 2003, with the Americans now in military control of Baghdad (though scarcely having a firm grasp on the country's postwar politics), the Bush administration called a second meeting to map out a post-Saddam political system. This time American officials invited three hundred Iraqis. Now the number of women included rose to five.[16]

What was notable about the three women eventually selected for membership in the Iraqi Governing Council was that they did not have access to the four bargaining chips crucial to effective political influence. That is, Raja Habib Khuzai and the other two women each entered the Governing Council without their own political parties, without their own militias, without their own treasuries, and without their own direct lines of communication to Washington.

Looking down the list of the twenty-five members of the Governing Council, what stood out was how their twenty-two male colleagues were identified. These men were identified not as individuals with their own professional credentials, but instead as leaders of this or that political party or public organization. Perhaps the three women were selected by the bargainers precisely because they could make the Council look minimally legitimate to the world, while not possessing the political resources needed to shape the Council's agenda. Maybe the three women would not even make common cause with each other. Masculinizing the internal culture of the new Governing Council thus could proceed undisturbed. Maybe.

It likely became difficult for any of the three women (or later two) on the Council to wield effective influence with either their fellow Council members or with the U.S. occupation authorities. Thus when the question arose about what steps should be taken to draft a new constitution for Iraq and reporters tried to figure out who among the Governing Council's members seemed to be wielding the most influence in that debate, the names of the "power brokers" mentioned were all male.[17]

Now an Iraqi beautician stands up. Dressed in snug-fitting pants and a flower-patterned top, she is Nimo Din'Kha Skander.[18] She describes her small business, the Nimo Beauty Salon, as a lively place. Just a single room in the busy Karrada neighborhood of Baghdad, the salon attracts women of several generations for haircuts, facials, and hair dyeing. Some of her customers wear head scarves, but many do not. The Nimo Beauty Salon is also a place where political affairs are regularly analyzed. Nimo Din'Kha Skander could be seen as presiding over a political forum.

While choosing hair colors, she and her customers talk about where the country is heading, whether male clerics could ever win a majority of Iraqis' votes, what the American occupiers ultimately intend. Like other Iraqi women and girls, they have heard harrowing stories of abductions and rapes of women since the lawlessness escalated after the collapse of Saddam Hussein's regime. They talk about the rapes in whispers. Stories of sexual assaults make many of them afraid to travel about the city. They know of some women and girls who have become afraid to leave their homes at all. There is no sign that the new U.S.-recruited-and-trained police force is being taught to take violence against women seriously. The police recruits selected by the U.S. occupation officials, furthermore, appear to be only men. The militias still controlled by some clerics and certain political parties also seem to be exclusively male.[19] This combination of masculinized security forces and a lack of gender-security-planning consciousness deprives Iraqi women of opportunities to be effective partic-

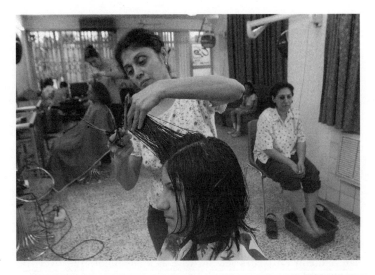

Iraqi women customers in a beauty parlor in October 2003. Women may talk with each other about the politics of security far from the fortified compounds of the Governing Council and the U.S. occupation authorities. (Photo: Laura Boushnak/AFP/Getty Images)

ipants in the emerging new political system. It is no wonder that only men appear at street demonstrations.[20]

Despite the political character of their conversations at the Nimo Beauty Salon, these women see "politics" as happening somewhere else, somewhere they are not. In this perception, Nimo Din'Kha Skander and her customers share a view commonly held by more influential political commentators. Everyone imagines a beauty parlor to be a feminized space, a private place. Politics couldn't, therefore, be going on here. It takes a feminist curiosity to see a beauty salon as a political forum — and to pay attention. Here is where the relationship between public and private power is being sorted out. Here the nature of the past's influence on the present is being weighed. Here the implications of sexual violence for enacting effective citizenship are being exposed. A feminized space is not the opposite of a political place. For many women, especially in a time of foreign military occupation, governmental flux, masculinized rivalries, and increasing sexualized violence, a feminized space may be the most secure political place for them to trade analyses and strategies.

Baghdad in the1990s was not Kabul in the 1990s. The Nimo Beauty Salon was never shut down by the regime of Saddam Hussein. In fact, Nimo Din'Kha Skander takes pride in having had Saddam Hussein's second wife as a customer. Yet, over the past decade, there have been changes in the constrictions faced by women, which many women have internalized.

The regime headed by Saddam Hussein was built on the strength of the Baathist party, a political party despised by both the young Afghan men who joined the Taliban and the Arab men who became followers of Osama bin Laden. The Baathist party was a secular, nationalist political party. Iraqi women first voted in 1980. Women's education, women's paid work, women's votes, all were encouraged by the Baathist-run government, not for the sake of democratization but for the sake of economic growth, to earn Iraq the status of being a "modern" nation and to maximize the regime's wartime mobilization. By 2000, 78 percent of school-age Iraqi girls were enrolled in primary schools.[21] However, after its 1991 defeat in the first Gulf War and during the subsequent decade of international economic sanctions, Saddam Hussein's regime sought to garner more regional aid by diluting its secular ideology and vaguely courting Islamic support. During the 1980s war with Iran, the Iraqi regime sought to attract more women into paid civil service jobs in order to replace the thousands of men it was drafting into its army. By contrast, during the 1990s, the regime, worried about dents in Iraqi men's sense of manly esteem after two devastating wartime defeats, promoted a more conservative brand of femininity. At the same time, many younger Iraqi women — now enduring postwar hardships and cut off from the outside world, not free to travel as their mothers and aunts had before them — began to adopt a more literal interpretation of Islamic femininity. To the dismay of many older urban Iraqi women, who had fought in earlier decades for women's right to live their lives as autonomous individuals, it became more common for young Iraqi women to adopt head scarves.[22]

Women's liberation in any country rarely follows a simple path "onward and upward." Women's status and political participation can vary surprisingly from one decade to another, from one generation to another. One's feminist curiosity, consequently, needs to have staying power. One cannot afford the luxury of turning away to follow the "next new thing" as soon as women in a country have won the vote, or as soon as a handful of women have been awarded cabinet portfolios, or even when many women have gained access to reproductive rights.

Progress in rolling back patriarchy can prove stunningly ephemeral. Older women are sometimes more literate, more worldly, more economically autonomous than their daughters and nieces. With some wars and postwartimes women's sphere of economic, social, and even political influence widens. With other wars and postwartimes those spheres dramatically shrink. The key causal factor here is whether the war-waging and postwar government is masculinist. If the government continues to privilege masculinity, then even those policies it may enact to widen women's spheres of activity can be reversed as soon as it decides such a reversal is politically convenient. This is a lesson that both Afghan and Iraqi women have learned. The broadening of women's autonomy is secure only when that broadening actually rolls back the masculinization of both local and foreign interventionist political cultures and government power.

Kawkab Jalil now rises to her feet. She is dressed in a fashionably tailored long black dress.[23] Her fingernails are hennaed. Her dark hair is uncovered. Kawkab Jalil, who is forty-six, explains that she only donned the scarf a year earlier due to social pressure, but recently put it aside when she decided that she did not have to prove her feminine respectability to strangers. She did not remove her head scarf to make Americans feel satisfied in their roles as "liberators." Jalil had stayed in Iraq during the eight-year war with Iran, the years of international sanctions, the era of increasing intimidation by the Baathist regime. She stayed even after being forced out of her long-standing job at the state electrical company when she refused to join the ruling party. In the wake of the fall of the Baathist regime and the confusion set off by the U.S. military conquest, Jalil says, "We need more courage, further boldness. We must reflect a bright future of Iraqi women. Not be oppressed, weak people who have no power."[24]

Kawkab Jalil was not a participant in the backroom bargaining sessions that produced the U.S.-appointed Governing Council. She instead joined a small number of Iraqi women in activating independent women's advocacy organizations designed to put pressure on both the Governing Council and the U.S. occupation authorities. Jalil herself has become a member of the Iraqi Women's League leadership committee. The League was founded in the 1950s but was forced underground during the Saddam Hussein era. By August 2003, five months after the American and British invasion, the League membership had risen to five hundred women, though Jalil and other women of the older generation noticed that many of the younger women who were now becoming active remained tentative. It was not a matter of their age, but rather of their historical generation. These younger Iraqi women had grown up with little chance to speak out or to learn organizational skills.[25]

Among the conditions that Jalil and other Iraqi activist women have tried to transform into political issues is the escalating violence against women. In August 2003 another women's group, the Organization of Women's Freedom in Iraq (OWFI), led a public demonstration in Baghdad to call for official action to stop the abduction of and assaults on women. Sixty people came out to demonstrate. One middle-aged woman who attended said, "This is my first demonstration for thirty-five years. . . . I came out here all by myself today to raise my voice, but where are all the women?"[26] A majority of the demonstrators, even on this issue so crucial to women, were men. The attendance gender profile says less about women's political consciousness than it does about how far — in any society — the threat of violence suppresses women's capacity to behave as fully participant political actors.

Insofar as the American occupation officials and their hand-picked Iraqi male advisors treated violence against women as a secondary matter, as something that could be dealt with later, the emerging Iraqi political system would become masculinized. Violence against women, as so many feminists — from the Congo to Kosovo to East Timor — have taught us, must be accorded urgent political attention if women are to gain the status of genuinely autonomous citizens.[27]

About the three women chosen behind closed doors to serve on the twenty-five-member Iraqi Governing Council, activist women such as Kawkab Jalil have expressed skepticism. At one strategy meeting, women kept telling an American reporter, "We do not know them . . . who are they?"[28] They noted that not one of the then-three women on the Council seemed to have an influential organizational support base of her own and thus would be unlikely to carry much political weight in either the Council's own deliberations or lobbying the American authorities. Warned a schoolteacher, "And if they're going to fail, that's it. They won't give this chance to women again."[29]

Then there is the serious matter of drafting Iraq's new constitution. Iraqi women activists, just like Afghanistan's women's rights advocates, decided that those chosen to draft, amend, and ratify the new constitution would shape women's lives for years to come. Thus women activists were dismayed at the composition of the committee chosen to draft the new constitution: of twenty-five members, all were men.[30] It appeared that the U.S. occupation authorities, their superiors in Washington, and the members of the Iraqi Governing Council all deemed women's future relationships to the state, to the law, and to male citizens well cared for in the hands of a small group of ethnically, religiously, and ideologically competitive men. But, these Iraqi activist women argued, this was a highly questionable supposition.

To bolster their political position, some Iraqi activist women therefore began to foster alliances with women activists outside Iraq. A group of exiled Iraqi women in Britain created the Iraqi Women's Rights Coalition (IWRC), which began to publish its own newsletter, *Equality Rights Now!* These British-based Iraqi women lent support to the women who, in June 2003, founded the Organization of Women's Freedom in Iraq.[31] One of the group's first efforts was to establish a shelter in Baghdad for Iraqi women suffering from domestic violence, including threats of "honor killings" by their own brothers, fathers, and uncles.[32] In August 2003 OWFI members wrote a formal letter to Paul Bremer, the chief U.S. occupation administrator in Baghdad, calling on him to use his authority to address the "unprecedented violence against women." He did not reply.[33]

In October 2000 the U.S. government voted, along with a majority of the UN Security Council, in favor of Security Council Resolution 1325. This groundbreaking resolution committed all agencies of the UN and every UN member state to ensuring that both women and women's concerns become integral to every new security institution and every decision-making stage in peacekeeping and national reconstruction in any area of armed conflict. Despite its vote for the historic SCR 1325, the U.S. government felt free to appoint an all-male constitution-drafting committee in occupied Iraq and to create newly remasculinized Iraqi police and security forces.[34]

CONCLUSION

In October 2003, one of the founders of OWFI, Yanar Mohammed, sought to raise the consciousness of Americans by traveling to New York. Yanar Mohammed, once active in Iraq's Communist party, a group banned by the Baathist regime, had spent her exile years in Canada. She returned to Iraq in the wake of the invasion to contribute to the new mobilization of women. Sponsoring her visit was a group of New York women who had created the Working Committee in Support of Iraq's Women.[35]

Women in colonized countries, women in militarily occupied countries, and women under local authoritarian rulers all have a long history of seeking alliances with those women abroad who seem sympathetic to their causes. The internationalization of women-to-women political alliances is not new. It began in the mid-1800s. There is plenty of evidence, garnered by feminist historians, to suggest that sustaining such alliances is hard political work.[36] There are the pulls and pushes of local women's own nonfeminist male potential allies. Men who oppose foreign occupation or foreign domination are not necessarily men who see the "sovereign nation" as composed of women and men living as equals in the family, the market, the courts, the universities, and the state's policy-making circles. Yet it is precisely those nonfeminist, even outrightly patriarchal, men with whom some women may believe they must make common cause, at least tactically. This can prove hard to explain to overseas feminist partners. Then there are the pitfalls of miscommunication. Mail now travels in a cybernetic flash, rather than via weeks of ocean voyage, but speed does not assure shared understanding of the terms and phrases. In fact, today any miscommunication can be spread far and wide with alarming quickness and so prove harder to undo. And there is burnout. Doing alliance-building among women, none of whom control abundant resources of time or money, can tax the most dedicated of internationally minded feminists.

In addition, as we have painfully learned, there is the perpetual temptation for women residing outside the war-torn or imperially occupied country to imagine that, by dint of their access to media and financial resources, those women residing in the affluent country also may have a superior understanding of what should be prioritized in the local women's struggle. And there is local women activists' complementary temptation to tailor their strategies and their discourses to reassure the seemingly well-endowed overseas supporters.

On the other hand, the step-by-step building of such dynamic cross-national alliances among women holds out the possibility that women in the imperially minded country will themselves gain a new understanding of their own government's policies and actions overseas, and this will prompt them to publicly question their government's official justifications for expansionist maneuvers carried out in their names. Moreover, if women pursue a genuine cross-national alliance of equals, it will involve a lot of intense listening, questioning, and rethinking. Such efforts, in turn, can sharpen activists' feminist understandings of what causes the perpetuation of masculinization in public life, not only "over there" but "here at home."

The intensity and variety of cross-national feminist interactions today are beyond anything seen before in the history of empires or international politics. These feminist interactions are producing fresh analyses of what is causing and perpetuating unequal international power and offering strategies to expose those causes and subvert them. Thus it would be a mistake, I think, to imagine that the latest version of empire-building in the name of "world order" or "global security" or "civilization" is an unstoppable steamroller.

Crafting a system of expansive, cohesive political influence — an empire — has always been a tricky enterprise. Only in retrospect do the earlier British, Ottoman, or Spanish empires look deceptively unavoidable. In practice, there were doubters and critics whom imperialists had to try to persuade or silence at home; there were rebels and recalcitrants they needed to co-opt or suppress in the occupied society. Silencing, suppressing, persuading, co-opting—these imperial activities have not guaranteed success over the long term. In large part, each is dependent on certain gender ideologies. And these ideologies, we have seen, are vulnerable to contradiction and challenge.

Masculinity has always been an essential tool wielded in this many-pronged process of empire-building. At home it has been necessary to convince both men and women that a militarized manliness (especially one allied with a manly sort of reason and a manly brand of commercial competitiveness) was a superior form of humanity. Both men and women have had to be persuaded that this construction of privileged masculinity endowed those actors who claimed to possess it with unique capacities to bring security and a sense of moral well-being to citizens at home, while it simultaneously conferred enlightenment, progress, and "civilization" on those abroad over whom they held sway. Security, moral satisfaction, progress, civilization—all are gendered. Subtract the politics of masculinity and the politics of femininity from one's investigation, and one is likely to produce an unreliable explanation of how empire-building proceeds—or falters.

For such militarized expansionism does falter, does lose its protective glow at home and among the co-opted and daunted abroad. It falters if the "civilizing" rewards promised turn out to fuel not the blessings of technocracy, order, and peace, but instead violence, corruption, and demoralization. Ambitious expansionism also stumbles if the performers of privileged masculinity appear self-serving or naive—or both.

The privileging of masculinity in general and certain forms of masculinity in particular thus need to be investigated. Making sense of the masculinized political cultures and masculinized political processes that legitimize and energize global expansionism, however, cannot be accomplished just by paying attention to varieties of men. Paying serious attention to women — to their experiences, their actions, and their ideas, in all their diversity; that is, wielding a feminist curiosity — is the only way to ensure that men-as-men and masculinity as an ideology can be seen with political clarity.

But what if we don't? No sustained curiosity about women means no discussion of the politics of femininity. No serious analysis of the politics of women and femininity converts into no concentrated public thinking about men and masculinities. No focused investigation of men and masculinities means no understanding of the genderings of international affairs. No curiosity about how and why international affairs have become reliant on particular ideas about femininity and masculinity produces little chance to make the global workings of unequal power fully visible. No visible rendering of internationalized gender means no possibility of instituting genuine and lasting change in those unequal power arrangements at home and abroad.

PART FOUR

Six Pieces
for a Work-in-Progress

Playing Checkers with the Troops

I grew up during World War II in an American suburb. Manhasset, Long Island, was a forty-five-minute commute from midtown Manhattan. Most of the fathers were driven every morning by the mothers to the local train station. At the time it seemed to be quite an ordinary girlhood. All the drama was taking place somewhere else. We heard about it on the radio.

But recently I've been wondering. I've been trying to think afresh about how the workings of militarization and ideas about femininity managed to insinuate themselves into this apparently ordinary girlhood. So I've been doing a sort of feminist archaeological dig into my own 1940s to 1950s girlhood. The six pieces here are just a beginning. The short lines aren't poetry. The phrases just seemed to come in this way.

1
A War without White Hats

When we played guns, there were no Good Guys, no Bad
    Guys.
We didn't designate any of us — Richie, Alfie, Tommy, or me —
to be the Indians or the Robbers or the Nazis.

We played Cowboys versus Cowboys, Soldiers versus Soldiers,
Commandos versus Commandos.

Often we didn't call ourselves anything.

It was the early 1940s, when the evening radio brought
wartime news and the Saturday matinee featured
sharp-shooting western heroes.

But as we shot at each other
from behind suburban pines, maples, and azalea bushes,
we seemed to have no need for
myths of White Hats, Civilization, or the Free World.
We needed only rules, our rules.

Kkhhgghh, kkhhgghh. You're dead.

Here are my neighborhood pals and me in 1947, just after World
War II. I'm on the right wearing a hat my father brought back
from Europe as a wartime souvenir. Alfie and Richie are next
to me. Tommy is in the back. We four were the "big kids." We
painted our faces only for a party, never for our serious everyday
games of "guns." (Photo courtesy of Cynthia Enloe)

2

Playing Guns

The weaponry wasn't important.
You just took your right hand, bent your last three fingers
in toward your palm. Then you pointed your first finger at
your intended target and straightened your thumb vertically.
You were armed.

In later years, when Hopalong Cassidy became popular,
Some of us did acquire guns and holsters.
Mine was of white leather, with blue and red glass studs.
It was a double-holster set, like Hopalong's.
I liked the feel of it around my ten-year-old waist,
the buckle shining in the middle, the holsters resting on
    either hip,
each weighted down with a silver six-shooter.

But they were for show, for dress-up,
not for a serious after-school game of Guns.
For that, one needed only a fast hand
and the right sound.

The sound was what took practice.
It was no good having your fingered pistol at the ready
if you couldn't make it fire convincingly.

Over the years, Tommie, Richie, Alfie, and I
perfected a credible sound.
It punctuated our play up and down the backyards
of Aldershot Lane.

Our sound resembled one derived from a foreign language.
We made it in the back of our youthful throats,

with our tongues arched upward.
The trick was to combine a spurt of air
with plenty of saliva, both in sync with
a little quick movement of one's pointed right finger
aimed at that afternoon's enemy.

Kkhhgghh, Kkhhgghh.

Kkhhgghh, Kkhhgghh.

3

Hitler Is a Jerk

Disney's *Snow White* came to the Manhasset movie theater
in the early years of the war.
Tickets were eighteen cents for the Saturday afternoon shows.
I think its animated predecessor, *Dumbo*, made a bigger impres-
    sion on me.
But the film did leave one enduring legacy.

All of us learned the Seven Dwarfs' catchy song,
"Whistle while you work."
A wartime wit had set it to more rousing patriotic lyrics.

"Whistle while you work,
Hitler is a jerk."
Richie and Alfie and Tommy and I liked the new version.
We sang it as we played in our driveway,
trying to get the orange basketball into
the hoop nailed above our garage door.

Bounce, throw, thud, bounce
"Whistle while you work,

Hitler is a jerk."
Bounce, throw, swoosh, bounce
"Mussolini is a meanie,"
Thud, bounce, bounce, bounce
"But the Japs are worse."

We were doing our bit for the war effort
as we sang and bounced the orange ball.
We didn't notice that we were tunefully
naming two dictators and then dismissing
an entire people.
We thought ourselves quite clever.

4

Leaden Soldiers

As I took them out of their boxes—
a special box for each regiment—
and stood them on their little flat bases,
I had the sense that I was looking at the world.
No two groups were alike. Each had
its own history, its own culture, usually its own royal allegiance.

Some wore kilts, others trousers;
some had turbans on their heads, others wore caps with tassels.
Their weapons were rudimentary: a rifle, a saber.
I was never attracted to heavy artillery.

Playing soldiers upstairs in my room meant
laying out all the colorfully attired three-inch men.
There might be roughly two sides.
Neither, though, tried to hide from the other.

No guerrilla warfare in my bedroom.
The leaden soldiers faced each other squarely.
Turbans confronted tassels.
Kilted men looked unflinchingly
into the eyes of their trousered foe.

I loved just looking at them, comparing them,
setting them out in varying arrangements.
I wasn't interested in waging battles.
The object was to keep all these little warriors
free from dents and chipped paint.

5

Gurkhas Wear Wool

I first saw Gurkhas with my own eyes in Kuala Lumpur.
Usually my Indian and Chinese Malaysian women friends
    and I
played field hockey there on the padang just beyond the
veranda of the Selangor Club. These women were generous
in their toleration of my baggy Bermuda shorts,
my mediocre stick work, and my stepping aside in the backfield
when rushed by the Sikh men we sometimes challenged.

On this day, however, it was the Gurkhas on parade
who occupied the field in the center of the capital.
It was noon, the sun was high.
The British woman standing next to me gazed at
the rifle-carrying, uniformed Nepali men in admiration.
"You can see how tough they are," she whispered.

"Only the Gurkhas would wear wool serge here
in the tropics."

I had heard about the Gurkhas' stalwartness since I
was a girl. My father's air commandos had
been stationed in Burma, behind the Japanese lines,
in a daring operation that brought together American,
Australian, British, and Nepali men.
Gurkhas were men whom other men could count on. They
took
pride in service to the empire (my father adopted
an Anglophilic appreciation of the Raj). Their short stature
belied
their strength and endurance. To fight well — once against
lowland Indians,
now against the Japanese, later against Communist
insurgents and Indonesians —
they (I was told) only needed to be effectively led
by British officers, men who appreciated their rare attributes.

In Burma my father took photos of Gurkha troops.
He brought home a tattered manual that instructed British
officers
in how to inspire these men of the empire.
When the remaining members of his commando unit,
men now in their eighties, came together in London for
a reunion
five decades after the war, my father was delighted that
their honor guard included young Gurkhas.
To him, it was a sign that they, gray, bent, uncertain in their step,
were still worthy of imperial respect.

6

The Cigarette

I've seen the small black-and-white photographs
of my mother smoking in Berlin.
My father took them shortly after they were married.
I think he found the effect of the cigarette smoke artistic.
These pictures were posed, set in their small apartment.
My mother looked slim and quite beautiful.
Despite their acute awareness of the dark clouds forming,
these were their happy years,
living on modest incomes,
surrounded by friends of disparate nationalities.

Ten years later my mother wasn't smoking anymore.
She was a suburban mother and housewife.
My father had enlisted soon after Pearl Harbor.
He was sent first to flight surgeon's school in Kansas,
then to India and Burma, and finally to London and Germany.
There were months on end when
my mother was the lone adult in our household.

When she described these months as a wartime single mother,
she didn't portray them as a time of hardship.
With one small exception.
Looking back, she would tell of the night when,
having put David and me to bed upstairs,
she had started longing for a cigarette.
There were always cigarettes in the house.
Kept not in their packages, but in a clear glass box,
the glass top etched with the name of a German hotel.

The visible layers of white cigarettes were there to welcome
any guest who might stop by.

That night she went into the living room.
I've pictured this happening in the winter.
Maybe she even had laid a fire in the fireplace.
Did she sit on the floor or in one of the upholstered chairs?
She never offered that much detail.
She recalled only how she thought that smoking a cigarette
would make her feel less lonely, would conjure up
the conviviality of those earlier Berlin days.
She told of lighting up the cigarette, of inhaling the smoke,
preparing for the sensual pleasure.
Then, in her telling, she would chuckle, and say,
"It tasted awful."

Notes

CHAPTER 1. THE SURPRISED FEMINIST

Cynthia Enloe's "The Surprised Feminist" was originally published in *Signs: Journal of Women in Culture and Society* 25, no. 4 (2000). © 2000 by the University of Chicago. All rights reserved. Reprinted by permission of the University of Chicago Press.

CHAPTER 2. MARGINS, SILENCES, AND BOTTOM RUNGS

Cynthia Enloe's "Margins, Silences, and Bottom Rungs: How to Overcome the Underestimation of Power in the Study of International Relations" was originally published in Steve Smith, Ken Booth, and Marysia Zalewski, eds., *International Theory: Positivism and Beyond* (New York: Cambridge University Press, 1996), 186–202. Reprinted with permission of Cambridge University Press.

1. Sandra Harding, ed., *The "Racial" Economy of Science* (Bloomington: Indiana University Press, 1993), and Nancy C. M. Hartsock, "Theoretical Bases for Coalition Building: An Assessment of Postmod-

ernism," unpublished paper, Department of Women's Studies, University of Washington, Seattle, 1994.

2. Octavio Paz, *The Other Mexico: Critique of the Pyramid* (New York: Grove Press, 1972).

3. Marjorie Griffin Cohen, *Free Trade and the Future of Women's Work* (Toronto: Garamond Press, 1987).

4. Judith Adler Hellman, *Crisis in Mexico* (New York: Holmes and Meier Publishers, 1983).

5. Rosario Castellanos, *The Nine Guardians* (London: Readers International, 1992).

6. Ibid., 19.

7. Amy Kaplan and Donald E. Pease, eds., *Cultures of United States Imperialism* (Durham: Duke University Press, 1993).

8. Castellanos, *The Nine Guardians*, 46.

9. Maureen Ahern, *Rosario Castellanos Reader* (Austin: University of Texas Press, 1988).

10. Castellanos, *The Nine Guardians*, 99–100, 105.

11. Ibid., 127.

12. Ibid., 128–29.

13. Ronald Nigh, "Zapata Rose in 1994," *Cultural Survival Quarterly* 18, no. 1 (1994): 10.

14. Duncan Earle, "Indigenous Identity at the Margin: Zapatismo and Nationalism," *Cultural Survival Quarterly* 18, no. 1 (1994): 26–30.

15. Nigh, "Zapata Rose," 10.

16. Zapatista National Liberation Army, "Communiqué from the Clandestine Indigenous Revolutionary High Command of the Zapatista National Liberation Army (CCRI-CF del EZLN)." First published in *La Jornada*, February 27, 1994; reprinted in a translation by Ronald Nigh in *Cultural Survival Quarterly* 18, no. 1 (1994): 12.

17. Neil Harvey, *Rebellion in Chiapas* (La Jolla: Center for U.S.-Mexican Studies, University of California at San Diego, 1994).

18. Americas Watch, *Human Rights in Mexico: A Policy of Impunity* (New York: Human Rights Watch, 1990).

19. Sara Lovera, "Se Constituye el Grupo Rosario Castellanos '23 de Marzo,'" *Doble Jornada*, February 7, 1994, 5.

20. Zapatista National Liberation Army, "Women's Revolutionary Law," trans. Mat Miscreant, distributed by Love and Rage, New York News Bureau, lnr@blythe.org (1994).

21. "Mexico," *Ms.* 4, no. 6 (May–June 1994): 16.

22. Anthony De Palma, "Rage Builds in Chiapas Village Where Land Is Life," *New York Times*, February 27, 1994.

23. Ibid.

24. Benedict J. Kerkvliet and Resil B. Mojares, eds., *From Marcos to Aquino: Local Perspectives on Political Transition in the Philippines* (Honolulu: University of Hawaii Press, 1992).

CHAPTER 3. THE GLOBETROTTING SNEAKER

Cynthia Enloe's "The Globetrotting Sneaker" was originally published in *Ms.*, March–April 1995, 11–15. Reprinted by permission of *Ms.* Magazine, © 1995.

This essay draws from the work of South Korean scholars Hyun Sook Kim, Seung-kyung Kim, Katharine Moon, Seungsook Moon, and Jeong-Lim Nam.

1. Jeong-Lim Nam, "Reforming Economic Allocations in the Family: The Women's Movement and the Role of the State in South Korea," *Women's Studies International Forum* 18, no. 2 (1995): 113–23.

2. Donald Katz, *Just Do It: The Nike Spirit in the Corporate World* (New York: Random House, 1994): 191.

3. Vernon Loeb, "$75 Nikes, 15 Cents an Hour," *Boston Globe*, December 30, 1991.

4. M. Goozner, "Nike Manager Knows Abuses Do Happen," *Chicago Tribune*, November 7, 1994. For more on Nike's operations, see Miguel Korzeniewicz, "Commodity Chains and Marketing Strategies: Nike and the Global Athletic Footwear Industry," in Gary Gereffi and Miguel Korzeniewicz, eds., *Commodity Chains and Global Capitalism* (Westport, Conn.: Greenwood Press, 1993); Katz, *Just Do It*; Verité, "Workers Win Independent Union in Mexico," *Monitor: Exploring the Dynamics of the Global Assembly Line*, no. 6 (Fall 2002): 12–13.

CHAPTER 4. DAUGHTERS AND GENERALS
IN THE POLITICS OF THE GLOBALIZED SNEAKER

Cynthia Enloe's "Daughters and Generals in the Politics of the Globalized Sneaker" was originally published in Preet S. Aulakh and Michael G. Schecter, eds., *Rethinking Globalization(s): From Corporate Transnationalism to Local Interventions* (London: Macmillan Press Ltd., 2000), 238–46. Reproduced with permission of Palgrave Macmillan.

1. This chapter is based on an oral presentation delivered at Michigan State University on April 3, 1998, as part of the conference "Globalization and Its (Dis)Contents: Multiple Perspectives," later published in Preet S. Aulalsh and Michael G. Schecter, eds., *Rethinking Globalizations* (New York: St. Martin's Press, 2000).

2. For an elaboration on this argument, see Cynthia Enloe, "Feminists Try on the Post–Cold War Global Sneaker," in Nancy Hewitt, Jean O'Barr, and Nancy Rosebaugh, eds., *Talking Gender* (Chapel Hill: University of North Carolina Press, 1996), 176 ff.

3. Seung-kyung Kim, *Class Struggle or Family Struggle? The Lives of Women Factory Workers in South Korea* (New York: Cambridge University Press, 1997).

4. See also Insook Kwon, "'The New Women's Movement' in 1920's Korea: Rethinking the Relationship between Feminism, Imperialism, and Women," *Gender and History* 10, no. 3 (November 1998): 358–80.

5. For an elaboration on this phenomenon, see Indrasari Tjandraningshih, "Between Factory and Home: Problems of Women Workers," in Jeff Ballinger and Claes Olsson, eds., *Behind the Swoosh* (Uppsala, Sweden: International Coalition for Development Action, 1997), 145–59.

6. Choi Soung-ai, "Whose Honor, Whose Humiliation? Women, Men, and the Economic Crisis," *Asian Women Workers Newsletter* (Hong Kong) 17, no. 2 (1998): 6–7.

7. On this and related points, see Ballinger and Ollson, *Behind the Swoosh*.

8. Ines Smyth and Mies Grijns, "*Unjuk Rasa* or Conscious Protest? Resistance Strategies of Indonesian Women Workers," *Bulletin of Concerned Asian Scholars* 29, no. 4 (1997): 13–22.

9. Diane Lauren Wolf, *Factory Daughters: Gender, Household Dynamics, and Rural Industrialization in Java* (Berkeley: University of California Press, 1992).

CHAPTER 5. WHOM DO YOU TAKE SERIOUSLY?

This essay was originally presented at the "Conference on Convergence and Diversity: Pacific Asia in the 2000s" at Victoria University of Wellington, Wellington, New Zealand, March 1–2, 1997.

1. Australian feminist Dale Spender began alerting us in the early 1980s to the tendency of teachers to (1) call on male students in class discussions more than on their young female classmates and (2) to pay attention to the boys' comments more often — e.g., to follow up on their comments. More recently numerous researchers in the United States monitoring American elementary and middle school classroom interactions have confirmed Spender's British findings. Even women teachers who are aware of these gender-biased patterns and who consciously try to break them have seen themselves on voluntary videotapings falling into these boy-privileging behaviors. See, for instance, Peggy Orenstein, *Schoolgirls: Young Women, Self-Esteem, and the Confidence Gap* (New York: Doubleday, 1994).

2. Although not myself a formal political theorist, ever since reading — and hearing — Hannah Arendt when I was an undergraduate, I have been deeply affected by her ideas. On the distinctiveness and value of public speech, see especially, Arendt's "Lying in Politics," "Civil Disobedience," and "On Violence," all collected in her *Crises of the Republic* (New York: Harcourt Brace Jovanovich, 1972).

3. For an assessment of Hannah Arendt and of listening as a political act, see Susan Bickford, *The Dissonance of Democracy: Listening, Conflict and Citizenship* (Ithaca, N.Y.: Cornell University Press, 1996).

4. For a collection of essays by feminist theorists coming to grips with Arendt, see Bonnie Honig, ed., *Feminist Interpretations of Hannah Arendt* (University Park: Pennsylvania State University Press, 1995).

5. One collection of comparative studies of suffragist movements,

which includes chapters on New Zealand, Australia, and several other Pacific societies, is Caroline Daley and Melanie Nolan, eds., *Suffrage and Beyond: International Feminist Perspectives* (New York: New York University Press, 1994).

6. For a worldwide mapping of women's refuges and shelters established to provide women with alternatives to remaining in abusive situations, a mapping that makes Fiji's Women's Crisis Center visible, see Joni Seager, *The Penguin Atlas of Women in the World*, 3rd ed. (New York: Penguin Books, 2003). For Okinawan feminists' ongoing critiques and mobilizing against U.S. military personnel's abusive acts and those of Japanese men, see the newsletter *Okinawa: Peace, Human Rights, Women, Environment*, published in the 1990s by the Okinawa Christian Center (Okinawa, Japan); its third issue was published in January 1997. Regarding the public discussion sparked by a major 1993 press exposé of the "epidemic" of violence against women in Melbourne, see Adian Howe, " 'The War against Women': Media Representations of Men's Violence against Women in Australia," *Violence against Women: An International and Interdisciplinary Journal* 3, no. 1 (February 1997): 59–75.

7. For a nuanced, detailed account of the dynamic politics of the early English gendered textile industry, see Judy Lown, *Women and Industrialization: Gender at Work in Nineteenth-Century England* (Minneapolis: University of Minnesota Press, 1990).

8. I have explored military personnel planners' attempts — sometimes confused — to recruit women in three of my books: *Does Khaki Become You? The Militarization of Women's Lives* (London: Pandora/HarperCollins, 1988), *The Morning After: Sexual Politics at the End of the Cold War* (Berkeley: University of California Press, 1993), and *Maneuvers: The International Politics of Militarizing Women's Lives* (Berkeley: University of California Press, 2000).

9. Among recent investigations of women factory workers' own strategizing is the work of Seung-kyung Kim, *Class Struggle or Family Struggle: The Lives of Women Factory Workers in South Korea* (New York: Cambridge University Press, 1997). For a fuller bibliography of works analyzing women factory workers' aspirations, coping strategies, and organizing

efforts, see my *Bananas, Beaches and Bases: Making Feminist Sense of International Politics,* 2nd ed. (Berkeley: University of California Press, 2000).

10. *Asian Women Workers Newsletter* is a quarterly published in Hong Kong by the Committee for Asian Women. The July 1996 issue (p. 17) carried a New Zealand women's group's definition of sexual harassment.

11. I am indebted to several scholars who have been investigating the ways in which rapes have been politically constructed by nationalists: on China in the 1940s, historian Robert Shaffer, and on South Korea in the 1990s, women's studies researcher Insook Kwon.

12. Among the women who have thought especially hard about this form of silencing are those who themselves were raped during the 1991–95 war in the former Yugoslavia and those who sought to support them. See, for instance, Alexandra Stiglemeyer, ed., *Mass Rape* (Lincoln: University of Nebraska Press, 1995); Beverly Allen, *Rape Warfare* (Minneapolis: University of Minnesota Press, 1996).

13. Among the several valuable collections of articles on feminism and human rights is Rebecca J. Cook, ed., *Human Rights and Women* (Philadelphia: University of Pennsylvania Press, 1994).

CHAPTER 6. FEMINIST THEORIZING FROM *BANANAS* TO *MANEUVERS*

"Feminist Theorizing from Bananas to Maneuvers: A Conversation with Cynthia Enloe (Interviewed by Marysia Zalewski, 9 September 1998)" was originally published in *International Feminist Journal of Politics* 1, no. 1 (1999): 138–46. Reprinted by permission of Taylor & Francis Group (http://www.tandf.co.uk).

CHAPTER 7. ALL THE MEN ARE IN THE MILITIAS, ALL THE WOMEN ARE VICTIMS

Cynthia Enloe's "All the Men Are in the Militias, All the Women Are Victims: The Politics of Masculinity and Femininity in Nationalist Wars" was originally published in Lois Ann Lorentzen and Jennifer

Turpin, eds., *The Women and War Reader* (New York: New York University Press, 1998), 50–62. Reprinted by permission of New York University Press.

1. The following material on Borislav Herak is derived from two journalists' interviews with Herak after he was captured and imprisoned by the Bosnian authorities. While awaiting trial on charges of murder and rape he was permitted to talk to a variety of foreign journalists; see John Burns, "A Serbian Fighter's Trail of Brutality," *New York Times*, November 17, 1991; and George Rodriguez, transcript of interview with Borislav Herak conducted for the *Dallas Morning News* at the Viktor Buban military prison, Sarajevo, in January 1993, reprinted in Alexandra Stiglmayer, ed., *Mass Rape: The War against Women in Bosnia-Herzegovina* (Lincoln: University of Nebraska Press, 1994).

2. John Burns, "Bosnia War Crime Trial Hears Serb's Confession," *New York Times*, March 14, 1993. For detailed reporting on the rapes of women that occurred from 1992 to 1995 in Bosnia, see Stiglmayer, *Mass Rape*; "Serbia's War against Bosnia and Croatia," *off our backs*, special supplement (May 1993); Ivana Balen, "Responding to War-time Rapes," *Helsinki Citizens Assembly Newsletter*, no. 6 (Winter 1993): 12–13; Cornelia Sorabji, "War Crimes: Crimes against Gender or Nation?" *War Report* (February–March 1993): 16–17; the United Nations War Crimes Commission report as described in Paul Lewis, "Rape Was a Weapon of Serbs, U.N. Says," *New York Times*, October 20, 1993; "Correction: Report on Rape in Bosnia," *New York Times*, October 23, 1993.

3. For those wishing to become acquainted with this literature, here are some starting places: Nira Yuval-Davis and Floya Anthias, eds., *Woman-Nation-State* (London: Macmillan, 1989); Floya Anthias and Nira Yuval-Davis, with Harriet Cain, eds., *Racialized Boundaries: Race, Nation, Gender, Colour and Class and the Anti-Racist Struggle* (London: Routledge, 1993); Roberta Hamilton and Michele Barrett, eds., *The Politics of Diversity: Feminism, Marxism and Nationalism* (London: Verso, 1987); Constance Sutton, ed., *Feminism, Nationalism and Militarism* (Fairfax, Va.: American Association of Anthropology, 1993); *Feminist Review*, special issues on "Nationalisms and National Identities" (Summer 1993) and "Thinking through Ethnicities" (Autumn 1993); Nanette Funk and

Magda Mueller, eds., *Gender Politics and Post-Communism* (New York: Routledge, 1993); Jan Pettman, *Living in the Margins: Racism, Sexism and Feminism in Australia* (Sydney: Allen and Unwin, 1992); Angela V. John, *Our Mother's Land: Chapters in Welsh Women's History, 1830–1939* (Cardiff: University of Wales Press, 1991); Hue-Tam Ho Tai, *Radicalism and the Origins of the Vietnamese Revolution* (Cambridge, Mass.: Harvard University Press, 1991); Andrew Parker et al., eds., *Nationalisms and Sexuality* (New York: Routledge, 1991); *Gender and History*, special issue, "Gender, Nationalism and History" (Summer 1993).

4. My own efforts to use feminist analysis to think freshly about nationalism include *The Morning After: Sexual Politics at the End of the Cold War* (Berkeley: University of California Press, 1993) and *Bananas, Beaches and Bases: Making Feminist Sense of International Politics*, 2nd ed. (Berkeley: University of California Press, 2000).

5. Women in Black, *Compilation of Information on Crimes of War against Women in Ex-Yugoslavia — Actions and Initiatives in Their Defence* (Belgrade: Women in Black, 1993). Women's presence in some militias on all sides was confirmed by Yugoslav scholars participating in the Conference on Gender, Nationalism and Democratization: Policy Initiatives for Central and Eastern Europe, sponsored by the Network of East-West Women, Washington, D.C., October 26, 1993.

6. Karl Kaser, "Ex-Yugoslavia, a Case Study," and Zarana Papic, "Ex-Yugoslavia, a Case Study," two papers presented at the Conference on Gender, Nationalism and Democratization: Policy Initiatives for Central and Eastern Europe, sponsored by the Network of East-West Women, Washington D.C., October 26, 1993.

7. See Women in Black, *Compilation of Information*. My own gender-ignorant examination of the ethnic politics shaping the Yugoslav military is included as part of *Ethnic Soldiers: State Security in Divided Societies* (London: Penguin, 1980). My brief attempt to understand the Yugoslav women's postwar meaning of having served in what they saw as a war of liberation is contained in *Does Khaki Become You? The Militarization of Women's Lives* (London and San Francisco: Pandora/HarperCollins, 1988).

8. Shireen Hassim, "Family, Motherhood and Zulu Nationalism: The Politics of the Inkatha Women's Brigade," *Feminist Review*, no. 43

(Spring 1993): 5–12. For an exploration of white and black South African men's and women's attitudes toward soldiering during the 1980s, a period of intense militarization, see Jacklyn Cock, *Women and War in South Africa* (London: Open Letters Press, 1992).

9. Christopher Browning, *Ordinary Men: Reserve Police Battalion 101 and the Final Solution in Poland* (New York: HarperCollins, 1992).

10. Ibid., 49.

11. Ibid., 185.

12. Ibid.

13. United States Department of Defense, *Tailhook Report* (New York: St. Martin's Press, 1993). A more extensive discussion of the "Tailhook affair" is included in Enloe, *The Morning After.*

14. Reprinted in Stiglmayer, *Mass Rape.*

15. A report of the United Nations War Crimes Commission is summarized in Lewis, "Rape Was Weapon of Serbs, UN Says." A clarifying afternote was added by the *New York Times* three days later: "Correction: Report on Rapes in Bosnia."

16. A Danish psychologist's study of how Middle Eastern and Latin American refugee women reacted to the traumas — including rape — of civil conflict is Inger Agger's *The Blue Room: Trauma and Testimony among Refugee Women* (London: Zed Books, 1994).

CHAPTER 8. SPOILS OF WAR

Cynthia Enloe's "Spoils of War" was originally published in *Ms.*, March–April 1996, 15. Reprinted by permission of *Ms.* Magazine, © 1996.

CHAPTER 9. MASCULINITY AS
A FOREIGN POLICY ISSUE

Cynthia Enloe's "Masculinity as a Foreign Policy Issue" was originally published in *Foreign Policy in Focus* 5, no. 36 (October 2000): 254–59. Reprinted by permission of Foreign Policy In Focus (Silver City, NM, and Washington, DC, http://www.fpif.org).

1. See briefs: Holly Burkhalter, "The Mine Ban Treaty," *Foreign Policy in Focus* 5 (July 2000): 21; Shannon McManimon and Rachel Stohl, "Use of Children as Soldiers," *Foreign Policy in Focus* 6 (October 2001): 6; Joe Stork, "International Criminal Court," *Foreign Policy in Focus* 3 (April 1998): 4.

2. See brief: Carlos Salinas, "Colombia in Crisis," *Foreign Policy in Focus* 5 (March 2000): 5.

CHAPTER 10. "WHAT IF THEY GAVE A WAR . . ."

Cynthia Enloe, Vivian Stromberg, and the Editors of Ms., "'What If They Gave a War . . .': A Conversation about Militarism, Women, Men, and the Superfluity of War" was originally published in *Ms.*, August–September 1999, 14–18, 21–22. Reprinted by permission of *Ms.* Magazine, © 1999.

CHAPTER 11. SNEAK ATTACK

Cynthia Enloe's "Sneak Attack: The Militarization of U.S. Culture" was originally published in *Ms.*, December 2001–January 2002, 15. Reprinted by permission of *Ms.* Magazine, © 2001.

CHAPTER 12. WAR PLANNERS RELY
ON WOMEN

This essay was originally published in Japanese in *Associe* (Tokyo), April 2003.

CHAPTER 13. FEMINISTS KEEP THEIR EYES
ON MILITARIZED MASCULINITY

This essay was circulated in Okinawa in February 2003 by Okinawan Women Act Against Military Violence.

1. Because his Democratic opponent had such an outstanding com-

bat record as a soldier in Vietnam, during the 2004 U.S. presidential electoral campaign the incumbent president, George W. Bush, was asked repeatedly about his military service record during the U.S.-Vietnam War of the late 1960s to early 1970s. Whether or not his family's connections won him a then-much-sought-after place in the Texas Air National Guard (whose members were unlikely to be deployed to Vietnam) and whether or not he actually fulfilled his service obligations in the National Guard became salient issues since militarized masculinity had become so tightly woven into the media's and voters' understanding of the U.S. presidency. See Elizabeth Bumiller and David M. Halbfinger, "Military Service Becomes Issue in Bush-Kerry Race," *New York Times*, February 4, 2004; Mimi Schwartz, "In Search of the President's Missing Years," op-ed, *New York Times*, February 27, 2004.

CHAPTER 14. BECOMING A FEMINIST

This interview with Cynthia Enloe by Ken Booth, Caroline Kennedy-Pipe, and Michael Cox was originally published in the *Review of International Studies* 27, no. 4 (October 2001): 649–66. Reprinted with the permission of Cambridge University Press.

1. Cynthia Enloe, *Maneuvers: The International Politics of Militarizing Women's Lives* (Berkeley: University of California Press, 2000).

2. Cynthia Enloe, *Ethnic Conflict and Political Development* (Boston: Little, Brown, 1973) and *Comparative Politics of Pollution* (New York: Longmans, 1975).

3. Cynthia Enloe, *Does Khaki Become You? The Militarization of Women's Lives* (London: Pluto Press, 1983; 2nd ed., London: Pandora Press, 1988).

4. Cynthia Enloe, *Bananas, Beaches and Bases: Making Feminist Sense of International Politics* (London: Pandora Press, 1989; 2nd ed., Berkeley: University of California Press, 2000).

5. Cynthia Enloe, *Ethnic Soldiers: State Security in Divided Societies* (London: Penguin Books, 1980).

6. See Enloe, *Bananas, Beaches and Bases; The Morning After: Sexual*

Politics at the End of the Cold War (Berkeley: University of California Press, 1993); and *Maneuvers*.

7. Christine Chin, *In Service and Servitude: Foreign Female Domestic Workers and the Malaysian "Modernity" Project* (New York: Columbia University Press, 1998).

8. Katharine H. S. Moon, *Sex among Allies: Militarized Prostitution in U.S.-Korea Relations* (New York: Columbia University Press, 1997).

9. See, for example, Judy Lown, *Women and Industrialization: Gender at Work in Nineteenth-Century England* (Minneapolis: University of Minnesota Press, 1990); Sheila Rowbotham, *Hidden from History* (New York: Vintage Books, 1974); Gloria T. Hull, Patricia Bell Scott, and Barbara Smith, eds., *All the Women Are White, All the Blacks Are Men, But Some of Us Are Brave: Black Women's Studies* (New York: Feminist Press, 1982); Kate Rushin, *The Black Back-ups* (Ithaca, N.Y.: Firebrand Books, 1993); Adrienne Rich, *On Lies, Secrets, and Silences: Selected Prose, 1966–1978* (New York: Norton, 1979).

10. Sandra Whitworth, *Men, Militarism and UN Peacekeeping: A Gendered Analysis* (Boulder, Colo.: Lynne Rienner, 2004).

CHAPTER 15. WOMEN AFTER WARS

Cynthia Enloe's "Women after Wars: Puzzles and Warnings" was originally published in Kathleen Barry, ed., *Vietnam's Women in Transition* (London: Macmillan Press Ltd., 1996), 299–315. Reproduced with permission of Palgrave Macmillan.

1. I had the good fortune to be part of a small group guided through the South Vietnamese Women's Museum in January 1993, thanks to arrangements made by Dr. Kim Quy, director of the Women's Studies Research Center of the Ho Chi Minh City Social Science Research Institute.

2. I have tried to think more about what adding a brothel display would do to a military museum's message about women's relationships to soldiers in "It Takes Two," in Saundra Sturdevant and Brenda Stoltzfus, eds., *Let the Good Times Roll: Prostitution and the U.S. Military in Asia* (New York: New Press, 1992), 22–29.

3. Among the most detailed and interesting accounts of efforts to weave prewar conventions of femininity into women's new wartime roles are Lois Browne, *Girls of Summer: In Their Own League* (New York: HarperCollins, 1992); Maureen Honey, *Creating Rosie the Riveter: Class, Gender and Propaganda during World War II* (Amherst: University of Massachusetts Press, 1984); Leisa D. Meyer, "Creating G.I. Jane: The Regulation of Sexuality and Sexual Behavior in the Women's Army Corps during World War II," *Feminist Studies* 18, no. 2 (Fall 1992): 581–602; Allan Berube, *Coming Out under Fire: The History of Gay Men and Lesbians in World War II* (New York: Plume, 1991); Ruth Roach Pierson, '*They're Still Women After All*': *The Second World War and Canadian Womanhood* (Toronto: McClelland and Stewart, 1986); Claudia Koonz, *Mothers in the Fatherland: Women, the Family and Nazi Politics* (New York: St. Martin's Press, 1987); Irene Staunton, ed., *Mothers of the Revolution: The War Experiences of Thirty Zimbabwean Women* (Bloomington: Indiana University Press, 1991); Sita Ranchod-Nilsson, "Women and Democratization in Southern Africa: The Legacy of Zimbabwe's Liberation War for Women's Politics after Independence," presented at the International Studies Association–Midwest Meeting, Michigan State University, November 20–21, 1992; Karen Kampwirth, *Women and Guerrilla Movements: Nicaragua, Guatemala, Chiapas, Cuba* (State College: Penn State University Press, 2002); Mary Ann Tétreault, *Stories of Democracy in Politics and Society in Contemporary Kuwait* (New York: Columbia University Press, 2000); Haya al-Mughni, *Women in Kuwait* (London: Seqi Books, 2001).

4. I am grateful to Duke University historian Sarah Deutsch, herself a researcher on women of several racial groups whose actions together helped create what is now thought of as the American West, for sharing with me some of the ideas that were discussed in the planning for this museum.

5. For a description of the debates about the nature of the family among Vietnamese male and female nationalists during the 1920s and 1930s, see Hue-Tam Ho-Tai, *Radicalism and the Origins of the Vietnamese Revolution* (Cambridge, Mass.: Harvard University Press, 1992).

6. D'Ann Campbell, *Women at War with America: Private Lives in a*

Patriotic Era (Cambridge, Mass.: Harvard University Press, 1984); Sarah Fishman, *We Will Wait: Wives of French Prisoners of War, 1940–1945* (New Haven: Yale University Press, 1991).

7. Judy Barrett Litoff and David C. Smith, *Since You Went Away: World War II Letters from American Women on the Home Front* (New York: Oxford University Press, 1991).

8. Thai Thi Ngoc Du, "The Situation of Divorce and Its Influences on Women and Families in Ho Chi Minh City," presented at the Seminar on Women and the Family, Ho Chi Minh City, January 1993. A revised version of this paper appears in Kathleen Barry, ed., *Vietnam's Women in Transition* (New York: St. Martin's Press, 1996).

9. Elaine Tyler May, *Homeward Bound: American Families in the Cold War Era* (New York: Basic Books, 1988), 185.

10. Ibid.

11. The following discussion is based on a number of feminist studies of World War II women industrial workers: Honey, *Creating Rosie the Riveter*; Miriam Frank, Marilyn Ziebarth, and Connie Field, *The Life and Times of Rosie the Riveter* (Emeryville, Calif.: Clarity Educational Productions, 1982); Sherna Berger Gluck, *Rosie the Riveter Revisited: Women, the War, and Social Change* (New York: Penguin Books, 1988); Studs Terkel, *"The Good War": An Oral History of World War Two* (New York: Ballantine Books, 1984).

12. One example of research so motivated, but focusing on American women who went into more professionalized, white-collar war jobs, is Adelaide Sherer Bennett, "'War Stories': Upper Middle Class Women in Worcester, Massachusetts," unpublished master's thesis, College of Professional and Continuing Education, Clark University, 1992.

13. I have discussed this practice of ethnically defined mobilization at length in *Ethnic Soldiers: State Security in Divided Societies* (London and Athens, Ga.: Penguin Books and University of Georgia Press, 1980).

14. Staunton, *Mothers of the Revolution*; Sita Ranchod-Nilsson, "Gender Politics and National Liberation: Women's Participation in the Liberation of Zimbabwe," unpublished Ph.D. dissertation, Northwestern University, 1992.

15. I have discussed this process at greater length in *The Morning*

After: Sexual Politics at the End of the Cold War (Berkeley: University of California Press, 1993).

16. Murray Hiebert and Susumu Awanohara, "Ready to Help: Agencies Prepare Their Menus of Projects," *Far Eastern Economic Review*, April 22, 1993, 71.

CHAPTER 16. DEMILITARIZATION — OR MORE OF THE SAME?

Cynthia Enloe's "Demilitarization — or More of the Same? Feminist Questions to Ask in the Postwar Moment" was originally published in Cynthia Cockburn and Dubravka Zurkov, *The Postwar Moment* (London: Lawrence and Wishart, 2002), 22–32. Reprinted by permission of Lawrence and Wishart.

For tutoring me on the subtle genderings of political life and the ongoing processes of militarization in postconflict societies, I am especially grateful to Dyan Mazurana, Suzanne Williams, Cynthia Cockburn, Venessa Farr, Angela Raven-Roberts, Sandra Whitworth, Wenona Giles, and Maja Korac.

CHAPTER 17. A FEMINIST MAP OF THE BLOCKS ON THE ROAD TO INSTITUTIONAL ACCOUNTABILITY

This essay was originally presented at the a conference of the National Council for Research on Women, New York, May 30, 2002.

CHAPTER 18. WHEN FEMINISTS LOOK AT MASCULINITY AND THE MEN WHO WAGE WAR

Carol Cohn and Cynthia Enloe's "A Conversation with Cynthia Enloe: When Feminists Look at Terrorists, 'Boring Men,' and International Politics" was originally published in *Signs: Journal of Women in Culture and Society* 28, no. 4 (2003). © 2003 by the University of Chicago. All rights reserved. Reprinted by permission of the University of Chicago Press.

We would like to thank Sandra Harding and Kate Norberg, editors of *Signs*, for inviting us to have this conversation and for offering such good ideas along the way.

1. Some of the papers from the forum were collected in Eva Isaksson, ed., *Women and the Military System* (New York: St. Martin's Press, 1988).

2. Cynthia Enloe, *Does Khaki Become You? The Militarization of Women's Lives* (London: Pandora, 1983). For Enloe's more recent work on women and the military, see her *Maneuvers: The International Politics of Militarizing Women's Lives* (Berkeley: University of California Press, 2000).

3. Cynthia Enloe, *Bananas, Beaches and Bases: Making Feminist Sense of International Politics* (Berkeley: University of California Press, 1990). See also Enloe's *The Morning After: Sexual Politics at the End of the Cold War* (Berkeley: University of California Press, 1993) and "Sneak Attack: The Militarization of U.S. Culture" (chap. 11 in this volume).

4. There is now a Feminist Theory and Gender Section in the International Studies Association. The journal launched in 1999 by its members, the *International Feminist Journal of Politics*, is an excellent location for exploring some of this new scholarship.

5. Carol Cohn, "Sex and Death in the Rational World of Defense Intellectuals," *Signs: Journal of Women in Culture and Society* 12, no. 4 (1987): 687–718, and "Wars, Wimps, and Women: Talking Gender and Thinking War," in *Gendering War Talk*, ed. Miriam Cooke and Angela Woollacott (Princeton, N.J.: Princeton University Press, 1993), 227–46.

6. The other five committees of the General Assembly are the First Committee (disarmament and international security), the Second (economic and financial), the Fourth (special political and decolonization), the Fifth (administrative and budgetary), and the Sixth (legal). The web site http://www.peacewomen.org has a very useful guide to the UN system. This web site is maintained by the Women's International League for Peace and Freedom.

7. Cynthia Enloe proposed these at "A Dialogue between Academics, Activists, and UN Officials" on women, peace, and security, held at the UN on April 11, 2002. The event was part of a larger, continuing NGO-academic-UN dialogue project organized by Sheri Gibbing at the Women's International League for Peace and Freedom (WILPF), which Carol Cohn has worked on. Other participants in the April 11 session on Security Council Resolution 1325 included Jennifer Klot (then senior governance advisor at UNIFEM [UN Development Fund for Women]), Ann Tickner (professor, School of International Studies, University of Southern California), Maha Muna (then at the Women's Commission for Refugee Women and Children, now at UNIFEM), and Iris Marion Young (professor of political science, University of Chicago). See Enloe's "Demilitarization — or More of the Same? Feminist Questions to Ask in the Postwar Moment" (chap. 16 in this volume).

8. Cynthia Enloe, *Ethnic Soldiers: State Security in a Divided Society* (London: Penguin, 1980).

9. Adrienne Rich, *Of Woman Born: Motherhood as Experience and Institution* (New York: Bantam, 1977).

10. Seung-Kyung Kim, *Class Struggle or Family Struggle: The Lives of Women Factory Workers in South Korea* (New York: Cambridge University Press, 1997); Diane Singerman, *Avenues of Participation: Family, Politics, and Networks in Urban Quarters of Cairo* (Princeton, N.J.: Princeton University Press, 1996); Anne Allison, *Nightwork* (Chicago: University of Chicago Press, 1994); Purnima Mankekar, *Screening Culture, Viewing Politics* (Durham, N.C.: Duke University Press, 1999).

11. Catherine Lutz, *Home Front: A Military City and the American Twentieth Century* (Boston: Beacon Press, 2001); Jennifer L. Pierce, *Gender Trials: Emotional Lives in Contemporary Law Firms* (Berkeley: University of California Press, 1995); Hugh Gusterson, *Nuclear Rites: A Weapons Laboratory at the End of the Cold War* (Berkeley: University of California Press, 1996).

12. Joni Seager, *The Penguin Atlas of Women*, 3rd ed. (New York: Penguin, 2003).

13. Hannah Arendt, *The Origins of Totalitarianism* (New York: Har-

court Brace, 1951), *On Revolution* (New York: Viking, 1963), *Men in Dark Times* (New York: Harcourt Brace, 1968), and *Crises of the Republic* (New York: Harcourt Brace, 1972).

14. Amy Waldman, "Kabul Brides Married Taliban for Better, Then for Worse," *New York Times*, December 31, 2001.

15. See Cynthia Cockburn and Dubravka Zarkov, eds., *The Postwar Moment: Militaries, Masculinities, and International Peacekeeping* (London: Lawrence and Wishart, 2002); Dyan Mazurana and Angela Raven-Roberts, "Gender Perspectives in Effective Peace Operations" and "Integrating the Human Rights Perspective," both in *Challenges of Peacekeeping and Peace Support: Into the Twenty-first Century*, ed. Annika Hilding-Norberg (Stockholm: Elanders Gotab, 2002); Dyan Mazurana, Susan McKay, Khristopher Carlson, and Janel Kasper, "Girls in Fighting Forces and Groups: Their Recruitment, Participation, Demobilization, and Reintegration," *Peace and Conflict: Journal of Peace Psychology* 8, no. 2 (2002): 97–123; Sandra Whitworth, *Men, Militarism and UN Peacekeeping* (Boulder, Colo.: Lynne Rienner, 2004); Julie A. Mertus, *War's Offensive on Women: The Humanitarian Challenge in Bosnia, Kosovo, and Afghanistan* (Bloomfield, Conn.: Kumarian, 2000); Suzanne Williams, "Conflicts of Interest: Gender in Oxfam's Emergency Response," in *The Postwar Moment*, ed. Cockburn and Zarkov, 85–102; Wenona Giles and Jennifer Hyman, eds., *Sites of Violence: Gender and Conflict Zones* (Berkeley: University of California Press, 2004).

16. See Carol Cohn and Sara Ruddick, "A Feminist Ethical Perspective on Weapons of Mass Destruction," in *Ethics and Weapons of Mass Destruction*, ed. Sohail Hashmi and Phillip Valera (Cambridge: Cambridge University Press, 2004).

CHAPTER 19. UPDATING
THE GENDERED EMPIRE

1. Among the most talked about have been Niall Ferguson, *Empire* (New York: Basic Books, 2003); Paul Kennedy, *The Rise and Fall of Great Powers* (New York: Vintage, 1989); Eric Hobsbawm, *The Age of Empire*,

1875–1914 (New York: Vintage, 1987); and Simon Schama, *The Embarrassment of Riches* (New York: Vintage, 1987).

2. Philippa Levine, *Prostitution, Race and Politics: Policing Venereal Disease in the British Empire* (New York: Routledge, 2003); Piya Chatterjee, *A Time for Tea: Women, Labor, and Post/Colonial Politics on an Indian Plantation* (Durham: Duke University Press, 2001); Kumari Jayawardena, *The White Women's Other Burden: Western Women and South Asia during British Rule* (New York: Routledge, 1995).

3. See Insook Kwon, "'The New Women's Movement' in 1920s Korea: Rethinking the Relationship between Imperialism and Women," *Gender and History* 10, no. 3 (November 1998): 358–80; Vron Ware, *Beyond the Pale: White Women, Racism and History* (London: Verso, 1991); Laura Wexler, *Tender Violence: Domestic Visions in an Age of U.S. Imperialism* (Chapel Hill: University of North Carolina Press, 2000); Amy Kaplan and Donald E. Pease, eds., *Cultures of United States Imperialism* (Durham: Duke University Press, 1993); Lora Wildenthal, *German Women for Empire, 1884–1945* (Durham: Duke University Press, 2001); Kristin L. Hoganson, *Fighting for American Manhood: How Gender Politics Provoked the Spanish-American and Philippine-American Wars* (New Haven: Yale University Press, 1998); Nupur Chaudhuri and Margaret Strobel, eds., *Western Women and Imperialism: Complicity and Resistance* (Bloomington: Indiana University Press, 1992); Louise Young, *Japan's Total Empire* (Berkeley: University of California Press, 1998); Mona Etienne and Eleanor Leacock, eds., *Women and Colonization* (New York: Praeger, 1980); Clare Midgley, ed., *Gender and Imperialism* (New York: Manchester University Press, 1998). See also two critically insightful novels by the pre–World War II Dutch writer Madelon H. Lulofs, set in 1930s colonial Indonesia: *Rubber* (New York: Oxford University Press, 1987) and *Coolie* (New York: Oxford University Press, 1987).

4. Anne E. Brodsky, *With All Our Strength: The Revolutionary Association of the Women of Afghanistan* (New York: Routledge, 2003).

5. For a feminist analysis of how Pakistani government officials, Afghan male party leaders in exile, and complying international agencies

and donors together have colluded to deepen the masculinization of the political, economic, and cultural power inside the refugee camps during the period from 1990 to 2003, despite women and children comprising a majority of the camps' residents, see Saba Gul Khattak, "In/Security: Afghan Refugees and Politics in Pakistan," *Critical Asian Studies* 35, no. 2 (June 2003): 195–208.

6. A detailed account of Ismail Khan's mode of provincial rule is contained in Barry Bearak, "Unreconstructed," *New York Times Magazine*, June 1, 2003, 40–47, 62–101.

7. For information on the abuse of women and girls in Herat, see "We Want to Live as Humans: Repression of Women and Girls in Western Afghanistan," report by Human Rights Watch, New York, December 2002; "Afghanistan Report," by Amnesty International, Washington, D.C., October 5, 2003. For a detailed journalistic account of the Taliban's and Al Qaeda's marriage politics, see Amy Waldman, "Kabul Brides Married Taliban for Better, Then for Worse," *New York Times*, December 31, 2001.

8. Bearak, "Unreconstructed," 62.

9. This account is derived from Carlotta Gall's article "Women Gather in Afghanistan to Compose a Bill of Rights," *New York Times*, September 28, 2003. In September 2003 she attended a small, unofficial conference in the southern city of Kandahar along with other women — lawyers, human rights specialists, and civil society leaders. They represented groups such as Women for Afghan Women and the Afghan women lawyers' association, groups of Afghan women who were literate. By contrast, according to feminist geographer Joni Seager, an estimated 80 percent of Afghan women (compared to 53 percent of men) were still unable to gain access to the tools that would allow them to learn how to read and write (Joni Seager, *The Penguin Atlas of Women in the World* [New York: Penguin Books, 2003], 113).

10. Preeta D. Bansal and Felice D. Gaer, "Silenced Again in Kabul," *New York Times*, October 1, 2003.

11. Gall, "Women Gather in Afghanistan."

12. Ibid.

13. Sonali Kolhatkar describes the Afghan *loya jerga*'s constitutional debates and its gendered dynamics and outcome in her article "Afghan Women Continue to Fend for Themselves," *Foreign Policy in Action*, March 2004, 1–9.

14. Patrick E. Tyler, "Attackers Wound an Iraqi Official in a Baghdad Raid," *New York Times*, September 21, 2003. Akila al-Hashimi died of her wounds.

15. Alex Berenson, "U.N. Chief Orders Further Reduction of Staff in Baghdad," *New York Times*, September 26, 2003. Just two months before being assassinated and shortly after being appointed to the Governing Council, Akila al-Hashimi had been one of three Council members to represent the interim government on a trip to New York to lobby members of the United Nations (Felicity Barringer, "U.N. Gives Iraqi Governing Council Qualified Welcome," *New York Times*, July 23, 2003).

16. Zainab Al-Suwaij, "Iraq's Silenced Majority," *New York Times*, May 23, 2003.

17. Patrick Tyler, "Iraqi Groups Badly Divided over How to Draft a Charter," *New York Times*, September 30, 2003.

18. Much of the following derives from Sabrina Tavernise, "Iraqi Women Wary of New Upheavals," *New York Times*, May 5, 2003.

19. Amy Waldman, "U.S. Struggles to Transform a Tainted Iraqi Police Force," *New York Times*, June 30, 2003.

20. Human Rights Watch, *Report on Women's Rights in Iraq* (New York: Human Rights Watch, July 2003); Neela Banerjee, "Rape (and Silence about It) Haunts Baghdad," *New York Times*, July 16, 2003.

21. Seager, *Penguin Atlas of Women*, 114–15.

22. Tavernise, "Iraqi Women Wary of New Upheavals."

23. Most of the following is derived from Sharon Waxman, "Facing the Future," *Washington Post*, June 17, 2003.

24. Ibid.

25. Lauren Sandler, "Veiled Interests," *Boston Globe*, August 31, 2003.

26. Ibid.

27. The women inside the United Nations and their allies in femi-

nist nongovernmental organizations have been most influential in pressing all international agencies and donor countries to take seriously the political implications of violence against women in war zones and in postwar reconstruction efforts. One of the closest monitors of these efforts is *PeaceWomen*, an electronically distributed newsletter published by the Women's International League for Peace and Freedom (www.peacewomen.org). See also UNIFEM's report on the chief conditions and official attitudes that obstruct women's effective participation in postconflict political life: Elisabeth Rehnand and Ellen Johnson Sirleaf, *World Progress of Women 2002*, vol. 1, *Women, War, and Peace* (Bloomfield, Conn.: Kumarian Press, 2003).

28. Sandler, "Veiled Interests."

29. Ibid.

30. Ibid.

31. See www.peacewomen.org, September 12, 2003.

32. E-mail announcement circulated by the New York–headquartered National Council for Research on Women (www.ncrw.org), October 10, 2003.

33. Lauren Sandler, "Veiled and Worried in Baghdad," *New York Times*, September 16, 2003.

34. For a feminist discussion of the strengths and weaknesses of UN Security Council Resolution 1325, see Carol Cohn, Helen Kinsella, and Sheri Gibbings, "Women, Peace and Security: Resolution 1325," *International Feminist Journal of Politics* 6, no. 1 (March 2004): 130–40.

35. E-mail from National Council for Research on Women.

36. See, for example, Claire Midgley, *Women against Slavery: The British Campaigns 1780–1870* (New York: Routledge, 1992); Lila Rupp, *Worlds of Women: The Making of an International Women's Movement* (Princeton, N.J.: Princeton University Press, 1997); Margot Badran, *Feminists, Islam, and Nation: Gender and the Making of Modern Egypt* (Princeton, N.J.: Princeton University Press, 1995). For case studies of contemporary efforts at creating genuine alliances of women across national boundaries, see Felicity Hill, Mikele Abotiz, and Sara Poehlman-Doumbouya, "Non-governmental Organizations' Role in

the Buildup and Implementation of Security Council Resolution 1325," *Signs* 28, no. 4 (Summer 2003): 1255–70; Pam Spees, "Women's Advocacy in the Creation of the International Criminal Court," *Signs* 28, no. 4 (Summer 2003): 1233–54; Sherrill Whittington, "Gender and Peacekeeping: The United Nations Transitional Administration in East Timor," *Signs* 28, no. 4 (Summer 2003): 1283–88; Mrinalini Sinha, Donna J. Guy, and Angela Woolacott, eds., "Feminisms and Internationalism" (special issue), *Gender and History* 10, no. 3 (November 1998).

· Index

cheap labor: as labor made cheap,
2, 55; politics hidden by, 60;
worker turnover and, 64–65.
See also daughters and daughterhood; factory workers; sneakers
Chiapas: civil society in, 143; gendered and racialized contradictions in, 27–28; marginal position of, 24–25, 27; NAFTA
viewed from, 35, 39–42; peasant
rebellion in, 34–37, 42; private
armies in, 34–35; race and class
hierarchies in, 32–33. *See also*
Mayan Indians
Chicago Tribune, 53
children: advertising that targets,
44; rights of, 124–25, 129; as
soldiers, 14; television viewing
of, 140. *See also* girlhood
Chile: politics in, 20, 230
Chin, Christine, 169–70
China: athletic footwear manufacturing in, 48–49, 50–51, 54, 55,
58; democratization movement
in, 71; violence against women
as public issue in, 80; wages in,
54
Choi Soung-ai, 66
cigarette smoking, 316–17
citizens: obstacles to, 65; postconflict categorization of, 221–22,
228–29; presumptions about
male and female, 210; responsibilities of, 176, 188, 287; speaking and listening as, 70–71
civilization: definitions of, 260
civil rights activism, 160
Clark University, 160, 164, 248–49
class: hierarchies of, 32–33; in
postwar military transformation,
211–12

Clinton, Bill, 53–54, 126, 209
CND (Campaign for Nuclear
Disarmament), 168
Cockburn, Cynthia, 261
Cohn, Carol, 237–67
Cold War: end of, 43; gendered
power structures in, 38–39;
modes of discourse in, 239;
sneaker manufacture in context of, 59; womanhood as
constructed in, 174
Colombia: military aid for, 127
Columbine High School massacre,
18
Committee for Asian Women
(CAW), 56, 79–80
comparative politics: ethnicity
considered in, 163; feminist
approach to, 163–64; presumptions in, 26; teaching of, 248–49
Comparative Politics of Pollution
(CE), 159–60
conflicts. *See* postconflict society;
war and conflicts
Confucianism, 46
Connecticut College, 157–58, 162,
252
consciousness: organizing and
militarizing of, 101–2
consciousness-raising, 47–48
constitution writing: in
Afghanistan, 286–89; in Iraq,
293–94, 300
constructionism, 90
Costa Rica: bananas from, 177; as
non-military model, 185
credibility: state's view of, 31–32;
status based on, 13–14; trivialization as undermining, 74. *See
also* authority
Croatia: war with, 108

Indexer: Margie Towery
Compositor: BookMatters, Berkeley
Text: 10/15 Janson
Display: Knockout, Janson
Printer and binder: Maple-Vail Manufacturing Group